J. M. Dillon is Regius Professor of Greek at Trinity College, Dublin. He is the author of *The Middle Platonists* (1977) and other works.

A. A. Long is Professor of Classics at the University of California, Berkeley. His earlier book, *Hellenistic Philosophy: Stoics, Epicureans, Sceptics* (second edition) is also available from the University of California Press, in cloth and paper.

Hellenistic Culture and Society, III

D1072009

The Question of "Eclecticism"

HELLENISTIC CULTURE AND SOCIETY
General Editors: Anthony W. Bulloch, Erich S. Gruen, A. A. Long, and
Andrew F. Stewart

Edited by
John M. Dillon
and A. A. Long

The Question of "Eclecticism"

Studies in Later Greek Philosophy

University
of California
Press

Berkeley
Los Angeles
London

University of California Press
Berkeley and Los Angeles, California

University of California Press, Ltd.
London, England

LIBRARY OF CONGRESS CATALOGING-IN-PUBLICATION DATA

The Question of "eclecticism."

    Includes indexes.
    1. Philosophy, Ancient.   I. Dillon, John M.
II. Long, A. A.
B335.Q47   1988   186'.3   87-10852
ISBN 0-520-06008-3 (alk. paper)

Printed in the United States of America

1   2   3   4   5   6   7   8   9

Contents

Preface

In the period 50 B.C.–A.D. 200, Greek philosophers belonged to an intellectual tradition that had persisted for five or six hundred years. They were more distant from their Ionian origins than we are today from the Reformation and the Copernican Revolution. How did they, and their interpreters (such as the Roman Cicero), regard that tradition and the schools to which they claimed allegiance? What contribution did philosophy make at that time to religious thought, to scientific methodology, or to the emergence of certain concepts we now take for granted? In what perspectives, viewing the period in general, should we regard the significance of Plato's philosophy, Aristotle, Stoicism, and Skepticism? These are some of the general questions addressed in the chapters of this book. The period that it covers is strongly in need of reexamination. It has tended to fall outside standard divisions of the history of philosophy, while its principal figures have generally been downgraded as "eclectics," indiscriminate assemblers of other thinkers' doctrines. The purpose of this book is revision and reassessment of this unhelpful notion, a goal it pursues by means of detailed case studies of some of the most interesting philosophers and concepts at work in the period.

The book began its life as a colloquium on later Greek philosophy held in Dublin, at Trinity College, as part of the quinquennial meeting of the Eighth International Classical Congress (F.I.E.C.) in August 1984. The colloquium was organized for F.I.E.C. by Anthony Long, who invited the participants to consider the theme of so-called eclecticism in the period from Cicero to about A.D. 200. Each chapter of the book was written as an original paper read to the colloquium, whose participants also included Frederick Brenk, Walter Chalmers, Joachim Classen, John Cleary, George Kerferd, Ian Kidd, Miroslav Marcovich, Paul Moraux, Reimer Müller, Ann Sheppard, Richard Sorabji, Gisela Striker, Gregory Vlastos, and Abraham Wasserstein. They and others have helped to shape the form the book has taken. The editors are particularly grateful to Doris Kretschmer of the University of California Press for her interest and advice at all stages of its production, and to the John Simon Guggenheim Memorial Foundation for the award of a Fellowship to A.A. Long, which facilitated the final stages of the editorial process. They also express their thanks to Thomas Chance and Jeff Purinton, who gave valuable research assistance.

Technical details, which any work of ancient philosophical interpretation requires, have been largely confined to footnotes. The main arguments of each chapter, where they depend on philology, are developed through translation of the Greek and Latin originals. Greek words, which are transliterated in the main text, are also explained in the Index of Greek and Latin Philosophical Terms. Thus the book is designed to appeal to as wide an audience as possible.

—J.M.D., A.A.L.

Notes on contributors

JACQUES BRUNSCHWIG is Professor of the History of Ancient Philosophy at the University of Paris X–Nanterre. His publications include the Budé edition of Aristotle, *Topics*, vols. 1–4 (1967), and articles on Plato, Aristotle, and Hellenistic philosophy. He is also editor of *Les Stoiciens et leur logique* (1978), and co-editor of *Doubt and Dogmatism* (1980) and *Science and Speculation* (1982).

JOHN M. DILLON is Regius Professor of Greek at Trinity College, Dublin. His books include *Iamblichi fragmenta* (1973), *The Middle Platonists* (1977), *A Classical Lexicon for Finnegan's Wake*, with B. O'Hehir (1977), *Two Treatises of Philo of Alexandria*, with David Winston (1983), and *Proclus on the Parmenides of Plato*, with Glenn Morrow (1987).

PIERLUIGI DONINI is Professor of Ancient Philosophy at the University of Turin. His publications on later Greek philosophy include *Tre studi sull'aristotelismo nel II secolo d.c.* (1973), *Le scuole l'anima l'impero: la filosofia antica da Antioco a Plotino* (1982), and studies on the problem of determinism.

JOHN GLUCKER is Professor of Classical Philology and Philosophy in Tel-Aviv University, Israel. He is the author of *Antiochus and the Late Academy* (1978), articles on Greek and Latin literature, ancient philosophy, and the methods and history of Classical philology; he has also written two books on the Presocratics and Plato in Hebrew.

CHARLES H. KAHN is Professor of Philosophy at the University of Pennsylvania. His books include *Anaximander and the Origins of Greek Cosmology* (1960), *The Verb "Be" in Ancient Greek* (1973), and *The Art and Thought of Heraclitus* (1979), and he is currently at work on a book on Plato and the Socratic dialogue.

A. A. LONG is Professor of Classics at the University of California, Berkeley. His books include *Language and Thought in Sophocles* (1968), *Hellenistic Philosophy* (1974; 2d ed. 1986), and *The Hellenistic Philosophers*, with D. N. Sedley, 2 vols. (1987), and he is the editor of *Problems in Stoicism* (1971) and co-editor of *Theophrastus of Eresus* (1985).

JAAP MANSFELD is Professor of Ancient and Patristic Philosophy at the University of Utrecht. His publications include *Die Offenbarung des Parmenides und die menschliche Welt* (1964), *The Pseudo-Hippocratic Tract Peri Hebdomadon Ch. 1–11 and Greek Philosophy* (1971), *An Alexandrian Platonist against Dualism*, with P. W. van der Horst (1974), and *Die Vorsokratiker*, 2 vols. (1983, 1986).

G. WATSON is Professor of Greek at St. Patrick's College, Maynooth, Republic of Ireland. He is the author of *The Stoic Theory of Knowledge* (1966), *Plato's Unwritten Teaching* (1973), and articles on other topics in Greek philosophy.

Abbreviations

The following abbreviations are used to refer to standard reference works and periodicals. Abbreviated references to ancient texts follow the conventions of LSJ and the *Oxford Latin Dictionary*.

ALGHJ	Arbeiten zur Literatur und Geschichte des Hellenistischen Judentums
ANRW	*Aufstieg und Niedergang der römischen Welt*
BICS	*Bulletin of the Institute of Classical Studies of the University of London*
CJ	*Classical Journal*
CPh	*Classical Philology*
CQ	*Classical Quarterly*
DK	*Die Fragmente der Vorsokratiker*, ed. H. Diels and W. Kranz
Dox. Graeci	*Doxographi Graeci*, ed. H. Diels
JRS	*Journal of Roman Studies*
LSJ	Liddell-Scott-Jones, *A Greek-English Lexicon*
OCT	Oxford Classical Text
RE	*Paulys Real-encyclopädie der classischen Altertumswissenschaft*

REA	*Revue des Etudes Anciennes*
REG	*Revue des Etudes Grecques*
REL	*Revue des Etudes Latines*
RPh	*Revue de Philologie*
RSF	*Rivista Critica di Storia della Filosofia*
SVF	*Stoicorum veterum fragmenta*, ed. H. von Arnim
TAPA	*Transactions of the American Philological Association*
Vig. Chr.	*Vigiliae Christianae*

Chronology

A.D.

ca. 4 B.C.–65	Seneca the Younger
ca. 1st century	"Longinus," author of *On the Sublime*
ca. 30–100	Quintilian, rhetorician
ca. 40–112	Dio Chrysostom, sophist and rhetorician
ca. 50–100	Moderatus of Gades, Neo-Pythagorean philosopher
ca. 50–120	Plutarch of Chaeroneia
ca. 55–135	Epictetus
ca. 70–150	Nicomachus of Gerasa, Neo-Pythagorean philosopher
ca. 81–150	Favorinus, Academic philosopher
ca. 83–161	Ptolemy, astronomer and geographer
ca. 100–160	L. Calvenus Taurus, Platonist philosopher
ca. 121–180	Marcus Aurelius
ca. 123–180	Apuleius of Madaurus, rhetorician, novelist, Platonist philosopher
ca. 125–185	Maximus of Tyre, sophist
ca. 129–199	Galen
ca. 130–180	Aulus Gellius, Roman encyclopaedist
ca. 150	fl. Numenius of Apamea, Platonist philosopher
ca. 150	fl. Albinus, Platonist philosopher
ca. 150–215	Clement of Alexandria, Christian theologian
170–ca. 245	Flavius Philostratus, sophist
ca. 175	fl. Atticus, Platonist philosopher
ca. 200	fl. Alexander of Aphrodisias, Aristotelian commentator
ca. 200	fl. Sextus Empiricus, Pyrrhonist philosopher
ca. 200	fl. Diogenes Laertius, author of philosophers' lives
205–270	Plotinus
ca. 225	fl. Ammonius Saccas, Platonist philosopher

232–ca. 305	Porphyry, Platonist philosopher
ca. 260–340	Eusebius of Caesarea, bishop
4th century	Calcidius, Platonist commentator
330–379	Basil of Caesarea, bishop
354–430	Augustine of Hippo

Introduction

There is a period in the history of Greek philosophy, covering roughly the first century B.C. and the first two centuries A.D., that has long been a source of embarrassment to intellectual historians. The immediately preceding period, now commonly called Hellenistic philosophy, had seen the emergence of three new movements, Stoic, Epicurean, and Skeptic, the last of which actually came to characterize Plato's successors in the Academy. The third century A.D. is marked by the development of that highly original interpretation of Plato that we call Neoplatonism and also by the flowering of the great tradition of commentary on Aristotle, ushered in by Alexander of Aphrodisias.

Between these two well-defined periods we find a series of thinkers whose contribution to philosophy has been disparagingly labeled *eclectic*. They include such well-known amateurs as the Romans Cicero and Seneca, but also such professional Greek philosophers as the Stoics Panaetius and Posidonius, the Platonists Antiochus, Plutarch, and Albinus, and doctors and scientists such as Galen and Ptolemy. In this period, it has seemed, it was no longer possible to be a "pure-blooded" follower of any of the traditional schools. This supposed merging of philosophical identities has been accounted for by another well-publicized opinion about this period: its decline of intellectual vigor and its loss of creativity. These negative features were often attributed to the heavy hand of Rome and its demands for an undifferentiated pabulum, consisting of a compromise between the doctrines of the warring schools and emphasizing moral edification rather than the cut and thrust of argument. This process might seem to be exemplified by the proconsul L. Gellius Poplicola, who in Athens in 69 B.C. "called together the philosophers of the time, and urgently advised them to come at length to some settlement of their controversies" (Cicero *De legibus* 1.53). One of the principal villains of the piece, in this scenario, is Cicero, whose hastily composed accounts of the Hellenistic movements may seem to deal a deathblow to any further innovations in those philosophies.

Such a view of intellectual history was given credence by the immense authority of Eduard Zeller, whose still indispensable account of the whole of Greek philosophy was heavily influenced by the Hegelian tendency to view intellectual history in terms of alternations between periods of high and low creativity. We would not wish to assert that there is no validity whatever in this view of history. Arguably, adventurous speculation did decline during this period. There can also be observed a growth of faith in authority, a seeking for "ancient" sources (leading to the proliferation of pseudepigrapha), and the domination of the concept of "the Classical." On the other hand, the work of philosophy should be seen as continuing, if in different modes. The dissemination and assimilation of established ideas and methodologies were a stimulus to critical reflection and innovation. If this period lacks an individual philosopher comparable to Plato, Aristotle, Epicurus, or Zeno, that is not a reason for hastily adjudging it to be second-rate, dull, and largely derivative from the past in its perspectives.

The purpose of the present collection of essays is to offer a series of studies that will provide the basis for a deeper understanding of the real intellectual character of that age. Such a collection, arising as it does from a set of colloquium papers, cannot aspire to be comprehensive. However, we do think that the movements and individuals constituting the key factors in this period are represented, even if not necessarily in proportion to their importance. If the Epicureans do not find much place here, that is no accident. They remain curiously peripheral, for reasons related to the introverted nature of their movement and the hostility it inspired in the schools directly influenced by Plato. Nevertheless, they do make their appearance in various connections, as the index will testify.

The dominant theme of this book is a critical reexamination of the traditional (since Zeller) characterization of this period, its "eclecticism." The dispiriting connotations of this term are nicely expressed in this quotation from the article on *Eclecticism* in the *Encyclopaedia Britannica* (14th edition):

> Eclecticism always tends to spring up after a period of vigorous constructive speculation, especially in the later stages of a controversy between thinkers of pre-eminent ability. Their respective followers, and more especially cultured laymen, lacking the capacity for original work, seeking for a solution in some kind of compromise, take refuge in a combination of those elements in the opposing systems which seem to afford a sound practical theory.

Actually, in reference to our period, where this definition is most at home, to characterize the Hellenistic age as "a period of vigorous constructive speculation" would have been a considerably higher estimate than was common at the time the article was written; it is only in the last generation or so that the study of Hellenistic philosophy has come into its own, and its exciting features have ceased to be overshadowed by the towering figures of Plato and Aristotle. As for controversy, that by no means comes to an end in our period, which witnesses the emergence of, among other things, a renewed Skepticism, under the aegis of Aenesidemus and his Neo-Pyrrhonism, whose vigorous scrutiny of the whole history of philosophy is charted in the pages

of Sextus Empiricus. As for compromise, it is true that some of
the thinkers in our period were impatient of the terminological
niceties and fine conceptual distinctions that had characterized
inter-school debates in the Hellenistic period. Toward the end of
that epoch, Antiochus of Ascalon had combined Platonic, Aristotelian, and Stoic concepts in his ethics, while discarding the
Stoic insistence on the absolute irrelevance of all bodily and external goods for happiness. We find Seneca and Plutarch equally
unwilling to go along with the more bizarre features of Stoicism.
Galen too, and Ptolemy, as Chapter 7 indicates, were more interested in the validity of empiricism in general terms than in
very precise justification of its detail. Sometimes such attitudes
do involve a fuzziness of thought. More often, however, they
point to a deliberate interest in establishing a theory or a concept
on the basis of the general consensus of a very long-standing
and tested intellectual tradition.

Eclecticism, then, in its pejorative sense, seems a less than useful term to capture the particular quality of intellectual life in this
period. Our studies should provide a number of suggestions for
replacing it with more informative and less complacent terminology. The reader who has followed us so far will have seen
how diverse are the thinkers it has been fashionable to call eclectic. To place the term and the concept in their historical perspective is the purpose of Pierluigi Donini's chapter, which begins
the book. There was a use for the Greek verb *eklegein* to signify
selecting the best from a group of things. But in philosophical
parlance neither the word itself nor the concept it expresses is
attested before the Roman period, and then only rarely, in notable
contrast to its free and mainly derogatory employment in modern
histories of philosophy.

This negative connotation of eclecticism, however, is also to
be contrasted with the way the term was used when it first became widespread in modern times. Jakob Brucker, the most in-
fluential historian of philosophy in the mid-eighteenth century,
regarded what he called the "eclectic method of philosophizing"

as characteristic of such seminal figures of recent philosophy as Hobbes, Descartes, and Leibniz. What Brucker was commending—and in this he was followed by Diderot—was the eclectics' refusal to submit to tailor-made and supposedly authoritative doctrines. As Diderot expressed it, "the eclectic goes back to the clearest general principles, examines them, discusses them, admits nothing except on the evidence of his own experience and reason." However, such ancient philosophers of our period as the Alexandrian Platonists were not considered to have been eclectics in this honorable sense. They were seen, rather, as "syncretists," whose efforts to reconcile different opinions had yielded a disorderly jumble. Under the influence of German idealism, the term *eclecticism* itself lost its connections with a critical and open approach to inquiry and assumed the opprobrious sense with which Zeller employed it. And via Zeller, as we stated at the outset, eclecticism has persistently been viewed as an objectively valid category for describing the philosophy of our period. Donini's survey, by tracing the origins of eclecticism in the history of Greek philosophy, confirms the inadequacy of the term to capture the variety and interest of the men and ideas discussed in this book.

Developments within the Academy during the first half of the first century B.C. played a major part in shaping the philosophical tendencies of the next two hundred and fifty years. Philo of Larissa sought to mitigate the extreme skepticism of his predecessors (Arcesilaus, Carneades, and Clitomachus) by claiming that the Academy, from Plato onward, had been united in its modest disavowal of human access to absolutely certain truths. This implausible thesis generated two opposite responses in the Academics Antiochus and Aenesidemus. Antiochus, renouncing all skepticism, put forward an alternative unitary tradition, that of Plato, Aristotle, and Stoicism, whose essential agreements on most points of doctrine he opposed to the New Academic support for "suspension of judgment about everything." Aenesidemus, in order to free Skepticism from its now-tarnished pedigree, abandoned the Academy and founded a Neo-Pyrrhonian philosophy. These schisms, for all their differences, exhibit a common interest in attaching the proper contemporary stance of philosophy, in its proponents' view, to an authoritative tradition. They also show how eclecticism and skepticism were alternative medicines for dealing with the same illness—a philosophical legacy that had become diffuse and multiform. Eclecticism, as in Antiochus, suggests that disagreements between philosophers are merely verbal and that at bottom the doctrines of superficially discrepant systems are compatible. Skepticism, by contrast, insists that the dogmatists' contradictions of one another indicate actually contradictory doctrines, which are not explicable as verbal or simply conceptual differences.

Our collection of "case histories" begins with that of Cicero, dealt with by John Glucker in "Cicero's philosophical affiliations." Cicero's philosophical position has generally been viewed as an ostensibly consistent adherence to the moderate skepticism of Philo's Fourth Academy, a stance which allowed him, in his later writings, to explore what could be said for and against alternative doctrines. A difficulty that this view of Cicero fails to meet is the absence of any support for skepticism in the *De re-publica* and *De legibus*, composed in the 50s B.C. The positive tone of these works, to say nothing of their deliberately Platonic titles, could be seen as deriving from Cicero's sympathy for the more doctrinaire teachings of Antiochus of Ascalon, with whom Cicero had studied in Athens in 79 B.C. On the other hand, however generous toward Antiochus Cicero shows himself to be in the main body of his philosophical writings, composed in the last three years of his life, he never commits himself in them to "Old Academic" dogmatism. Glucker seeks to solve these problems by arguing that there were in fact three stages in Cicero's philosophical development: an initial adherence to Philo was followed by an affiliation lasting over thirty years (79–46 B.C.), to the doctrinaire Platonism of Antiochus, which was in turn succeeded, in Cicero's final years—his most fertile period of philosophical composition—by a return to the position of the Philonian New Academy. Glucker's thesis directs sharp attention to a number of passages in which Cicero gives indications of his philosophical position, some of which have been underemphasized at the expense of others. Cicero's readers have been reluctant to take him seriously enough as a philosopher to credit him with genuine changes of school allegiance; but if one is willing to grant him that honor, Glucker's scenario is certainly the best explanation of the evidence.

As a philosophical writer, Cicero sees himself as providing his Roman readers with an entire conspectus of the Greek philosophical tradition. The case of the Jewish philosopher Philo of Alexandria is comparable, though very different in its assessment and use of that tradition. Philo's position is remarkable in that he regards Moses, *qua* divinely inspired author of the Pentateuch, as the first philosopher and the Greeks as presenting mere reflections of his teaching, distorted to a greater or lesser degree. Above all, the study of the philosophy of the schools is to be subordinated to the exegesis of Scripture. Jaap Mansfeld, in Chapter 3, presents an illuminating account of how Philo uses a doxographic parade of the doctrines of the various schools as a foil for his exposition of the Mosaic philosophy. He divides his essay into two parts, each investigating a different strategy of Philo's. The first demonstrates how Philo uses various opinions, particularly Stoic and Peripatetic ones, to set up a sequence of "literal" and "allegorical" interpretations of a scriptural passage. The second exploits the Skeptic technique of constructing a *dissensio*, or disagreement, by arranging the theories of the philosophers in polar opposition, again in order to provide a foil for the doctrine of Moses. Instead of using these disagreements as grounds for suspension of judgment, Philo invokes them as evidence of human fallibility. Inspired by God, Moses transcends the doubts of those who rely on purely human wisdom.

Either Cicero or Philo may fairly be denominated *eclectic*, at least in their strategies. (Whatever we believe about Cicero, it is still reasonable to claim that Philo's own Mosaic philosophy is a fairly coherent brand of Middle Platonism.) But the next two chapters address figures who would claim to be professional school philosophers and who would be greatly distressed to think that they deviated from school orthodoxy. In Chapter 4 John Dillon looks at what *orthodoxy* can signify in a situation where there is no longer any central validating authority, but simply a rather vague tradition. He concludes that orthodoxy, although an ideal much striven for, is essentially a state of mind, permitting Antiochus to break with his predecessors and "return" to dogmatism, Plutarch to challenge the prevailing consensus on the issue of the creation of the world in time, Albinus to adopt freely much Peripatetic doctrine, and Atticus in turn to inveigh bitterly against this, while himself adopting Stoic formulations. The Neo-Pythagoreans are a special case, with their own peculiar relationship to Plato and their own doctrinal squabbles, particularly on the question of whether the Indefinite Dyad is primordial or is derived from the One. Their preoccupation with such relatively esoteric questions alerts us to the fact that, alongside the blurring of philosophical identities, there were some who were much concerned with validating their orthodoxy within a closed tradition.

Pierluigi Donini, in Chapter 5, focuses on one particularly interesting essay of Plutarch's, to show how he, though an "orthodox" Platonist according to his lights, could freely use scientific doctrine borrowed from other schools to elucidate a problem of natural philosophy ("What is the moon made of?"), but with a sting in the tail. The myth of the *De facie* "corrects" the scientific section in various ways: it shows that scientific explanation (such as the Peripatetics or Stoics would offer) can provide the *material* cause of the moon's existence, but is inadequate to address the *final* cause, the true purpose of the moon. This can only be done by means of a Platonist myth. To this extent Plutarch too is "using philosophy," rather in the manner of Philo of Alexandria. Donini's treatment vindicates the unity of the *De facie*, which has frequently been impugned, arguing that Plutarch's supposed eclecticism has a serious philosophical purpose.

In his study of Sextus Empiricus, Jacques Brunschwig starts from the data common to skepticism and eclecticism (see p. 6 above) and then considers the intricate problems the skeptic faced in his analysis and refutation of the criterion of truth. Writing in about A.D. 200, Sextus was the legatee of a concept that had been utilized and interpreted in many different ways over the five preceding centuries. In order to justify his strategy of pitting one dogmatic doctrine against another, Sextus as a skeptic must assume that he and his opponents all have the same *notions* and use the same *words* to express them, for without this assumption he has no basis for indicating actual contradictions over doctrines. But the skeptic is also tempted to expose disagreements between dogmatists over their definitions of the same terms. This approach, because it rejects the assumption of a common conceptual legacy, is incompatible with the former one. Brunschwig finds Sextus combining these two methodologies in his treatment of the criterion of truth. Sextus starts from an apparently univocal notion of *kritērion*, according to which this term stands for something that provides "immediate knowledge" (*prodēlos*). His subsequent discussion, however, includes inappropriate attempts to expose conceptual disagreements over the division of the *kritērion* into different aspects and also introduces a quite different conception of it as that which tests nonevident matters (*adēlos*). These two conceptions seem to belong to different traditions, the prodelic to Stoicism, the adelic to Epicureanism. Sextus says nothing to indicate that in his discussions he is shifting about between these two notions. He may, however, have thought himself justified in doing so, on the ground that elimination of the prodelic *kritērion* disposes of the immediate evidence necessary for the operation of the adelic *kritērion* of the Epicureans.

While it suited skeptics to represent doctrinaire philosophers as proponents of radically discrepant opinions, practicing scientists had an interest in playing down fine differences between concepts or theories whose general tenor they could appropriate as underpinning for their methodology. Highly instructive in this regard, though neglected, is Ptolemy's short essay *On the Criterion and Commanding-Faculty*. A. A. Long gives an account of this work in Chapter 7 that seeks to place Ptolemy's position on these concepts in its intellectual context and to assess its bearing on his researches. Ptolemy, who owed no allegiance to any school of philosophy, analyzes the criterion of truth in terms that reveal his indebtedness to the tradition drawn upon by Sextus Empiricus. Like Sextus, he analyzes different aspects of the criterion and builds much of his account on a distinction between sense-perception and intellect. Unlike Sextus, he does not treat these as rival claimants to the role of decisive cognitive faculties, which can be set against one another or eliminated in turn, but attributes positive functions to them conjointly. Completely ignoring the issues that had generated skepticism, Ptolemy strikes a balance between empiricism and rationalism in a manner which he could expect would win general support from all the doctrinaire schools of philosophy. His "eclecticism," manifested in the ground he shares, or implicitly claims to share, with competing epistemologies, would be better termed a methodology of optimum agreement. As such, it can be interpreted as the reverse of the skeptical strategy of refuting all doctrines by exposing them as contradictory to each other. Ptolemy's synthetic stance on the criterion of truth and his refusal to engage with questions of terminology or fine-tuning is exactly the same as that of his contemporary scientist, Galen. Both men opted for an epistemology that granted due weight, as they saw it, to the reciprocal importance of controlled observations and theoretical postulates. The use they made of their philosophical inheritance enabled them not only to resist the skeptical exploitation of "disagreement," but also to stake a middle ground in the controversies between extreme rationalists and empiricists that were issues in medicine, for Galen, or in harmonics, for Ptolemy. What we witness in these strategies is an innovative manipulation of traditional concepts in the interests of a new kind of philosophy of science.

Our earlier studies have exhibited philosophers using their philosophical inheritance in various ways, either for the enhancement of their positions or for the more exact definition of them. We turn finally to two chapters in which concepts are seen to take on new depth and complexity through cross-fertilization between philosophical traditions.

Imagination, as the concept of a mental faculty capable of producing what its possessor has never experienced, is not identified by any specific term in Classical Greek philosophy. Philostratus, however, in the third century A.D., uses the term *phantasia* (compare our "fantasy") to describe the artist's ability to create something which the eye has never seen (contrast *mimēsis*), but the mind has conceived. G. Watson investigates the largely uncharted route which transformed *phantasia* from its original Platonic relation to fallible opinion (*doxa*) and sense-perception (*aisthēsis*) into a term for the creative imagination. Without extraneous influence, he argues, one who accepted Plato's strictures on the cognitive weakness of the senses would scarcely elevate *phantasia* to the status of mental illumination. Yet such a usage occurs not only in the Platonic-sounding contexts of Philostratus but also in earlier and similar passages of Cicero, "Longinus," Quintilian, and Dio Chrysostom. One clue to the mediating influences is the tendency for such writers to make literature superior to the visual arts. In Stoicism, the capacity to "make a transition" from the seen to the unseen is a distinctive feature of human *phantasia*, and this was closely linked with *lekta*, the "incorporeal" meanings of sentences. The presumption of such a Stoic background helps to explain how writers of a Platonic cast could begin to view *phantasia* approvingly, thanks to its connection with the domain of reason (*logos*) and "meanings" that are not reducible to physical things. A second factor that points in the same direction is the intense interest Platonist writers of our period took in the question of human access to the divine nature. The key text was Plato's *Timaeus*, where the divine creator is pictured as a craftsman who models the world on intelligible Forms. For Plato himself, divine creativity was not an exercise of *phantasia*. Stoics, who accepted the craftsman image of God but rejected Plato's two-world metaphysics, helped to suggest that the artist, working creatively with *phantasia*, is like God. Hence it became possible for Platonist writers, under Stoic influence, to treat an artist's vision as similar in kind, though cognitively inferior, to the divine vision of perfect Beauty.

A second modern notion that was facilitated by a striking convergence of different philosophical traditions is that of the will. As formulated by Aquinas, *voluntas* is an essentially spiritual power that exercises decisive control over voluntary actions. Working as he did with an Aristotelian theory of the soul, Aquinas incorporated all the concepts Aristotle used in his account of human action. In Aristotle, however, these concepts—what is "up to us," the voluntary, desire for the end (*boulēsis*), and deliberate desire for the means (*prohairesis*)—are not tied together by a single notion of will, as *voluntas* unites them in Aquinas. Charles Kahn, in Chapter 9, makes these points, in order to show that "our" concept of the will can be viewed from a number of different perspectives, in selecting one of which a historian will incline to emphasize particular philosophers and traditions. By studying a wide range of concepts and thinkers from Aristotle to Augustine, he shows that Albrecht Dihle in his recent book *The Theory of Will in Classical Antiquity* laid undue weight on the theological and biblical perspective, highly important though this was for Augustine and Aquinas. Kahn identifies four historical stages that cumulatively shaped modern (i.e., from Descartes onward) notions of the will: (1) the early Stoic theory of human action, in which the mind's "assent" and responsibility for its "impulses" are developed; (2) the translation into Latin of Greek philosophical terms which, as with *voluntas* and *liberum arbitrium*, acquired a resonance absent from the Greek originals; (3) the later Stoic interest in a concept of moral character or moral identity—an introspective self bent on conformity with the "will of God"—where this is expressed by Epictetus in the term *prohairesis* and by Seneca with *voluntas*; (4) the Augustinian notion, influenced on the one hand by Neoplatonism and on the other by his meditations on Scripture, of a spiritual realm to which the human will belonged. Kahn allows that the concept of the will as an overall attitude of obedience or disobedience to the will of God was only "figuratively" anticipated in the later Stoic tradition. But that tradition, in conjunction with the other factors he isolates, played its part in shaping the thought of Augustine and Aquinas.

□□□

The issues we have outlined here are sufficient, we believe, to provoke renewed attention to this curious but fascinating chapter of intellectual history. "Renewed attention," since our Renaissance predecessors needed no encouragement to find food for reflection in their study of Cicero, Plutarch, Philo, Galen, Ptolemy, and so on. And here, perhaps, is where we reach something like a proper use for the term *eclectic*. Every culture is both selective and synthetic in its approach to the tradition it acknowledges as its own; and the fact of acknowledgment itself involves the promotion of this or that idea or thinker and the demotion of other parts of the tradition. The period surveyed in this book was unusually rich in its cultural resources. Further patterns of thought are certainly waiting to be recovered there, obscured merely by a lack of discrimination in our present cultural perspectives.

—J.D., A.A.L.

PIERLUIGI DONINI

1

The history of the concept of eclecticism

Antiquity knew both the concept of eclectic philosophy and the term itself, but both were much less widespread than their popularity in modern times would lead one to think. The idea that a philosophy could show the combined influence of other thinkers was by no means unusual in the classical world: we need only be reminded of the way Aristotle explains Plato's thought in the first book of *Metaphysics* as a creative blend of the philosophies of Parmenides, Heraclitus, Socrates, and the Pythagoreans (A6.987a29ff.). Likewise, the idea that a particular doctrine or philosophical statement could be the result of the combination of two or more others was fairly common.[1] But the ancients never

In writing this paper I have been greatly helped by the discussion that followed my first draft, read at the FIEC Congress in Dublin; I would like to thank all those who took part in that debate. I am particularly grateful to the late Professor Paul Moraux, who allowed me to see important parts of his second volume on Greek Aristotelianism before publication; to Jaap Mansfeld, who generously made available to me much valuable material on the history of eclecticism; and to Tony Long. I alone of course am responsible for the interpretation offered here.

1. Cf., e.g., Aristotle *An.* 1.2.405a1, μίξαντες; Philo Alex. *Aet.* 7, μιχτὴ δόξα; *Commenta Lucani*, p. 290 Usener (= *SVF* 2.817), *mixtum*

labeled these two kinds of mixture *eclecticism*. When this term is employed, it has an entirely different meaning: it means a philosophy whose structural character is that of deliberately planning to select some doctrines out of many philosophies and fit them together.

There are, however, only a few known examples of the use of the term in this sense. The most important one is in Diogenes Laertius, who says that "an eclectic school was introduced by Potamo of Alexandria, who made a selection from the tenets of all the existing sects" (1.21, trans. Hicks, Loeb Classical Library), the meaning of the Greek verb *eklegein/eklegesthai* being precisely "to choose, to make a selection." In connection with Diogenes' statement about Potamo it is very interesting to find that an "eclectic philosopher" from Alexandria is mentioned in an inscription from Ephesus which has recently been published.[2] Another instance of the term is provided by the Christian writer Clement of Alexandria: he calls his own ideal of the philosophical method *eklektikon* (*Strom.* 1.37.6). Finally, it should be remarked that Galen twice speaks of a medical school which is called *eklektikē* by some people.[3] Unfortunately, we are not in a position to say whether the name was first given to this medical school and then transferred to Potamo's philosophy or whether the reverse happened.

---

dogma. In Cicero the idea that two notions, sometimes originating from different philosophers, may be combined so as to form a third notion is frequent: e.g., *Fin.* 2.19 (*iungere, coniungere*); cf. *Fin.* 5.21f.

2. The inscription is no. 789 in *Inschriften Griechischer Städte aus Kleinasien.* Vol. 13: *Die Inschriften von Ephesos*, part 3, H. Engelmann, D. Knibbe, and R. Merkelbach, eds. (Bonn, 1980): ἡ βουλὴ [καὶ ὁ δῆμος] | ἐτίμησαν Π [. . . . . . .] | | ’Αλεξανδρέα ἀπὸ [τοῦ Μουσείου] | [φ]ιλόσοφον ἐγκλεκ[τικόν]. I owe this piece of information to Tony Long, whose comments are worth quoting: "I know nothing about the dating of this, but I imagine it is probably early Christian period. The restoration of *eklektikon* looks certain, and the mention of Alexandria is especially interesting, in view of Potamo."

3. Galen 14.684 Kühn, 19.353 Kühn.

If eclecticism has by this date become a relatively technical notion, its origins, in the sense used by Clement—constituting a corpus of theories by selecting from many doctrines—have roots at least as far back as Xenophon. He makes Socrates speak of readings from the works of ancient wise men, "which we select [*eklegometha*] on the basis of whatever we perceive good" in them; and there are other examples of this use of the term.[4] But until the Roman period neither this idea nor the term *eklegein* may yet have established a regular place in philosophy. A fragment of Epicurus's work *On Nature* is particularly interesting, because it seems to contain a distinction between the constructive use of someone else's doctrines and the "confused mixture" of ideas deriving from different sources;[5] but neither here nor in an apparently similar passage of Theophrastus is the verb *eklegein* or any of its derivatives employed.[6] Nor, it seems, is such a distinction familiar to other ancient writers.

4. *Mem.* 1.6.14. Cf. Aristotle *Top.* 1.14.105b12; Galen 19.13 Kühn (= *Scripta min.* 96.5ff. Marq.), Achilles *Is.* 1.3, pp. 31.27ff. Maass (= 7B1a DK). On the other hand, ἐκλέγειν seems to indicate an arbitrary and forced choice of scriptural passages in Irenaeus 1.19.1 (cf. 2 *Praef.*, 2.24.3). Finally, there is an interesting but disputable passage in D.L.8.6 (= 22B129 DK). I owe this reference, as well as many others, to Jaap Mansfeld.

5. Epicur. *Nat.* [29] [28–31], pp. 272–77 Arrighetti, esp. [28] line 8, συμπεφορημένος, and [31] line 2, συμπεφορῆσθαι. The adverb συμπεφορημένως is also found in Theophrastus *Phys. op.* fr. 2, p. 477 Diels (= Diog. Apoll. 64A5 DK).

6. In particular, for "a confused and casual combination" Epicurus uses the perfect tense of the verb συμφορεῖσθαι (cf. previous note). H. Diels in *Dox. Graeci* (in his comment on the Theophrastus passage [previous note]) adopts without hesitation the translation *eclectica ratio* both for Epicurus and for Theophrastus (cf. also his note to the text of Diogenes of Apollonia in DK); and in the "Prolegomena" he remarks that when Potamo founded the "eclectic sect," "he seems to have inaugurated a name, not a thing, since the word συμπεφορημένος was in use previously" (p. 81 n. 4). It seems to me that he does not notice that between συμφορεῖσθαι in Theophrastus and Epicurus and ἐκλέγεσθαι in Potamo there is also a complete change in meaning, from negative to positive; if this is so, it can hardly be said also that the "thing" remains the same. I do not suppose that Potamo and Clement would ever have admitted this.

To sum up, we may say that the very few ancient thinkers who described their own philosophy as "eclecticism" gave a clearly positive meaning to this term, that these authors did not represent schools of major importance, and, finally, that there are traces of a distinction between a good and a bad mixture of doctrines emanating from divergent origins.

When compared with the very limited evidence from antiquity, the many references in modern histories of philosophy to eclecticism or eclectics as typical features of later Greek thought may thus seem excessive. Even more remarkable is the fact that the use of these terms in modern times has not reflected the same point of view, but has undergone many changes from the Renaissance to the present. Nowadays everyone agrees that eclecticism, viewed as a general feature of a stage of ancient thought, was a very bad thing; that philosophy from the end of the second century B.C., or from the first century B.C. to Plotinus, was bad, and that it was bad above all because it was eclectic, is a widespread conviction even among Classical scholars. But few among them seem to be aware that there was a long period in philosophical historiography and in European thought in which eclecticism was nothing less than the ideal toward which philosophy aimed and which was accepted as a model by intellectual historians. In the chief monument of this historiography in the eighteenth century, Jakob Brucker's *Historia critica philosophiae*, one discovers that "the eclectic method of philosophizing, long approved by intelligent men and practiced by philosophers of the greatest ability," produced its greatest works in seventeenth- and eighteenth-century Europe, thanks to the great philosophers who founded modern thought by fighting against sectarian ideas and the principle of authority[7]; so Brucker presents philosophers

7. *Eclectica philosophandi methodus, dudum viris prudentibus commendata et a maximi ingenii philosophis culta: Historia critica philosophiae a mundi incunabulis ad nostram usque aetatem deducta* (Leipzig, 1742–1744). The quotation is from vol. 4, part 1, 190, of the 2d ed. (Leipzig, 1766–1767).

such as Giordano Bruno, Francis Bacon, Campanella, Hobbes, Descartes, Leibniz, and Christian Thomasius as "men who renewed the universal eclectic philosophy."[8] The article *Eclectisme* written by Diderot for the *Encyclopédie* contained a flattering definition of an eclectic which, like most of the article, is in fact derived from, or almost translated from, Brucker.[9]

> The eclectic is a philosopher who, trampling underfoot prejudice, tradition, antiquity, general agreement, authority—in a word, everything that controls the minds of the common herd—dares to think for himself, returns to the clearest general principles, examines them, discusses them, admits nothing that is not based on the testimony of his experience and his reason; and from all the philosophies he has analyzed without respect and bias he makes for himself a particular and domestic one which belongs to him. . . . There is no leader of a sect who has not been more or less eclectic. . . . The Eclectics are among the philosophers who are the kings on the face of the earth, the only ones who have remained in the state of nature, where everything belonged to everyone.
>
> (trans. A. A. Long)

In these authors, so great is the praise of eclecticism as a philosophical attitude opposed to dogmatism, to sectarian ideas, and

---

8. *Restauratores philosophiae eclecticae universae*: ibid., vol. 4, part 2, 3–543.

9. "L'éclectique est un philosophe qui foulant aux piés le préjugé, la tradition, l'ancienneté, le consentement universel, l' autorité, en un mot tout ce qui subjuge la foule des esprits, ose penser de lui-même, remonter aux principes généreux les plus clairs, les examiner, les discuter, n'admettre rien que sur le témoignage de son expérience et de sa raison; et de toutes les philosophies qu'il a analysé sans égard et sans partialité s'en faire une particulière et domestique qui lui appartienne . . . il n'y a point de chef de secte qui n'ait été plus ou moins éclectique . . . les Eclectiques sont parmi les philosophes ce qui sont les souverains sur la surface de la terre, les seuls qui soient restés dans l'état de nature, où tout étoit à tous" (*Encyclopédie*, art. "Eclectisme," vol. 5 [Paris, 1755]). This definition may be compared with *Historia Critica*, vol. 4.2, 4; for Diderot's dependence on Brucker in the philosophical articles of the *Encyclopédie* cf. J. Proust, *Diderot et l'Encyclopédie* (Paris, 1962), esp. 247–84 and 548–55.

to the principle of authority that they state that anyone who becomes a faithful disciple of an eclectic philosophy loses by this very fact the right of being considered eclectic.

Brucker and Diderot were not even innovators; their praise of philosophical eclecticism was the result of long studies and positive evaluation of the concept of eclecticism which began to develop in Europe from the late Renaissance. Some works on the history of philosophical historiography which have appeared recently in France and Italy[10] enable us to follow fairly clearly the development and the growing popularity of this concept between the sixteenth and the eighteenth century; this popularity is not necessarily linked with that of the philosophy of the Enlightenment, as is seen in the works of Italian historians of the first part of the eighteenth century. There we even find eclecticism being praised for apologetic purposes, and specifically to further Catholic apologetics.[11] Even the Catholic opponents of the *Encyclopédie* thought that a positive and Christian interpretation of eclecticism was possible.[12] It seems therefore reasonable to conjecture that in all these cases the greatest influence was the tradition of Christian eclecticism as it had been specified by Clement of Alexandria.[13] In any case, in Brucker himself religious problems have decisive importance; the quarrel against dogmatism is aimed only against Catholicism and is strongly influenced by Protestant theology.

10. L. Braun, *Histoire de l'histoire de la philosophie* (Paris, 1973); G. Santinello, ed., *Storia delle storie generali della filosofia*. Vol. 1: *Dalle origini rinascimentali alla "historia philosophica"* (Brescia, 1981); Vol. 2: *Dall'età cartesiana a Brucker* (Brescia, 1979).

11. E.g., in Giambattista Capasso, author of a *Historiae philosophiae synopsis* (Naples, 1728), on which cf. Santinello, ed. (n. 10 above), vol. 2, 306ff., esp. 308–9.

12. Proust (n. 9 above), 257f.

13. At least Edoardo Corsini (author of a *Historiae philosophicae synopsis* included in the massive *Institutiones philosophicae ac mathematicae* [Florence, 1731–37]) explicitly looks back to him; cf. Santinello, ed. (n. 10 above), vol. 2, 323.

But for historians of ancient thought it may be particularly interesting to note that in Brucker and Diderot the high estimate of eclectic philosophy was not at all connected with a similar evaluation of ancient eclecticism. *This* eclecticism, they said, had been professed by Alexandrian Platonists, starting with Ammonius Saccas and Plotinus, i.e., by those whom we now call Neoplatonists. (The link between Ammonius and Potamo, who was the only person ancient tradition undeniably called an eclectic, was, besides, very difficult to prove.)[14] But the Platonic eclectics of Alexandria had not really been eclectics, for it could not be denied that they had formed a real sect. Moreover, instead of choosing the best doctrines and seeking the truth, they had, rather, aimed to *reconcile* widely different opinions and had succeeded only in producing a "heap" (*massa*), a "largely shapeless mass" (*chaos magnam partem informe*).[15] They therefore deserved to be called *syncretistae*, syncretists, far more than eclectics. Ancient philosophy, then, had produced the name rather than the practice of eclecticism. And antiquity had known only the "plague" of syncretism,[16] that "diseased reconciliation of doctrines and opinions which are utterly discrepant" (*malesana dogmatum et sententiarum toto caelo inter se dissidentium conciliatio*) which later on afflicted modern philosophy as well in various ways. Even in determining the only feature of the Alexandrians that could still be considered really eclectic (namely, the unwillingness to follow blindly the authority of a master), Brucker was able to repeat his very unfavorable judgment of their philoso-

14. The difficulty was largely due to the existence of the name of one Ποτάμων in Porphyry *Vita Plot.* 9 (however, after Wyttenbach many editors print Πολέμων). See the discussions in Brucker (n. 7 above), vol. 2, pp. 193–203 and Diderot, "Eclectisme," 273b–274a of the *Encyclopédie* (n. 9 above).

15. Brucker (n. 7 above), vol. 2, 190; cf. 362 *rectius Henotici vel Syncretistae dici meruissent*. Brucker derived the name *syncretism* from Plutarch *De frat. am.* 490B, although he knew very well that in antiquity the term had not had this meaning. Cf. vol. 4, part 1, 750.

16. Ibid., vol. 4, part 1, 750.

phy.[17] Diderot was perhaps only slightly less harsh in his general remarks on syncretism.[18] But the total judgment which historians in the period of the Enlightenment passed on eclectic philosophy in antiquity remained very unfavorable; and it determined the outlook of later historians.

However, in the last decades of the eighteenth century, while the popularity of the *Historia critica* in Europe continued, the change of philosophical outlook in Germany prepared the way for a radical change in the evaluation of eclecticism. After Kant, eclecticism could no longer be a philosophical or historiographical ideal.[19] At the end of the century the negative opinion on ancient eclectic philosophy, which had already been sanctioned by the Age of Enlightenment, was thus reconciled with the recent depreciation of the very concept of eclecticism: a discredited name could now without difficulty be given to a bad philosophy. This situation lasted throughout the nineteenth century, almost without exceptions.[20] In particular, it is presupposed by E. Zeller's *Philosophie der Griechen*, the work that was to influence most deeply the whole trend of subsequent studies of ancient thought.[21]

In order to discuss Zeller's views with some accuracy we ought

17. "In this respect alone something eclectic is found in them—that none of them has so taken an oath to his master as to refrain from rubbing off his own intellectual fancies and nonsense on a new system, and thus adding new discoveries to a senseless kind of philosophy" (*In hoc tamen uno eclecticum quid in iis deprehenditur, quod nullus inter eos ita in magistri verba iuraverit, ut non propria ingenii commenta nugasque novo affricaret systemati, sicque ineptum philosophiae genus novis inventis adaugeret*): ibid., vol. 2, 190.

18. "Syncretism is at most an apprenticeship of eclecticism" ("Le syncrétisme est tout au plus un apprentissage de l'éclectisme"): Diderot (n. 9 above), vol. 5, 271a.

19. On the changes in German philosophy and historiography, cf. Braun (n. 10 above), 159ff., 205ff., and esp. 222 ("refus définitif de l'éclectisme").

20. The most notable exception is probably Victor Cousin's "eclectic" philosophy.

21. *Die Philosophie der Griechen in ihrer geschichtlichen Entwicklung*, 3.1, 4th ed., rev. E. Wellmann (Leipzig, 1909), 547–64.

also to consider other developments which had taken place in the meantime in philosophical historiography. One was the popularity of the term *Neoplatonism* and the distinction between the Neoplatonic school and eclecticism. (Thus in Zeller Neoplatonism was no longer eclecticism, although somehow eclecticism had prepared the way for it.) Another development was that, while being impoverished by separation from the independent philosophical tradition of Neoplatonism, eclecticism in a looser sense expanded and came to stand for a general feature of philosophical thought from the end of the second, or from the first, century B.C. up to Plotinus. It is obviously impossible to explain in detail all this change as well, but anyone who reads Zeller's account of the general features of eclecticism can have no doubts about his strongly unfavorable judgment. We find a great number of expressions such as "the dying out of a scientific outlook," "scientific decline," "a merely exterior connection between different positions," and "uncritical philosophizing." It is tempting to say that Zeller calls eclecticism what Brucker called syncretism, yet the meaning of the judgment remains exactly the same. It is striking, however, that Zeller does not even attempt to define philosophical eclecticism exactly; he seems to assume that its existence, as well as the scope of the concept, is obvious. Yet when Zeller uses the term *eclecticism* as a huge generalization, making no attempt to establish a precise link with the only ancient philosophical tradition for which the name is attested, he may well seem guilty of carelessness. But the worst is to come.

Instead of providing a definition of eclecticism, Zeller preferred to give two principal explanations of the origin of the phenomenon, in a section with the significant title "Origin and Character of Eclecticism" ("Entstehungsgründe und Charakter des Eklekticismus"). One reason was intrinsic to the development of Greek philosophy; the other he derived from the general historical situation. According to Zeller, the intrinsic reason was the protracted debate among the philosophical schools. It is extremely important to note here that the only ones concerned are the three great Hellenistic schools, Stoicism, Epicureanism, and Academic Skepticism. Though Zeller never stated this presupposition fully or even explicitly,[22] the subsequent parts of his discussion make it quite obvious. The "very nature of things" (these or similar words occur frequently in the chapter in question, with eclecticism appearing in the end as the logical result of a natural process) entails this consequence: as the debate dies out between the founders and upholders of different systems, each of whom was eager to stress his own point of view and to underline divergences from other schools, and as quarrels abate, those points that the different doctrines have in common emerge; all the more so, since these doctrines had originated from a common ground. (This is an unmistakable hint of the origin of eclecticism from the three great Hellenistic philosophies.) Once this happens, the typical refusal of the Skeptics ("neither this nor that") changes into the eclectic reconciliation of different positions: "both this and that."

Several points in this reconstruction cause misgivings. In the first place Zeller stresses the role of Academic Skepticism as really paving the way for eclecticism and believes that the idea of "immediate knowledge," which is the fundamental principle of eclecticism, goes back to skeptical attitudes. He therefore believes that it was "not at all accidental" that it was precisely "the successors of Carneades" who were the chief source from which eclectic attitudes developed.[23] It is clear, however, that he consid-

22. Cf., however, the beginning of the chapter: "That form of philosophy which appeared about the beginning of our period had, in the course of the third and second centuries, perfected itself in its *three* principal branches. These *three* schools had hitherto existed side by side" (trans. S. F. Alleyne of *Zeller's Eclectics* [London, 1883], 1 [my italics]; cf. also Zeller [n. 21 above], 550).

23. Of course, the "Prinzip des unmittelbaren Wissens" also had for Zeller "a very limited value," because in questions of philosophy it allowed "immediate," though not "philosophical," knowledge to have the last word; moreover, such knowledge could appear "immediate" precisely because a clear scientific knowledge was lacking. Therefore "this return to the directly

ers some Stoics who go as far back as the second century B.C., such as Boethus and Panaetius, to be eclectics, and one therefore wonders how these men, who can hardly be included among Carneades' successors, could have become eclectics. But Zeller's theory has an even more objectionable limitation in that it attempts to trace the origins of eclecticism solely to the interaction among the three major Hellenistic philosophies. This theory would have point only if so-called eclecticism had been a contact between and a mixture of the doctrines of the Stoic, Epicurean, and Academic schools. But it is well known that events turned out quite differently. Epicureanism remained almost completely free from external influences, and it did not influence in an eclectic manner any important thinker (with the exception of Seneca, who was a completely peculiar and isolated instance). Moreover—and this is the most important point—we do not know of a single instance of a mixture only of Stoic, Epicurean, and Academic positions. From the time of Zeller himself, in fact, eclecticism is a completely different phenomenon from the one postulated in this theory. It is, rather, the contact and mutual interaction between the Hellenistic philosophies, particularly Stoicism, and three other philosophies which went back to a previous age and indeed had undergone a considerable decline in the Hellenistic period: dogmatic Platonism, Aristotelianism, and Pythagoreanism. Zeller's theory has no explanation to offer for this renewal of philosophies whose origin was earlier than the Hellenistic age, for the contact between them and their reaction to Stoicism—in short, for everything that actually happened between Panaetius and Alexander of Aphrodisias.

Equally questionable is the second reason adduced by Zeller, the external cause. In his view this was the influence of the Roman frame of mind, whose typical feature was a highly practical

certain is so far to be regarded primarily as a sign of scientific decay, an involuntary evidence of the exhaustion of thought": Zeller (n. 22 above), 19. For the "successors of Carneades," see Zeller (n. 21 above), 550.

and moral outlook. (This view of the Roman frame of mind seems to be one of the most successful *fables convenues* in Classical studies.) If such influence had really existed and had had a really decisive effect on philosophy, eclecticism would necessarily have turned out to be a sort of moralizing Stoic-Skeptical-Epicurean *lingua franca*. In fact it is well known that precisely in the Roman period, philosophies with metaphysical interests or foundations, such as Platonism, Aristotelianism, and Pythagoreanism, emerged again and helped to create a new vision of the world in which metaphysics had an ever-growing role. It is also well known that precisely in that period the pre-Hellenistic ideal of pure speculation (*theōria*) reappeared and became widespread. (It is remarkable that one of the first vigorous confirmations of this ideal is found in the Roman, Seneca.) Thus Zeller's theory on the origin and nature of eclecticism is a typical example of *a priori* argument; it explains wonderfully what never happened, while leaving what actually happened totally unexplained. The time has come to think again about the real problem: the sudden reappearance, almost at the same time, of dogmatic Platonism and Aristotelianism, as well as Pythagoreanism, and the interaction of these three philosophies with Hellenistic philosophy, especially Stoicism.

It has not been pleasant to criticize a historian to whom every student of ancient thought is still enormously indebted. Nevertheless, this was necessary. Zeller was chiefly responsible for disseminating a negative and unfavorable concept of eclecticism which until a few years ago almost completely prevailed in the study of ancient philosophy.[24] No one who used this concept

---

24. There is certainly no need to prove this fact—which every scholar knows—with a long list of titles. I remark only that the obviously negative connotation the term has today becomes particularly manifest when it is used to depreciate the thought of a philosopher whose activity does not take place within the chronological limits assigned to the age of eclecticism: thus, e.g., according to F. Wehrli *eclecticism* sums up the inferiority of the philosophy of Strato of Lampsacus (*Die Schule des Aristoteles*, vol. 10, 2d ed. [Stuttgart, 1969], 101).

after Zeller reexamined its theoretical foundations, and no one noticed that it was unable to keep close to the actual evidence. This, however, does not mean that things have not changed at all from Zeller's time to the present day. Some developments in subsequent studies in the long run weakened the foundations of Zeller's theory.

The point that seems to have caused most dissatisfaction among scholars was the excessively generic nature of the concept of eclecticism, its application without distinction to several centuries of the history of thought. It soon became clear that undifferentiated eclecticism ignored the many differences between thinkers in the period from Panaetius to Plotinus. Further distinctions were therefore devised to do justice to these.

There is not much to say on the attempt made by some scholars to put forward again the old distinction between eclecticism and syncretism. According to the definition given by the most explicit upholder of this distinction,[25] syncretism is only "the superficial and unauthentic agreement of the heterogeneous and disparate elements whose irreducible differences are blurred"; eclecticism, according to him, shows a greater degree of conceptual accuracy, since it is "the reunion by juxtaposition of reconcilable philosophical theses. The eclectic chooses, makes a selection," even though he still lacks a synthetic and organizing point of view that can create a unity which is more than a mere juxtaposition. As one can see, however, this is not exactly Brucker's or Diderot's distinction. Not even the term eclecticism has a fully positive meaning here: it betokens a degree of confusion and superficiality that is only slightly lower than that of syncretism. Nor does the distinction reflect the substance of the text of Epicurus mentioned above (p. 17). But the absence of ancient supporting evidence is not its greatest fault. Basically it errs in being completely divorced from the intentions of the ancient authors

25. P. Thévenaz, "De la philosophie divine à la philosophie chrétienne," *Rév. de Théologie et de Philosophie* 3, 1 (1951), 4–20. The quotations in the text come from p. 10 n. 1 and p. 13, respectively.

and in relying completely on the intuitions of modern interpreters, who in each instance have to decide whether a given philosopher should be included among eclectics or be confined to the shameful circle of syncretists. Finally, the distinction has the weakness of not being generally accepted by historians of philosophy; the word *syncretism* is largely used now as a technical term in the history of religion, and, above all, ancient religions;[26] when it is still used in the history of philosophy it seems on the whole not to differ from *eclecticism*.[27]

The distinction between eclectic and orthodox philosophers, which Karl Praechter invented,[28] was far more widespread. According to this point of view those philosophers could be considered orthodox who strove to remain loyal to an original core of doctrines held to be essential to, and typical of, the school from which they drew their name, and who in many cases were hostile to the intrusion of alien doctrines. Those who had no such concern and were open to extraneous influences were eclectic. A considerable advantage of this distinction was its applicability to all philosophical schools: thus among Platonists, Atticus and Taurus were typically orthodox, whereas "Albinus" and Apuleius were definitely eclectic; among Stoics, Epictetus was orthodox, while Seneca was absolutely eclectic and Marcus Aurelius was eclectic to a lesser extent; among Aristotelians, Alexander was orthodox and contrasted with the eclectic Aristocles.

Clarity and the ease with which it could be applied are doubtless qualities in favor of Praechter's classification. Yet in this case

26. Cf. M. Nilsson, *Geschichte der griechischen Religion* (Munich, 1950), 555.

27. This may be seen, e.g., in Ph. Merlan's use of the two terms in *The Cambridge History of Later Greek and Early Medieval Philosophy*, ed. A. H. Armstrong (Cambridge, England, 1967), 13–132, esp. 53, 63ff., 73, 84. In Merlan it is also clear that the two terms have in themselves neither a positive nor a negative meaning: they simply express a fact.

28. *Die Philosophie des Altertums*, 13th ed. (Graz, 1953), 32f., 487, 524f., 557.

too the defects in the end turn out to be greater than the virtues. The absence of any recognition of just this distinction from Classical philosophy is not particularly serious; one could say that when Atticus rejects Aristotelian doctrines he in fact contrasts his own orthodox Platonism with his opponents' eclectic interpretation. But such a suggestion could not be the basis for a reasonable classification of all Platonists (or of all the philosophers of the other schools) under the two headings of eclectic and orthodox. What good reasons are there for accepting Atticus as the standard of Platonic orthodoxy? By treating him as such (as Praechter did), we would simply adopt in an uncritical manner his own point of view, without taking into account the fact that Atticus himself was considered by later Platonists to have been a philosopher who had abandoned the school's tradition.[29] We would also be guilty of serious injustice to the intentions of the other side. Most so-called eclectics were honestly persuaded that they were loyal to the school's tradition;[30] on the other hand, even so-called orthodox philosophers were often exposed to external influences whose importance was underestimated by Praechter and his followers.

For these reasons Praechter's distinction appears today less and less convincing, and several suggestions for correcting the worst faults of the previous approaches are now available.[31] The

29. This was a typical (and, in my opinion, very good) argument of H. Dörrie's; cf., e.g., "Die Platonische Theologie des Kelsos in ihrer Auseinandersetzung mit der Christlichen Theologie, auf Grund von Origenes c. Celsum 7.42ff.," *Nachr. d. Akad. Göttingen*, no. 2 (1967), 19ff. and esp. 53 n. 1 (now in *Platonica minora* [Munich, 1976], 229ff.).

30. This is the argument of C. Moreschini in his essay "La posizione di Apuleio e della scuola di Gaio nell'ambito del medioplatonismo," *Annali della scuola normale superiore di Pisa* 33 (1964), 17–56 (reprinted in *Apuleio e il platonismo* [Florence, 1979]). The argument is taken up and developed by P. Moraux, *Der Aristotelismus bei den Griechen*. Vol. 2: *Der Aristotelismus in I und II Jh. n. Chr.* (Berlin, 1984), xxi–xxvii, 432ff., 447.

31. Thus, e.g., Moreschini (n. 30 above) suggests a distinction within Middle Platonism between more rationalistic philosophers and others who were more religious. (A short review of the opinions that have been ex-

most recent is also the one that has been most carefully thought out. In his introduction to the second volume of his monumental work on Greek Aristotelianism, Paul Moraux proposes a distinction between de facto orthodoxy and intentional orthodoxy: the latter would then also apply to nearly all the philosophers who are traditionally considered eclectic, such as "Albinus," insofar as they at least appear sincerely convinced that they are presenting the genuine version of their school's doctrine, even when they insert elements of different origins. Moraux, however, makes it important to show that external elements are accepted only when they are considered useful in clarifying, completing, or defending the doctrine of the school. Examples of this are the acceptance by Aristotle of Mytilene of Stoic doctrines and of Aristotelian ones by "Albinus." Similarly, Moraux seems to achieve a more precise definition of the concept of eclecticism. Although he continues to speak of "undeniable" or "effective" eclecticism[32] with regard to authors who accept doctrines not belonging to their own schools, he is careful to distinguish this eclecticism, which may very easily be reconciled with full and loyal membership in a philosophical school, from Galen's eclecticism stated as a guiding principle: the latter consists in a refusal to belong to any previously established system, either of philosophy or medicine, and has nothing to do with "a more or less casual and arbitrary combination of elements coming from different sources." "Galen's choice ... is seen as always having scientific foundations. Galen's eclecticism is the immediate result of his strict scientific ideal." Other scholars in recent times have already noted Galen's quite special position.[33] Thus a fully positive and honorable sense of eclecticism has reappeared in the history of philosophy.

---

pressed in recent years may be seen in my book *Le scuole l'anima l'impero: la filosofia antica da Antioco a Plotino* [Turin, 1982], 20–22.) Moraux's remarks summarized in the text below are found on xxi–xxvii, 429–34, and 447; on Galen see xxii, 433, and 687–808 in general.

32. "Unleugbarer Eklektizismus," p. xxiv; "tatsächlicher," xxvii.

33. Cf. especially the study of M. Frede, "On Galen's Epistemology," in V. Nutton, ed., *Galen: Problems and Prospects* (London, 1981), 65–86.

This review shows that the term *eclecticism* has been used by modern historians (after Zeller) to indicate different philosophical attitudes with a number of different senses. Let us try to enumerate these for the sake of clarity.

1. There is first of all the negative meaning of the term, originating chiefly from Zeller and denoting a combination of heterogeneous elements that is substantially uncritical and more or less deliberate. In this sense the term has undergone a strong decline in recent years. (In the sense employed by Praechter, involving the antithesis between eclecticism and orthodoxy, the term is indeed dying out.) The more penetrating the interpretation of individual authors once contemptuously defined as eclectic becomes, the more inadequate this sense of eclecticism appears. After the most recent studies it seems very difficult to dismiss and condemn as eclectic authors such as Arius Didymus, Plutarch and the Middle Platonists in general, or even, I should like to add, Seneca.[34]

2. The term may be used as a statement of fact, without any positive or negative implications: it simply states that the doctrine of a philosophical school is combined in an author's thought with elements of a different origin.

3. *Eclecticism* is also defined as the more or less arbitrary attitude of authors who accept into the doctrine of their own school extraneous elements because they are honestly convinced that these are compatible with, and indeed helpful in explaining or defending, their own doctrine.

4. The eclectic attitude of Potamo and Clement, which is completely deliberate and stated at the outset, can obviously continue to be described as eclecticism.

5. More recent discussions indicate, however, that this attitude must be distinguished from another one, which chooses among doctrines with the same deliberate program but whose spirit is strongly anti-dogmatic and anti-sectarian. The typical example is Galen.

34. See the bibliography in Donini (n. 31 above).

6. Finally, although it has not yet been mentioned, there is a sixth attitude, which must be distinguished as absolutely different from all previous ones and which is often called eclectic. It is the posture of Antiochus of Ascalon, who tried to prove the basic agreement between Platonism, Aristotelianism, and Stoicism and tended to make these three schools coincide and form a single common doctrine. Now even if the results obtained by Antiochus may seem similar to those of eclecticism of types (1) and (3), his point of departure is completely idiosyncratic. Was there anyone who really adopted it after him? Platonists open to Aristotelian influence may in a certain sense be considered his heirs. But who among them was equally open to Stoicism as well? To conclude, it seems that Antiochus's position is indeed very personal, and it is better to consider it sui generis.

So we have available today no fewer than six different interpretations of the concept of eclecticism: this may cause some dizziness. Other interpretations are perhaps possible and may have escaped me; others will probably be suggested by this book. If, however, I may be allowed to state what lesson I think I have learned from the account just given, my impression is that it is now wise to use great caution in applying such an ambiguous term. The history of the discussion seems to produce an exhortation to employ the term sparingly: in fact, as was said above, sense (1) is already disappearing, and according to some scholars, sense (6), namely Antiochus, has in fact nothing to do with eclecticism.[35] A further widening of senses (4) and (5) seems difficult in the light of the warning, often proclaimed in recent years,[36] that eclecticism as a deliberate plan was a rare and un-

35. E.g., O. Gigon, "Eklektizismus," in *Lexikon der alten Welt* (Zürich, 1965). E. Bréhier, an author who was well aware of the history of terms and concepts, as is shown by the *Introduction* to the *Histoire de la philosophie*, vol. 1.1, 8th ed. (Paris, 1963), 17f., carefully refrained from defining Antiochus as an eclectic and preferred to speak of his philosophy as a "dogmatisme syncrétiste" (vol. 1.2, 364).

36. Cf. A.H. Armstrong, *An Introduction to Ancient Philosophy*, 3d. ed.

usual position in antiquity and essentially foreign to the traditions and philosophical customs of the Hellenistic and Roman ages, where the desire to look back to a well-defined school or tradition is always evident. In fact Potamo and Clement had no followers in pagan philosophy. As for Galen's anti-dogmatic eclecticism, it is difficult to find even one ancient philosopher who reproduces his features exactly. Perhaps Seneca alone might be compared with him on account of his critical attention to themes of contemporary Platonism and Epicureanism and his frequent claims of intellectual freedom and independence; but in fact he remains different. In my judgment there is either no eclecticism in Seneca or there is a hint of a further widening of the meaning of the term.[37]

It seems therefore that only senses (2) and (3) may be effectively and widely applied. However, the former of these is also open to objections. While it is true that it seems rather harmless and comfortable, perhaps it is innocent only because it has not much capacity to explain things: it registers the facts but does not make their qualities and causes clear. When we acknowledge that a doctrine is composite, we can hardly avoid asking ourselves *how* and *why* it was put together. We shall then inevitably be compelled to answer the question by changing our innocent eclecticism into another one, for the most part belonging to sense (1) or (3).

(London, 1957), 142 (of the 1969 reprint); also Moraux (n. 30 above), xxv–xxvii.

37. The essential difference lies, in my view, in the fact that Galen is guided by a clear scientific ideal, whereas Seneca never accepts Stoicism or any other idea, philosophical or otherwise, as a firm criterion for judgment.

JOHN GLUCKER

2

Cicero's philosophical affiliations

CICERO AND THE PHILOSOPHICAL
SCHOOLS OF HIS AGE

Let us start with *affiliations*. I have chosen the term quite deliberately. Another contender, *allegiance*, is medieval and feudal and
involves no free choice. *Affiliation*, also medieval and feudal in
origin, is derived from Latin *filius* and may remind us of *filius-
familias*—but it does denote, in our modern languages, a free
adoption into a society of a member who is thereafter free to end
his membership or "change his affiliation."

This is no mere wordplay. In a famous passage, Seneca (*NQ*
7.32.2) writes: "Therefore so many communities [*familiae*] of
philosophers have perished without a successor," and he specifies: "Academics both older and younger [*et veteres et minores*],
Pyrrhonians, Pythagoreans, Sextians." Cicero himself (*ND* 1.11),
writing in August of 45 B.C., long after the demise of the Acad-

This is a shortened and edited version of the paper as originally drafted. In
my original version fuller quotations were supplied and all quotations were
in the original Greek and Latin. A section on *probo, probare*, their Latin
cognates and Greek counterparts, was omitted as too technical for this
volume.

emy as an institution,[1] has a similar "familial" expression: "which [Academy] I understand in Greece itself is practically bereft [*orbam*]." Abandoning one philosophical school for another is "moving back into an old house from a new one" (Cicero *Acad.* 1.13). A claim to be heir to the traditions of the Academy is called "living off [*depasci*] the ancient estate of the Academy" (Cicero *Leg.* 1.55).[2]

Philosophy, then, is no mere assemblage of people: rather, it is a community made up of communities; and the label of a school is of far greater importance than purity of doctrine or degree of eclecticism. Antiochus, in his final incarnation, was Stoic in his epistemology[3] and a Peripatetic of sorts in his ethics. For the modern historian, he is an eclectic (or Eclectic). For Cicero? ... "He was called an Academic, but was in fact, if he had made a very few changes, the purest Stoic" (*Luc.* 132).[4] The first of the "eclectic" philosophers—as modern scholars have commonly viewed them—Panaetius was "a lover of Plato and Aristotle" (fr. 57 Van Straaten), who "was always ready with a quotation from Plato, Aristotle, Xenocrates, Theophrastus, or Dicaearchus" (Cicero *Fin.* 4.79). Yet he was elected head of the Stoic school in Athens, and probably justified his Academic and Peripatetic borrowings by claiming a Socratic and Platonic descent for the early Stoa.[5] The term *eklektikos* does not seem to

1. See my *Antiochus and the Late Academy* (Göttingen, 1978) (henceforth referred to as *Antiochus*), passim, esp. chap. 8, 330–79.

2. Although Plato and his successors never possessed the grounds of the Academy, which was a piece of public property; cf. *Antiochus*, chap. 5, 226–55.

3. Cicero *Acad.* 1.35–43, esp. 43, where Antiochus calls the Stoic adoption of sense-perception as the criterion of truth a mere "correction of the Old Academy." On Panaetius as the possible source of this view, see *Antiochus*, 28–30.

4. By *Luc.* I refer in this chapter to Cicero's *Lucullus*, the title of the second of Cicero's Academic books, surviving only in its first version and commonly referred to as *Acad(emica)* 2 or *Academica priora*—both titles being inventions of modern editors.

5. On all this, see *Antiochus*, 28–30 again.

be used before Galen, or much after him;[6] and even Galen is at least as interested in explaining how people become affiliated to the more definable "sects" (*haireseis*).[7] Potamo of Alexandria is the only one described as representing both—an *eklektikē hairesis* (*Suda* s.v. *Potamon*, 2126 Adler; Diogenes Laertius 1.21).[8] If, as the *Oxford Classical Dictionary* tells us, he was the "founder of the Eclectic School," we hear nothing of the subsequent fortunes of that "school."[9]

Even when the old institutions begin to disintegrate, one does not cease to claim affiliation to their traditions and to belong to a *hairesis*, *secta*, or *disciplina*.[10] Cicero, who stands on the dividing line between the Academy as a school and Academic Skepticism as a "school of thought," justifies his support for it as for an apparently "deserted and derelict school," whose doctrines, however, have not ceased to exist with the demise of their exponents (*ND* 1.11). A century later, one can already be a Stoic, Epicurean, or Platonist anywhere in the Empire, belonging to no institution;[11] and Marcus Aurelius's chairs of philosophy in Athens are instituted in the four major "sects." But affiliation to one of these "sects" remains a crucial matter of philosophical identity throughout the ancient world. One can no more be a "mere" philosopher than call oneself, in our modern world, a "mere" Christian; and the chairs of Platonic, Stoic, or Epicurean philosophy are not unlike the chairs of Catholic, Evangelical, or Jewish theology in modern universities.[12]

Affiliations change, of course, in philosophy just as in politics,

6. Cf. Donini, Chapter 1 above.
7. *Antiochus*, pp. 188–91; cf. Galen *Sect. intr.*, 65 Kühn.
8. On Potamo see Long, Chapter 7 below.
9. The error, of course, is based on interpreting *hairesis* as a "school" in the institutional sense: see *Antiochus*, chap. 4, 159–225.
10. *Antiochus*, 98–120.
11. *Antiochus*, chap. 4, 159–220.
12. Although there was no "University of Athens"—only endowed, but separate, chairs in the various philosophies and in rhetoric; see *Antiochus*, 147ff.

albeit not so often.[13] Arcesilaus, at first a pupil of Theophrastus, was lured away into the Academy by his friend Crantor (Diogenes Laertius 4.29–30). Antiochus changed his affiliation, as I believe, twice;[14] and his pupils Dio and Aristo defected to the Peripatos.[15] What happened in Greece could—and did—happen in its cultural province, Rome. Cicero's famous letter to Trebatius Testa of February of 53 B.C. (*Fam.* 7.12) begins with the words: "I'm wondering why it is that you have stopped sending me letters. My friend Pansa has informed me that you have turned Epicurean."[16] The rest of the letter, despite its jocular style,[17] draws serious conclusions from this "conversion" as to the conduct of Trebatius's private and public life. The Epicurean injunction not to engage in politics was seriously followed by Atticus himself most of his life. By adopting an Epicurean affiliation, Trebatius was bound to change his whole outlook and conduct just like any Greek follower of a philosophical sect.

What, then, of Cicero himself? Modern scholarship tends either to emphasize his continuous loyalty to Academic Skepticism and its last representative, his teacher Philo of Larissa, or to dwell on his "eclectic" inconsistency, especially in the field of

13. The reason is probably that there were no fixed political parties in the ancient world, whereas the philosophical schools and sects had a more permanent tradition.

14. The crucial text is Cicero *Luc.* 69–71. For Antiochus's early apprenticeship in the Stoic school of Mnesarchus and Dardanus, cf. *Antiochus*, 28–30, esp. 28 n. 52.

15. *Antiochus*, 95–96.

16. This, although I have not seen it noticed by commentators, is probably the first joke in this letter. An Epicurean, "who measures everything by his own pleasure," no longer feels obliged to answer letters. This is of course a travesty of Epicurean egoism, forgetting their idea of friendship and Atticus's untiring correspondence with Cicero.

17. For a convincing argument that the report itself is not a joke (as had been maintained by C. Sonnet), but is based on a fact, see A. Momigliano, review of B. Farrington's *Science and Politics in the Ancient World*, *JRS* 31 (1941), 149–57, esp. 152.

ethics.[18] But despite such slight deviations, and with a few honorable exceptions to which we shall soon return, Cicero's lifelong

18. I shall only provide a selective doxography. E. Zeller, *Philos. d. Gr.*[2],
vol. 2.1 (Leipzig, 1865), 574, treats Cicero as an adherent of the New Academy from the time when he was first introduced to it by Philo and regards
his position as "only in general an eclecticism founded on skepticism," on
577 (unchanged in the 5th, most recent, edition revised by Wellmann [Leip-
zig, 1923], 672, 675). F. Ueberweg, *Grundriss d. Gesch. d. Philos.*, vol. 1 (Berlin, 1863), 149: Cicero is an eclectic, tends toward the skepticism of the New
Academy, but incorporates Stoic elements in his ethics; see also 152. (The
same passages are reproduced, with slight variations, in the revised edition
by M. Heinze [Berlin, 1894], 305, 309.) Ueberweg-Praechter of 1926, 465,
repeats the same eclectic recipe but begins with the words: "The new Academy was embraced by . . . Cicero and Varro" (and speaks of Varro, the pupil
of Antiochus, whom he represents in Cicero's *Academici*, and of Posidonius,
as a "new Academic"!). W.S. Teuffel, *Gesch. d. röm. Lit.*, 6th ed. by W. Kroll
and F. Skutsch (Leipzig, 1916), 401: Cicero is an eclectic, and even the Academic Skepticism, "which he often embraced," is something he had learned
in its milder form from Philo, not to mention Antiochus's influence. W. Win-
delband, *Gesch. d. abendl. Philos. im Altertum*, 4th ed. (Munich, 1923), 256–
57: Cicero counted himself as an Academic Skeptic but was influenced
mainly by Philo. R. Philippson, *RE* 7A1 (*M. Tullius Cicero, philosophische
Schriften*), col. 1181: "One thing remains firm, that from his early writings
onward he always embraced the Skepticism of the new Academy"; cf. also
col. 1175. K. Büchner, *Cicero* (Heidelberg, 1964), 41: "Cicero maintained
allegiance to Philo and the Skeptical Academy throughout his entire life,
even when he seemed to incline to other directions. The evidence for this is
the . . . Academica" (which, presumably, were written by Cicero "throughout his entire life"!). E.J. Kenney and W.V. Clausen, eds., *The Cambridge
History of Classical Literature*, vol. 2, Latin Literature (Cambridge, England,
1982), chap. 11, "Cicero," by L.P. Wilkinson, 230: "Philo of Larissa, head
of the 'New' Academy, visited[!] Rome and it made a deep impression on
him. . . . So when Cicero, later, visited Athens to study he chose to join the
Academy[!]." In a footnote, we are told that the Academy, "now under Antiochus of Ascalon, . . . had become eclectic . . . but Cicero remains true to
Philo's undogmatic spirit of discussion." I find it invidious but necessary to
remark that *Antiochus* had been available since 1978. A.A. Long, *Hellenistic
Philosophy* (London, 1974), 230, describes Cicero as "professing to be an
adherent of the moderate skepticism of Philo of Larissa"; but his section
(229–31) deals exclusively with Cicero's later philosophical writings. Not so
Walter Burkert, in his classic article "Cicero als Platoniker und Skeptiker,"
Gymnasium 72 (1965), 175–200, esp. 181, where he maintains that Cicero

loyalty to Philo and Skepticism is taken for granted. The reason is not far to seek.[19] As a contemporary scholar who is well aware of the importance of affiliations reminds us, we find declarations of allegiance to the Skeptical Academy both in Cicero's earliest theoretical work, *De inventione*, written about 81 B.C., and in his last work, *De officiis* (2.7–8), written in the last few months of his life.[20]

The passage in *De inventione* is sharp and clear. One identifies in it immediately such Academic Skeptical terms as *affirmatio* (*apophasis*), *quaerentes dubitanter* (*skeptomenoi*), and *assentior* (*sunkatatithemai*), and its last sentence is a strong promise of lifelong allegiance. But promises—in philosophy just as much as in religion or politics—are often made to be broken. In 81 or 80 B.C., when he wrote *De inventione*,[21] Cicero was young, relatively unknown, and still under the strong and fresh influence of Philo of Larissa. A year or two later, in 79, he studied in Athens itself under Antiochus. His subsequent career, especially after his prosecution of Verres in 70 and his consulate in 63, turned him into

---

opted decisively for Philo's brand of Academic Skepticism from his first encounter with philosophy, embracing it in *De inv.* and repeating this allegiance in almost all his philosophical writings. And on 182: "Yet he remained loyal to Philo, although he thereby stood alone in Rome." It may not be accidental that he quotes *ND* 1.6 as *desertae disciplinae et iam pridem relictae patrocinium esse susceptum*, omitting not only *a nobis*, but also the awkward *necopinatum*. See also n. 20 below. (The quotations from works in German have been translated into English by A. A. Long.)

19. One partial exception is M. Schanz and C. Hosius, *Gesch. d. röm. Literatur*[4] (Munich, 1927), 528: "The New Academy, of which he was an adherent not without fluctuations and deviations...." But when we come to the evidence for this on the following page, we find only references to Cicero's allegiance to the Skeptical Academy from his late writings.

20. Alfons Weische, *Cicero und die neue Akademie* (Münster, 1961; repr. 1975), 9 and n. 23. This is repeated by P. L. Schmidt, *Die Abfassungszeit von Ciceros Schrift über die Gesetze* (Rome, 1969), 175.

21. W. Kroll in *RE* 13 (1939), cols. 1091–95 (M. Tullius Cicero, *Rhetorische Schriften, De inventione*).

one of the leading orators and statesmen in Rome, a *pater patriae* despite his equestrian origins. Such a career called for resolute action and firm convictions—at least in ethics and in political theory—rather than doubt, an open mind, and constant deliberation and vacillation.

Having already anticipated a later stage, let us now jump to Cicero's later philosophical writings. Cicero never tires of speaking about himself, and the philosophical writings of his last years are just as full of self-revelations as any of his speeches and letters. Many of these passages are often quoted in modern research in support of the prevailing view that Cicero owed a lifelong allegiance to Academic Skepticism. Two crucial passages are rarely discussed or mentioned, and in such cases they are misunderstood. I therefore quote them in full:

> Tum ille: "istuc quidem considerabo, nec vero sine te. sed de te ipso quid est" inquit "quod audio?"
> "Quanam" inquam "de re?"
> "Relictam a te veterem Academiam"[22] inquit, "tractari autem novam."
> "Quid ergo" inquam "Antiocho id magis licuit nostro familiari, remigrare in domum veterem e nova, quam nobis in novam e vetere? certe enim recentissima quaeque sunt correcta et emendata maxime . . ."
>
> (*Acad.* 1.13)

> "I will deal with your point," he rejoined, "although I shall require your assistance. But what is this news I hear about yourself?"
> "What about, exactly?" I asked.

22. Bentley's *Academiam* for *iam* of all the mss. is so obvious that one wonders how so many generations of editors, including Cratander, Paulus Manutius, Lambinus, Turnebus, and Davis (two editions), could go on reading *veterem iam* assuming an ellipsis, and with *iam* in the wrong place. Reid, at least, noticed that *iam* could not stand here and accepted Madvig's *illam*; but I find his reason—"the 'Academia' is so permanently before the mind of the ancient reader"—rather feeble.

"That the Old Academy has been abandoned by you, and the New one is being dealt with."

"What then?" I said. "Is our friend Antiochus to have had more liberty to return from the new school to the old, than we are to have to move out of the old one into the new? Why, there is no question that the newest theories are always most correct and free from error . . ."

(trans. adapted from Rackham,
Loeb Classical Library)

Multis etiam sensi mirabile videri eam nobis potissimum proba-tam esse philosophiam, quae lucem eriperet et quasi noctem quandam rebus offunderet, desertaeque disciplinae et iam pridem relictae patrocinium necopinatum a nobis esse susceptum.

(*ND* 1.6)

Many also, as I have noticed, are surprised at my choosing to espouse a philosophy that in their view robs the world of daylight and floods it with a darkness as of night; and they wonder at my coming forward out of the blue to take up the case of a derelict system and one that has long been given up.

(trans. adapted from Rackham,
Loeb Classical Library)

I start with the second of these pieces of evidence, if only because I have found it quoted nowhere. The philosophy that takes away the daylight, covers all in darkness, and is now deserted and aban-doned even in Greece itself (*ND* 1.11) is, of course, Academic Skepticism, or—to use Cicero's expression—that of the *Academ-ici* (*ND* 1.1, 11).[23] It is no new method (*ratio*); it has endured since Socrates (*ND* 1.11). Yet Cicero has taken up its case (*pa-*

---

23. Since he had by now accepted Philo's view that there had always been only one Academy, with a continuous skeptical tradition and, as a consequence of this, rejected Antiochus's claim to represent the doctrines of the early Academy; see *Acad.* 1.13, 46, and *Antiochus*, 102–6.

trocinium . . . susceptum, ND 1.6; *patrocinium suscepimus, ND* 1.11), in his own words, "out of the blue" (*necopinatum*).[24]

We return to our first passage, *Academica* 1.13. Any unprejudiced reader would take it to mean just what it says. Varro is accusing Cicero of having recently deserted Antiochus's "Old Academy" for what he—and Antiochus—called the "New Academy." The parallel with Antiochus in Cicero's answer makes it quite clear: both Cicero and Antiochus before him had deserted one type of Academy and "migrated" to another. In the eighteenth century, when the floodgates of modern secondary literature had not yet been opened, and scholars could still read and reread their ancient texts with the proper attention, this was quite clear to Conyers Middleton, who wrote:

> This it was that induced Cicero, in his advanced life and ripened judgement, to desert the Old Academy, and declare for the New, from a long experience of the variety of those sects, who called themselves the proprietors of truth, and the sole guides of life, and through a despair of finding any thing certain, he was glad, after all his pains, to take up with the probable.[25]

Middleton quotes as his evidence our passage of *Academica* 1 as well as *Tusculans* 1.17 and *Orator* 237. Modern scholarship, in the person of James S. Reid, cannot ignore the first of these

24. It would not do to quote the following sentence in 1.6: "As a matter of fact, however, we have not suddenly [*subito*] taken up philosophy, nor have we devoted any small amount of time and energy to it in the early period of our life." This sentence, with its *subito*—and everything that follows down to the end of 1.9—is an answer, not to the question in our sentence, but to the sentence that preceded it; to the questions of those "who have wondered about this sudden [*subito*] enthusiasm of ours for philosophy." It is only in 1.11 that Cicero answers the question posed in the passage I have quoted as evidence: why has he taken up the defense of the Skeptical Academy, of all things?

25. Conyers Middleton, *The Life of M. Tullius Cicero* (new edition, revised, London, 1837; first edition, 1741), 712. The passage may also be a reflection on the unfortunate experiences of the author's academic life and theological controversies. On Middleton, see Leslie Stephen, "Middleton, Conyers," *Dictionary of National Biography*, vol. 37 (1894), 343–48.

passages. But Reid is obviously disturbed by the plain sense of that passage. When, in his great commentary, he reaches the word *tractari* ("to be dealt with"), he comments with relief: "*tractari*: it is important to notice that this implies a reference to some *writings* of Cicero, which can only be the 'Academica' itself (cf. Introd. p. 15). The illusion of the dialogue is not here carefully preserved."[26] Let us turn, then, to page 15 of the Introduction:

> It has been supposed by many scholars,[27] on the strength of certain passages in the *Academica Posteriora*,[28] that Cicero had for a time abandoned the views he learned from Philo, and resumed them just before the *Academica* was written. In 13, Varro charges Cicero with deserting the Old Academy for the New, and Cicero seems to admit the charge. But one of the phrases used by Varro (*tractari autem novam*) points to a solution of the difficulty. Varro evidently means that Cicero, having in earlier works copied the *writings* of the "Old Academy" philosophers, is about to draw on the literary stores of the New Academy.[29]

We have already seen that this is hardly the sense of our passage—or of the other piece of evidence, *ND* 1.6, where the word

---

26. *M. Tulli Ciceronis Academica* (London, 1885; repr. Hildesheim, 1966), 106. Even on Reid's interpretation, the illusion of the dialogue could still be maintained. Cicero had already published his *Hortensius* which, we shall soon see, contained some clear allusions to his renewed skepticism. At the same time as the Academic books, he was also composing *De finibus*; cf. *Antiochus*, 407–15, with references to Cicero's letters of the period and to modern literature.

27. Reid was a far better Ciceronian than any of us can ever hope to be. But I have examined numerous earlier editions of Cicero's Academic books as well as older works on Cicero or on the history of ancient philosophy, and apart from Middleton and Wyttenbach (n. 67 below), I have found no scholar who took Cicero's words seriously.

28. That is, what Plasberg has taught us to call *Academicus Primus*. Note that Reid does not mention *ND* 1.6 and 11. (Nor, for that matter, does Middleton.)

29. As, for example, the doctrines of Antiochus himself, expounded by Cicero's Lucullus in his namesake dialogue and by Varro in ours; or the doctrines of Stoics, Epicureans, and Antiochus in *Fin.* and *ND*; or Panaetius's in *Off.*

tractari is not used and the terminology of affiliation is quite clear. But what of Reid's "solution," his new interpretation of *tractari* (for which he adduces no evidence)?

In late medieval and Renaissance Latin, *tractare* does indeed mean "to treat in writing," and one could fill bookshelves with books called *Tractatus de* . . . But to the best of my knowledge, this is not Classical Latin,[30] and certainly is not Ciceronian.[31] For Cicero, *tractare* is simply "to deal with," and if writing is involved as a matter of fact, it is no part of the sense. Thus the orator, he says (*Or.* 118), "should be in possession of all the topics familiar to and treated by [*tractatos*] philosophy," and when he delivers his speech he should be able to "deal with the subject-matter" (*rem tractare, De or.* 2.114, 116; cf. *argumenta tractare, De or.* 2.117). More frequent and specific is *causam* (or *causas*) *tractare* (*Cluent.* 50), often coupled with *agere* (*De or.* 1.70; 3 *Verr.* 10) or with *agitare* (*Cluent.* 82; *Planc.* 4): i.e., take up a case and deal with it thoroughly as counsel, a sense reminiscent of our "taken up its case" (*patrocinium . . . susceptum*) of *ND* 1.6, 11. Another Ciceronian idiom, not peculiar to him,[32] is *personam tractare,* "to act someone's part" (*Arch.* 3, *Q. Rosc.* 20, *Off.* 3.106).

Take or leave either of these Ciceronian senses. Cicero is accused by Varro either of taking up as a lawyer the cause of the "New" Academy (his own *patrocinium . . . susceptum*), or of representing in his own person, as an actor in the dialogues of his

30. The only example given by Lewis and Short for *tractatus* in the sense of "treatise, tractate, tract"—Pliny *NH* 14.4.5 and 45—is subsumed by the *Oxford Latin Dictionary* under "the act or process of dealing with a subject or problem, treatment, discussion." *OLD* has no entry for the senses of written work, tractate, and the like.

31. The *tractatio literarum* of *Brut.* 15 is no exception. Cicero is speaking of his own reading and study of Atticus's *Liber annalis.* A. E. Douglas in his commentary on *Brutus* (Oxford, 1966), 10, s.v. *ipsa mihi,* rightly comments: "The mere renewal of interest in literature benefited Cicero."

32. *OLD, tractare,* 7b: "(of an actor) to render, perform (the part of a character)." Cf. Horace *Ep.* 1.18.14, and Gellius 2.23.13.

own composition, the view of that sect—as he does, indeed, in *Fin.* 5 and has most probably done in the lost *Hortensius.* And, whatever the sense of *tractari* in *Acad.* 1.13, the expression "the Old Academy has been abandoned by you" (*relictam a te veterem Academiam*) in it is highly reminiscent of "a derelict system and one that has long been given up" (*desertaeque disciplinae et iam pridem relictae*) of *ND* 1.6, accompanied, as it is, by "my coming forward out of the blue to take up the case" (*patrocinium necopinatum a nobis susceptum*).[33] Cicero is not a careless writer.

So much should be clear even from our two passages. It was clear to Rudolf Hirzel in 1883—two years before the appearance of Reid's edition—and his footnote 1 on pp. 488–89 of the third volume of his monumental *Untersuchungen zu Ciceros philosophischen Schriften* is a model of lucidity, brevity (in a book not distinguished for that quality), and good sense. Hirzel reads correctly our passage of *Academica* 1 (although he makes no reference to *ND* 1.6 and 11), and deduces from it that before his later volte-face (and probably ever since 79 B.C. and Antiochus in Athens), Cicero regarded himself, and was regarded by others, as a follower of Antiochus's "Old Academy." But the evidence he adduces for that period (*Att.* 5.10, *Fam.* 15.4, 6, *Leg.* 1.39) is only part of what is available. Since Cicero's espousal of the "Old Academy" in a period between *De inventione* of 81–80 B.C. and *Academica* 1 of 45 B.C. is my *demonstrandum,* I shall deal with his own evidence in some detail.

Our first piece of evidence comes from *Pro Murena* 63–64, of the year of Cicero's consulate, 63 B.C. Cicero is comparing his own milder brand of philosophy with the harsher approach of

---

33. Joseph B. Mayor, *M. Tulli Ciceronis De natura deorum,* vol. 1 (Cambridge, England, 1880), 73 (s.v. *desertae et relictae*), comments: "*Des.* refers to desertion by an adherent, such as Antiochus; *rel.* to general neglect." His comment is quoted with approval by A. S. Pease *ad loc., M. Tulli Ciceronis De natura deorum liber primus* (Cambridge, Mass., 1955). Our *Acad.* 1 passage would not bear out this interpretation, and *desertarum relictarumque rerum* of 1.11 would tend to confirm that we have here a mere hendiadys.

the Stoic Cato. (My footnotes to the passage will serve as comments on the sort of philosophy represented [*tractata?*] here by Cicero.)

> Those men of our school, I say, descending from Plato and Aristotle,[34] being moderate and restrained people, say that with the wise man gratitude counts for something; that it is characteristic of the good man to feel pity;[35] that there are distinct types of crimes, with different penalties attached to them;[36] that there is a place for forgiveness with the consistent man;[37] that the wise man himself often holds some opinion with respect to what he does not know;[38] that he is sometimes angry;[39] and is open to persuasion and mollification;[40] that he sometimes alters what he has said, if it proves to be better so; that he on occasion departs from his opinion;[41] that all his virtues are controlled by a kind of mean.[42]

Except for one short sentence, everything in this passage represents Antiochus's "Old Academy."

34. A basic tenet of Antiochus's "Old Academy," that the early Academy and the Peripatetics were one and the same school: *Acad.* 1.17–18.

35. Cf. *Luc.* 135, *Tusc.* 4.46.

36. Cf. *Luc.* 133: "The Stoics hold that all sins are equal; but with this Antiochus most violently disagrees."

37. Cf. *Luc.* 135, *Tusc.* 4.46.

38. This (*Luc.* 59) is one version of Carneades' position. Arcesilaus agreed with Zeno in taking the opposite view (*Luc.* 66–67), and Antiochus (in the person of Lucullus) returned to this position, because it was Zeno's, not because of Arcesilaus. This, then, is the only place in our passage where the view of a Skeptical Academic is admitted and accepted.

39. One of the "motions of the soul" of *Luc.* 135; but see mainly *Tusc.* 4.43.

40. Cf. *Luc.* 135, *Tusc.* 4.46.

41. A regular feature of the dialectic of Plato's dialogues—especially what we call the later dialogues—which anyone who counted himself a follower of Plato would accept. After all, Antiochus himself (*Acad.* 1.30–43) accepted the criticism of Aristotle and his contemporaries of Plato's theory of Forms, as well as Zeno's epistemology, as a "correction of the Old Academy."

42. The famous Aristotelian doctrine of the "ethical virtues" as intermediaries between two extremes, accepted by Antiochus's "Old Academy": *Luc.* 135, *Tusc.* 3.22ff.

Our next piece of evidence comes from the lost *De consulatu suo* of 60 B.C. Cicero himself (*Div.* 1.17–22) has preserved for us, from the second book, a long speech addressed to himself by the Muse Urania. These are the relevant lines:[43]

> Haec adeo penitus cura videre sagaci
> otia qui studiis laeti tenuere decoris
> inque Academia umbrifera nitidoque Lyceo
> funderunt claras fecundi pectoris artis.
> e quibus ereptum primo iam a flore iuventae
> te patria in media virtutum mole locavit.
>
> Such were the truths they beheld who, painfully
>   searching for wisdom,
> gladly devoted their leisure to study of all that was
>   noble,
> who, in Academy's shade and Lyceum's dazzling
>   effulgence
> uttered the brilliant reflections of minds abounding
>   in culture,
> torn from these studies, in youth's early dawn, your
>   country recalled you,
> giving you place in the thick of the struggle for
>   public preferment.
>
> (trans. Falconer, Loeb Classical Library)

Cicero, of course, never studied in the umbriferous Academy, which was deserted during his stay in Athens (*Fin.* 5.1–2) and in which we have no evidence that Antiochus ever taught.[44] Nor could he have studied in the nitid Lyceum, since Aristotle's school had, by that time, almost certainly ceased to exist.[45] The references are metaphorical and poetical. The combination of Academy and Lyceum signifies Cicero's philosophical ancestry at the time he was called back in a hurry by his country; it is that

---

43. W. Morel, *Fragmenta poetarum Latinorum* (Leipzig, 1927), 70 (Cicero fr. 11 [3], lines 69–76).

44. *Antiochus*, 111, 242.

45. J.P. Lynch, *Aristotle's School* (Berkeley and Los Angeles, 1972), 201–7.

combination of early Academy and early Peripatos which was the hallmark of Antiochus's school.

Ten years after the *De consolatu*, Cicero could still declare himself a votary of the Ancient Philosophy. I refer to the peroration of his letter to Cato (*Fam.* 15.4, 6), written in December of 51 or January of 50 from his proconsulate in Tarsus:

> Haec igitur, quae mihi tecum communis est, societas studiorum atque artium nostrarum, quibus a pueritia dediti et devincti soli prope modum nos philosophiam veram illam et antiquam, quae quibusdam oti esse ac desidiae videtur, in forum atque in ipsam aciem paene deduximus, tecum agit de mea laude.

> This community of studies and disciplines which you and I share, to which being practically alone devoted and bound since childhood, we have drawn that true and ancient philosophy, thought by some to be a matter for leisure and relaxation, into the public sphere and practically into the line of battle—this summons you to embark on my praise.

"Since childhood" reminds us of "in youth's early dawn" from our last passage—that is, Cicero's studies in Athens under Antiochus. The expression "that true and ancient philosophy" should leave no doubt. Not only is "ancient" an obvious allusion to Antiochus's "Old Academy," harking back to "the philosophy of the ancients" (*antiquorum ratio, Acad.* 1.43), but calling such a philosophy "true" could not have been the act of a Skeptic.

We come now to *De legibus* 1.39:

> Perturbatricem autem harum omnium rerum Academiam, hanc ab Arcesila et Carneade recentem, exoremus ut sileat; nam si invaserit in haec, quae satis scite nobis instructa et composita videntur, nimias edet ruinas; quam quidem ego placare cupio, summovere non audeo.

> As for that disrupter of all these matters, this recent Academy of Arcesilaus and Carneades, let us plead for its silence. For if it makes an assault upon those things which we find elegantly enough set out and arranged, it will cause too much destruction.

For my part, I would seek to placate it, since I dare not try to dispose of it.

Hirzel, in the footnote I have referred to, and Pohlenz[46] took it for granted (with reservations on Hirzel's part, on which more later) that at the time of writing Cicero was still a follower of Antiochus. Meanwhile, a controversy has raged about the date of composition of *De legibus*, some scholars putting it as late as 44–43 B.C. This controversy has been largely settled now by P.L. Schmidt's thorough and convincing treatment of most of the issues involved, returning the work to its traditional milieu, the late 50s B.C.[47] But when it comes to our passage, Schmidt's discussion is rather disappointing.[48] He is quite aware of the view of Hirzel[49] and Pohlenz.[50] Yet he rehearses the old tale of Cicero's lifelong allegiance to Skepticism, quoting again our two old friends, *Inv.* 2.10 and *Off.* 2.7ff., in support of this view.[51] How does it happen, then, that we have in our passage such a severe criticism of the Skeptical Academy? "If we just ignore *Inv.* 2.10, Cicero was not faced by any necessity from themes in the works of the 50s to represent himself as a New Academic, and still less so by the tenor of our work."[52]

This will not do. It is not just that Cicero does *not* represent himself as a "New" Academic; he criticizes the "New" Academy

46. Max Pohlenz, *Die Stoa* (Göttingen, 1949), vol. 2, 126, n. on vol. 1, 243f.

47. Schmidt's book is cited in n. 20 above. See also Elizabeth Rawson, "The Interpretation of Cicero's *De legibus,*" *ANRW* 1 (1973), 334–56, and R.G. Tanner, "Cicero on Conscience and Morality," in J.R.C. Martyn, ed., *Cicero and Virgil: Studies in Honour of Harold Hunt* (Amsterdam, 1972), 87–112, esp. 104–6.

48. "Skepsis und Dogma" (n. 20 above), 174–79.

49. Although he refers only to the brief and unimportant footnote in Hirzel's *Untersuchungen*, vol. 3, 471 n. 2, and not to the more fundamental one on 488–89.

50. Pohlenz is cited in n. 46 above.

51. Schmidt (n. 20 above), 175.

52. Ibid., 177 (translated from the original German by A.A. Long).

as severely as only an outsider can do (although also as respectfully as only an old alumnus would). Even the words of *Rep* 3.9, "make your reply to Carneades, who is in the habit of casting ridicule on the best causes by his talent for misrepresentation," are not quite as harsh; and at least they are not spoken by Cicero in his own person. No, our passage of *De legibus*—just like the refutation of Carneades' speech "against justice" which follows on Philus's "advocacy of immorality" (*improbitatis patrocinium*, *Rep.* 3.8)—could hardly have come from Cicero's last years when, as a born-again Skeptic, he was an admirer of Carneades. It belongs to the period when he was still an avowed follower of Antiochus.[53]

□□□

When did Cicero change his philosophical affiliations and take up again the case of the Skeptical Academy? For a long time I believed that the moment of truth came in July of 51 B.C. when, on his way to his Asian proconsulate, he stayed for a while with Aristus, Antiochus's brother and successor, in Athens and may have become finally disillusioned with the "Old Academy" and its doctrines. The text of the relevant passage, *Att.* 5.10.5, is hopelessly corrupt. Its first sentence, "Athens powerfully pleased me," etc. (*valde me Athenae delectarunt . . .*), is fairly secure. But the crucial sentence is the next one. Tyrrell and Purser read: "sed multum†ea†philosophia sursum deorsum, si quidem est in Aristo,

---

53. In his later philosophical writings, Cicero rejects the appellation "New Academy," invented by Antiochus, and is only prepared to use it as a gesture of courtesy to Varro (*Acad.* 1.13, 46). He uses this terminology without reservations only in *De or.* 3.68 ("more recent") and in *Leg.* 1.39. *De oratore* is no later than November 55 B.C. (*Att.* 4.13.2), that is, during Cicero's Antiochian period, a point I should have noticed in *Antiochus*, 104 and n. 27. His use of this odd Antiochian term in the other passage strengthens the general assumption that *De legibus* belongs to the same chronological milieu—and especially the choice of "more recent" rather than "new" in both passages.

apud quem eram." They take it that Cicero's strictures on the topsy-turvy state of Athenian philosophy (the mss. agree on this part of the text) are meant to include, if not to single out, Aristus, of whom Plutarch (*Brut.* 2) is also critical.[54] Shackleton Bailey, however, emends: "sed mu<tata mul>ta. philosophia sursum deorsum. si quid est, est in Aristo, apud quem eram." He translates: "But many things have changed, and philosophy is all at sixes and sevens, anything of value being represented by Aristus." His comment is: "I do not believe that Cicero wrote this of his *hospes et familiaris* [host and friend] (*Brut.* 332), particularly as slighting criticism of a friend of Brutus . . . might have jarred upon his correspondent. *Agroikia* [boorishness] was not among his failings."[55]

This argument would not make me lose much sleep. Cicero's correspondent is not Brutus but Atticus, on whose perfect discretion he can rely; and in other letters to Atticus, he says much more damaging things about Brutus himself and about many another "host and friend." But even if he were disappointed with Aristus, this does not imply giving up his advocacy of Antiochus's school. After all, his letter to Cato from Tarsus which we have just noted, *Fam.* 15.4.6, was written later, and in it he still adheres to "that true and ancient philosophy." As to his disputation with Aristus recorded in *Tusc.* 5.22—whether it took place on the same occasion or on his way back from Asia[56]—it is the

54. R. Y. Tyrrell and L. C. Purser, *The Correspondence of M. Tullius Cicero*, vol. 3 (Dublin, 1914), 39–43, with a number of alternative suggestions for emending the more problematic parts. (In *Antiochus*, 112, I still took a position similar to theirs.) Watt's *OCT* reads *siquidem aestimes Aristo*, which makes little difference to the sense.

55. *Cicero's Letters to Atticus*, vol. 3 (Cambridge, England, 1968), 26 (text), 27 (translation), 205 (comments).

56. Shackleton Bailey (n. 55 above) claims that although Cicero calls himself *imperator* in *Tusc.* 5.22, and the title was only conferred on him in Cilicia, it is clear from *Att.* 6.9 that on his way back (October 50), Cicero lodged in the "citadel" (*arx*) of Athens, not with Aristus. See also his remarks on 6.9 on page 277. But Cicero reached Piraeus on 14 October 50

same old argument he had held "frequently with Antiochus," whose echoes we hear in his discussion with Piso in *Fin.* 5.79ff., and on which, as he tells us in *Luc.* 134, he had never been able to make up his mind: the choice between the logical consistency of the Stoics and the realism of the Peripatetic and Antiochian "three kinds of goods." No new matter here.

More to the point is the language of our first two pieces of evidence, *Acad.* 1.13 and *ND* 1.6, 11. "But what is this news I hear about yourself" and "out of the blue" both sound like recent news. The earliest evidence for Cicero's renewed allegiance to Academic Skepticism comes at the end of his *Orator* (237, on which more later). The first clear evidence in a properly philosophical work can be found in two fragments of his *Hortensius*, from February of 45 B.C. The first fragment (Augustine *C. Acad.* 3.14.31) reads: "If therefore there is nothing certain, and it is not for the wise man to hold an opinion, the wise man will never approve anything." A. Grilli[57] ascribes this sentence to Hortensius of the dialogue and takes the passage of Augustine, *C. Acad.* 1.3.7—formerly printed by Plasberg as a fragment of Cicero's *Academicus* 2[58]—to be Cicero's answer to Hortensius.[59] His arguments seem to me utterly convincing. Since the second fragment is readily available in Plasberg's edition of the Academic books of Cicero, I shall not quote it here. The reader can see for

---

(*Att.* 6.9.1, 7.1.1). He was at Brundisium only on 25 November or later (7.21.1). Even assuming a week or ten days for the journey, he still had a good month in Athens, during which he could stay at the citadel on his arrival as imperator, but also spend some time with Aristus, his "host and friend."

57. *M. Tulli Ciceronis Hortensius* (Milan, 1962), fr. 51, p. 31.

58. M. Tullius Cicero, *Academicorum reliquiae cum Lucullo* (Leipzig, 1922), p. 21 lines 10–14. In his Teubner editio maior of *Paradoxa Stoicorum, Academicorum reliquiae cum Lucullo* (Leipzig, 1908), 59 *ap. ad* 5, Plasberg comments that although he formerly regarded it as a fragment of *Hortensius*, he had been convinced by Hirzel's arguments to transfer it to the Academic books.

59. Grilli (n. 57 above), fr. 107, p. 50, and commentary, pp. 145–50.

himself that the position taken in it is clearly that of the Skeptical Academy—and, since Augustine introduces it with the words "in our Cicero's opinion" (*placuit Ciceroni nostro*), it is by now also Cicero's.

Cicero, then, changed his affiliations twice: once, from a youthful enthusiasm for Philo of Larissa and Academic Skepticism to Antiochus's "Old Academy"—albeit with reservations and with a lingering respect for the Skeptical tradition[60]—and then, some time in 45 B.C., back to the Skepticism of Carneades and Philo. Cicero's own evidence seems so overwhelming that one wonders what it is that made so many scholars ignore it, or feel uncomfortable when faced with it and attempt to find an unsatisfactory solution to an imaginary difficulty.

The combination of Cicero's early statement in *Inv.* 2.10 with his repeated statements of allegiance to Skepticism in his later philosophical corpus is one reason for this. It has caused even some of our contemporary experts such as Weische and Schmidt, both fully aware of the significance of philosophical affiliations, to ignore the rest of the evidence or to try to get around it.[61] But one other possible cause for the persistent adherence of so much of modern scholarship to this picture of the ever-faithful Cicero may be the "evidence" of Plutarch in his *Life of Cicero* 4 (862C–D):

60. Hirzel, in his footnote 1 referred to above, has noted that the last sentence of *Leg.* 1.39 shows "a certain wavering in him." I would rather compare it to *De or.* 3.67–68, where a favorable passage concerning the "more recent Academy" is included in a doxography which is Antiochian in its essentials; or with the words of Lactantius *Epit.* 50.8 (Cic. *Rep.* 3.11) on Carneades' speech against Plato's and Aristotle's (i.e., the "Old Academics'," in Antiochian terms) idea of justice, which are probably based on some statement of Cicero's: "not because he [*sc.* Carneades] thought that justice should be maligned, but to show that its defenders had nothing certain or firm to say about it." For the same sentiment, see also *ND* 3.44. That is, even during his Antiochian period, Cicero did not go so far as a wholesale repudiation of the Skeptical Academy.

61. Cf. nn. 20 and 47–52 above.

On coming to Athens he attended the lectures of Antiochus of Ascalon and was charmed by his fluency and grace of diction, while not approving of [*ouk epainōn*] his innovations in doctrine. For Antiochus had already fallen away from what was called the New Academy, and abandoned the sect [*stasis*] of Carneades, either swayed by clarity [*enargeia*] and sensations or, as some say, by a feeling of ambitious opposition to the disciples of Clitomachus and Philo to change his views and cultivate in most cases the Stoic viewpoint. But Cicero loved [*ēgapa*] those things [*sc.* the stance of Carneades] and devoted himself the rather to them, intending in case he was altogether driven out of a public career, to change his way of life away from the Forum and the state, and live quietly in the company of philosophy.

(trans. adapted from Perrin,
Loeb Classical Library)

Plutarch has always been one of the most popular authors both with Classical scholars and with the general public, read in the original or in one of the numerous translations produced ever since the Renaissance. But what is the value of his "evidence"?

No independent court or jury would accept his testimony as against the clear evidence of the numerous passages of Cicero himself. But other points in his passage show clearly that it is far from being historical. Plutarch claims that Cicero continued his philosophical studies ever since his youth, with the express purpose of retiring into a life of philosophy if he were to be removed from politics. Not only does Cicero, *ND* 1.7–8, see things differently even in retrospect—for he says there that because he had been ejected from public life, he was now applying himself to philosophy. But in *Leg.* 1.9ff., having been asked by Atticus (5ff.) to apply himself to writing history, he replies that if he has the time on his retirement from the Republic, he intends to employ it, like his teacher Mucius Scaevola, in giving free legal advice to people. This, by the way, is another proof that Cicero could not have written *De legibus* in the last years of his life, when forced retirement from politics was no longer a remote prospect and when he was dedicating his time to philosophical works. But it also shows that as late as 50 B.C., Cicero had no plan of that retirement into a philosophical *otium*; how much less so, then, in 79 B.C.?

Plutarch, of course, is no more reliable than his sources; and when it comes to Roman affairs, his understanding of the information and the background of his sources is likely to be deficient, especially if he relies on Latin sources and his own imperfect command of Latin.[62] It has been the prevailing view, most probably ever since A. H. L. Heeren's *De Fontibus et auctoritate Vitarum parallelarum Plutarchi* of 1820, confirmed on this point by Hermann Peter's *Die Quellen Plutarchs in den Biographien der Römer* of 1865, that Plutarch's main source for his *Life of Cicero* was the Greek biography written by M. Tullius Tiro.[63] But it was argued as long ago as 1902, by Alfred Gudeman in a little-known work called *The Sources of Plutarch's Life of Cicero*,[64] that Plutarch's source or sources could not have been Tiro or any other contemporary or near-contemporary like Sallust or Livy (for no one would dream of accusing Plutarch of having read the various writings of Cicero in the original for himself—as Gudeman need only mention),[65] but a post-Augustan source, *and in Latin.* Gudeman opts for Suetonius's lost *Life of Cicero*, which is not unlikely. What concerns us here is that the source is most prob-

62. For a specimen of Plutarch's misunderstanding of Latin sources, with examples of other mistranslations from Latin and a discussion of the modern literature on this issue, see *Antiochus*, Excursus 1, "Plutarch, *Lucullus* 42.3–4," 380–90.

63. In *Antiochus*, 15 n. 6 and subsequently, I also accepted this view without referring to later discussions.

64. Publications of the University of Pennsylvania, Series in Philosophy and Literature, vol. 3, no. 2.

65. In fact, R. Flacelière and É. Chambry, the editors of the Budé text of Plutarch's *Life of Cicero*, do claim that it is "incontestable" that Plutarch consulted various writings of Cicero directly; see *Antiochus*, 385 and n. 22. With Plutarch's knowledge of Latin being what he tells us it was in *Demosthenes* 2.3, I still find such a hypothesis highly improbable.

ably Latin and late, and thus liable to confuse issues and chronology.

An attempt to translate Plutarch's passage back into Latin would repay the effort. Many of his expressions have exact, or almost exact, parallels in Cicero's extant writings.[66] The presumed later Latin source clearly drew on passages in Cicero's writings. I shall take as one example Plutarch's words "But Cicero loved [*ēgapa*] those things." If this is meant to refer to the views of Clitomachus and Philo—or even to the general view of the Skeptical Academy—this is hardly clear or very good Greek. But a Ciceronian parallel, *Luc.* 2.9, could illustrate what may be lurking behind it: "but somehow or other most men prefer to go wrong, and to defend tooth and nail the system for which they have come to feel an affection [*adamaverunt*]."[67] Another example: Plutarch's "his innovations in doctrine [*dogmata*]" would make no sense, as it stands, in a Ciceronian text. Antiochus, after all, could introduce no innovations into the *dogmata*

66. E.g., ἀφικόμενος εἰς Ἀθήνας: *cum venissem Athenas, sex menses cum Antiocho . . . fui* (*Brut.* 315); Ἀντιόχου διήκουσε: *cum audissem Antiochum* (*Fin.* 5.1); τῇ εὐπορίᾳ τοῦ λόγου αὐτοῦ καὶ τῇ χάριτι: *quoniam in doctrina atque praeceptis disserendi ratio coniungitur cum suavitate dicendi et copia* (of the Academics, *Brut.* 20); ὥς φασιν ἔνιοι, φιλοτιμίᾳ: *quod erant qui illum gloriae causa facere dicerent* (*Luc.* 70). One could add more Ciceronian echoes, where the phrases are similar but the context is not quite as close.

67. D. Wyttenbach, ΕΚΛΟΓΑΙ ΙΣΤΟΡΙΚΑΙ (Leipzig, 1827), 329 *ad* ἐκεῖνα ἠγάπα, writes: "This should not be taken, as most do, as referring to the New Academy, but, rather, to the study of philosophy in general, which is the sense supported by what follows. Cicero did not attach himself to the New Academy until much later in life, in his old age"—quoting *Acad.* 1.13 in evidence. He is followed by B. Büchsenschütz, *Plutarch Demosthenes und Cicero* (Berlin, 1857), 67 *ad loc.* But the force of δέ and of ἐκεῖνα seems to indicate that this is, indeed, what Plutarch means—especially since it follows immediately on Antiochus's dogmatic innovations as against the skeptical Academy. This is also what most translators, from Amyot onward, take it to mean. The awkwardness of ἠγάπα in Greek and my Ciceronian parallel might lend some support to this interpretation. Wyttenbach is right, of course, as to Cicero's affiliations. (Wyttenbach's words have been translated by the editors from his original Latin.)

of the Skeptical Academy, since it had—and Cicero is one of our main sources for this—no *dogmata*. But the source might have misunderstood Cicero's own statement (*Luc.* 132), "he was called an Academic, but was in fact, if he had made a very few changes, the purest Stoic," to mean that Antiochus did, indeed, introduce some changes into the doctrines of the Academy. Here it is possible that the misapprehension arose already in Plutarch's source. In the case of "while not approving" (*ouk epainōn*) the error is clearly Plutarch's own.

The "synchronization" of events that occurred (more or less) in various periods of Cicero's life may have been already the work of Plutarch's source, or it may have been done by Plutarch himself.[68] Whoever did this telescoping may already have anticipated the error of modern scholarship and combined Cicero's statement in *De inventione* with his frequent references to his Skeptical affiliations in his later writings. Be that as it may, Plutarch's testimony is in no way a piece of reliable evidence, to be preferred to Cicero's own genuine and datable statements. It is, in the best case, the result of a misunderstanding of earlier sources by Plutarch or his source or both, and in the worst case, an ancient piece of speculation which is no better than any modern speculation when faced with Cicero's own words. Even if it were a smoother and a more consistent piece of narrative, it could hardly outweigh our firsthand evidence.

2. CICERO'S TWO PHILOSOPHICAL CORPORA

What, if any, were the effects of Cicero's changes in philosophical affiliation on the nature of his philosophical writings of the various periods? Since Cicero wrote no philosophical works at the

68. For an example of such telescoping by Plutarch, see *Antiochus*, 17 and Excursus 1, 380–90, esp. 380–83.

period of *De inventione*, we have to deal with two sets of works only: *De oratore*, *De republica*, and *De legibus* of the late 50s B.C., and Cicero's later philosophical writings of 46–43 B.C.

That there is a difference between the two sets is now generally acknowledged—but what sort of difference? In a recent article, P. L. Schmidt writes, "His philosophical works fall into two great contrasting cycles, depending on the changed political conditions," and explains that the works of the 50s were written when Cicero still believed he had an active political role to play, whereas the later works were already written from the standpoint of a private individual philosophizing at his leisure.[69] This is correct as far as it goes, and gives us one likely biographical reason for the change in attitude and affiliations, but it is still far from describing the essential nature of the difference in philosophical outlook. Gallus Zoll, in his detailed study of the form of Cicero's dialogues,[70] has noticed that the dialogues of the 50s display more Platonic imitation both in form and themes, whereas the dialogues of the last years are more avowedly Aristotelian.[71] But on the question of whether this may have anything to do with "an internal change in Cicero's artistic intentions," he seems to falter. Although he would have preferred to answer in the affirmative, the equal quantity of references to Plato and Aristotle in works of both periods, and with the same complimentary epithets, seems to convince him that this is merely a matter of adopting a different literary genus to suit different literary themes. He calls the earlier dialogues *Bildungsdialoge* ("educational dialogues") and the later dialogues *Wissensdialoge* ("scientific dialogues"), and takes this to be the source of their differences.[72]

The Platonism of Cicero's cycle of the 50s was a favorite

69. P. L. Schmidt, "Cicero's Place in Roman Philosophy: A Study of His Prefaces," *CJ* 74 (1978–1979), 115–27, esp. 119–20.

70. *Cicero Platonis Aemulus: Untersuchung über die Form von Ciceros Dialogen, besonders De oratore* (Zurich, 1962).

71. As Cicero himself says in *Att.* 13.19.4.

72. Zoll (n. 70 above), 147–53.

theme in studies of these works published in the generation before and after the Second World War. Much of this literature is mentioned and discussed in two well-known articles, one by Pierre Boyancé and one by Karl Büchner, each of which has the word *Platonism* in the title.[73] Büchner's article marks the beginning of a reaction against the "Platonizing" fashion. He points out that Cicero's arguments against community of property, marriage, and children among the Guardians in *De Rep.* 4 are not an isolated case of a criticism of Plato. Cicero's whole approach to the very essence of the state, which he bases on the historical experience of the Greeks and Romans, is the exact opposite of Plato's "geometrical construction" of the state, in his *Republic*, out of general characteristics of human nature. Büchner also touches on the sore point of *De oratore*. Plato's denial of the very existence of an *ars rhetorica* requires no elaboration. It is also clearly an exaggeration to speak of "Platonism in Rome." However much Cicero, Brutus, and, to some extent, Varro may have been admirers of Plato, they hardly instituted a school or a movement like Ficino's "Platonic Academy" of Florence; Cambridge Platonism; American Transcendentalism, with its emphasis on Plato and the later Platonists; neo-Kantianism; British Hegelianism—or, indeed, the movement in late antiquity that we call Neoplatonism.

But even in speaking merely of Cicero's Platonism we should be cautious. Quintilian's tag of *Platonis aemulus*, "Plato's counterpart," coming as it does in his comparative catalogue of Greek and Latin classics (10.1.123), is tendentious. That Cicero is unusually well versed in Plato, as his translations of *Timaeus* and

73. P. Boyancé, "Le Platonisme à Rome: Platon et Cicéron," *Assoc. Guillaume Budé. Congrès de Tours et Poitiers: Actes du Congrès* (Paris, 1953), 195–221, reprinted in Boyancé's *Etudes sur l'humanisme cicéronien* (Brussels, 1970), 222–47; K. Büchner, "Zum Platonismus Ciceros: Bemerkungen zum vierten Buch von Ciceros Werk De re Publica," *Festschrift Hermann Gundert* (Amsterdam, 1974), reprinted in Büchner's *Studien zur römischen Literatur*, vol. 9, 76–99.

Protagoras and the innumerable quotations and references in his writings show, is admitted. These Platonic *loci* have been collected by Thelma B. DeGraff in a well-known article.[74] But all it proves is Cicero's intimate familiarity with Plato and his comprehension of the plain meaning of Plato's Greek text. What matters, as Walter Burkert has emphasized,[75] is how and through whose interpretation Cicero read his Plato. After all, Plato's writings have always been available, and there had been numerous "Platonisms" even by Cicero's time. Cicero may have changed his view of the essence and orientation of Plato's philosophy when he changed his philosophical affiliation around 46 B.C. Serious work on this issue has never, to my knowledge, been done—perhaps because the change in Cicero's affiliation has not so far received the attention it deserves. This, however, is not the place to launch such a project. All we can do here is point to an obvious change in philosophical orientation between the writings of the 50s and those of the 40s. Put briefly, the writings of the 50s are "dogmatic," while those of the 40s are Skeptical.

I shall not go into *De oratore*. A dialogue on the art of rhetoric by a master of the trade can hardly be expected to present us with a Skeptical orientation—although *Orator* does end exactly on such a Skeptical note. But *De republica* is hardly the work of a Skeptic. We have already seen that Carneades' Roman speech against Plato's and Aristotle's idea of justice, defended by Philus in Book 2 as "the advocacy of immorality," is immediately refuted by Scipio. As to *De legibus*, we have already noted and discussed the offending passage, 1.39, where Cicero uses the strongest language in any of his writings against the Academy of Arcesilaus and Carneades. Such things could hardly be expected—and are never found—in the philosophical writings of the 40s.

This is not to say that in the works of the 50s Antiochus is

74. "Plato in Cicero," *CPh* 35 (1940), 143–53.
75. "Cicero als Platoniker und Skeptiker" (n. 18 above).

always or usually Cicero's source, or that his philosophy is represented by Cicero's persons of the dialogues. Max Pohlenz has already adduced some very cogent evidence against the thesis of Hoyer, Reitzenstein, and Theiler that Antiochus is the source of *De legibus*.[76] Nor is *De republica*, with its emphasis on Roman history and experience, more likely to be based on a work by Antiochus. In the best case, some parts of it, like the refutation of Carneades in Book 3 or the arguments against Plato's communalism among the Guardians in Book 4, may be partly drawn from Antiochian materials. By the late 50s, a whole generation had passed since Cicero's studies with Antiochus in Athens in 79 B.C.; and there were issues on which Cicero had never seen eye to eye with Antiochus and his school.[77] What matters is that in these writings Cicero is still highly critical of Arcesilaus, Carneades, and the *recentior Academia* and that his philosophical orientation is still positive and dogmatic.

Cicero's constant and recurring statements of allegiance to the Skeptical Academy in his later philosophical works are a commonplace. We have already seen that these declarations of renewed allegiance start as early as *Orator* of 46 and *Hortensius* of February 45. They continue unabated until *De officiis* of the last year of his life.[78]

This is not just a matter of formal and sporadic self-revelations: the new attitude affects the form and purport of these works. We do not have Cicero's *Hortensius*, and it is inconceivable that in such a protreptic, Cicero would have emphasized his Skeptical views to the exclusion of any statements concerning the assets and consolations of philosophy. There are indeed two fragments in which Cicero seems to point out that some positive

76. N. 46 above.

77. See p. 53 above.

78. It would be tedious to enumerate all of Cicero's many explicit and implicit allusions to his adherence to the Skeptical Academy in his later writings. A few references will suffice: *Or.* 237, *Hort*, frr. 51, 107 Grilli; *Tusc.* 4.7, 5.22, 33, 82, *Fat.* 4, *Off.* 1.2, 38, 2.7–8, 3.20, 33.

philosophical ideas can be accepted even by the Skeptic.[79] But we have also noticed that even in that dialogue Cicero himself represents or defends a Skeptical position. The Academic books, in both versions, are of course a manifesto of the Skeptical tradition in the Academy against Antiochus and the Stoa. Nor are *De finibus*, *De natura deorum*, and *De divinatione* the kind of works that would warm the heart of a dogmatic. Anyone who receives the impression that at the end of the *Tusculans* Cicero has settled to his own and his interlocutor's satisfaction the problems of death, suffering, the perturbations of the soul, or the self-sufficiency of virtue must have forgotten Hirtius's words, addressed to Cicero himself, in *De fato* 4: "Moreover, your *Tusculan Disputations* show that you have adopted this Academic practice of arguing against the thesis advanced." Even *De officiis*, in which Cicero admittedly follows Panaetius, is full of Skeptical declarations such as 2.7–8 and 3.20.

If it is true that *De officiis*, *Tusculans*, and even the last book of *De finibus* have a slightly more "dogmatic" ring to them and leave the reader with a far less devastating impression than, say, *De divinatione*, the explanation of this has always been available in some statements of Cicero himself. One may as well quote again one of the most famous and most widely cited of them, *Off.* 3.20: "Moreover, our Academy gives us great leeway, so that we may legitimately defend whatever turns out most plausible [*probabile*]."

The sentence is widely quoted and discussed, but mostly out of context, which is Cicero's preference for the Stoic formula that "whatever is honorable seems to be useful, and nothing is useful which does not seem honorable" over the distinction between *honestum* and *utile* drawn "by the old Academics and by your

79. Grilli (n. 57 above), frr. 58–59.

Peripatetics, who were once the same as the Academics."[80] Marcus Cicero, as a pupil of the "dogmatic" Cratippus, may have to be faithful to the doctrines of his school. His Skeptical father can pick and choose whichever doctrine seems to him to be more *probabilis* at the time, whatever its ancestry.

Even then, he has no obligation to stick to the doctrine that appears to him to be *probabilis*: "With others, who argue on the basis of fixed rules, this is the case: we live from day to day." A skeptic like Cicero can change his mind from day to day—and from work to work.

Eclecticism? One might, at first sight, interpret that way the statement of Cicero's interlocutor in *Tusc.* 5.82: "Since no chains of any definite doctrine constrain you, and you sip from all of them, whatever principally moves you with the appearance of truth ... " But even here, the picture is not that of a well-organized body of eclectic philosophy like that of Antiochus (or Potamo?), but of the bee flitting from flower to flower and choosing according to its taste and mood at the time. "We live from day to day" is no recipe for a consistent body of eclectic doctrine.

That this is Cicero's practice, and no mere matter of programmatic declarations never carried out, is clear to any reader of these late philosophical works. *De finibus* 4–5 bring out this matter quite forcefully. In Book 4 Cicero uses against Cato—albeit in an ampler form—arguments dangerously similar to those used by Piso against Cicero himself in 5.76ff.; and again, Cicero's own arguments in Book 5 against Piso are very similar to those used by Cato against Cicero in Book 4. There is, to be sure, a differ-

80. "Your," of course, is in reference to Cicero the younger, now a pupil of Cratippus the Peripatetic in Athens. The description of the early Academics and Peripatetics as flowing from the same Platonic source and being both *antiqui* is historical and not particularly Antiochian—as long as one does not claim (as Varro, representing Antiochus, does in *Acad.* 1.17–18) that they shared the same doctrines and that their doctrines represent the true philosophy of Plato.

ence of a good few years between the dramatic dates of Books 4 and 5.

The problem discussed there—the sufficiency of virtue for happiness and the status of the "external goods"—is, as we have already noted (p. 52 above), one that had exercised Cicero's mind ever since his studies with Antiochus in Athens. At that time, and also during his visit to Athens in 51 or 50 B.C. when he argued about the same problem with Aristus of Ascalon, he was far from happy with Antiochus's "Peripatetic" solution. His wavering between the Stoic and Peripatetic-Antiochian positions in *Fin.* 4–5 is beautifully described by Cicero himself in *Luc.* 134, written about the same time: "I am dragged in different directions—now the latter view seems the more plausible, now the former; and yet I firmly believe that unless one or the other is true, virtue is overthrown." At the end of *Tusculans* (5.120), he seems to have adopted a compromise based on a ruling by Carneades.[81] Yet when he reaches *Off.* 3.20, he seems to opt once more for the Stoic equation between "honorable" and "useful," which is essentially a species of the same argument. "We live from day to day" almost in the literal sense.

That this practice is no invention of Cicero's is clear from his own words. It is a "liberty" (*licentia*) given him and others of the same school of thought (*nobis*) by "our Academy" (*Off.* 3.20). It is a privilege given "to us alone in philosophy" (*Tusc.* 4.83); it is "we" who "live for the day . . . and so are alone free" (*Tusc.* 5.33); "but we . . . say some things are plausible, others the op-

---

81. The whole of this issue, whether the difference between the Stoics and Peripatetics on this problem is based on "a disagreement of words, not of things" (Antiochus's view, *Leg.* 1.54–55, and in his book which he sent to Balbus, *ND* 1.16), or whether it is (as Balbus the Stoic maintains there, and Cato throughout *Fin.* 4) "a very large disagreement of things, not a small one of words," requires a new investigation in the light of this final section of the *Tusculans*. If this issue had already been settled by Carneades in a fashion similar to that of Antiochus, why are we not told this clearly until we reach *Tusc.* 5.120, and why, in *Fin.* 3.41, do we have this crucial "judgment of Carneades" only referred to in passing?

posite" (*Off.* 2.7). If in doubt as to that "we"—which could, after all, be a polite reference to Cicero himself—the end of that long passage, *Off.* 2.7–8, should reassure us: "but these things have been set out carefully enough, I think, in our *Academics*." Whatever the sources of Cicero's own speeches in his Academic books,[82] the views he expresses there are not his own peculiar views—not even those peculiar to Philo[83]—but the traditional views of Arcesilaus and Carneades and their followers.

This practice of accepting for the time being what seems to one "chiefly plausible" (*maxime probabile*) was (admittedly, on Cicero's own evidence; but why distrust it when it concerns the school he supports?) already that of Carneades. The Antiochian Lucullus (*Luc.* 60) describes the method of the Skeptical Academy as "speaking *pro* and *contra* everything"—not only *contra* everything, but also *pro* everything. If we want an example of Carneades at work, we have it in *Luc.* 131 and 139. In 131 we read: "Carneades used to put forward the view—not that he held it himself but in order to combat the Stoics with it—that the chief good was to enjoy those things that nature had recommended as primary."[84] But in 139 we have: "so that I should follow Calliphon, whose opinion indeed Carneades was constantly defending with so much zeal that he was thought actually to accept it (although Clitomachus used to declare that he had never been able to understand what Carneades did accept)." Clitomachus was an industrious, but not an unduly perspicacious, pupil. He was that paradoxical animal, an orthodox Carneadean,[85] which, to a more intelligent follower of the Skeptical Academy, would be tantamount to an attempt to be a dogmatic skeptic.

Carneades' practice was, in principle, just like that which we

---

82. On which see *Antiochus*, Excursus 3, 391–423, esp. 406–20.
83. *Antiochus*, 84–88.
84. Cf. *Fin.* 5.20 (as part of the *Carneadea divisio*), 2.42 (where this position is treated as well-known).
85. *Antiochus*, 75ff.; 303–4.

have observed in Cicero's later writings: to defend whichever available or possible doctrine appealed to him for the time being—whether it was merely for the sake of argument, or in a more "positive" fashion, as *probabilis*. That this involves constant changes of mind and position is only natural. What Clitomachus did not grasp and Cicero, in his later stage, does is that as long as you have not given up your basic Skeptical orientation and methods, these constant vacillations, far from being alien to your approach, are of its essence. Cicero's "day-to-day eclecticism" is therefore far from being his own invention.

In his philosophical corpus of the 50s, then, Cicero rejected the Skepticism of Carneades and adopted some positive doctrines. It is highly likely, as Schmidt[86] has suggested, that this has something to do with his renewed hopes, after his return from exile and with the new political constellation being formed in Rome, of a return to political activity, if only as an *éminence grise*. I would hazard a guess that, throughout the period between his studies in Athens in 79 B.C. and his forced retirement from politics after Pharsalus, Cicero required some positive doctrines to correspond to the positive role he played as a statesman and orator. Antiochus's approach, even if not his exact doctrines, suited Cicero to the hilt. He could claim for himself a respectable Platonic pedigree, more ancient than Cato's Stoic one and far less severe.

During his final years of political excommunication, divorce, the failure of his second marriage, and the death of Tullia, his doubts and hesitations turned him naturally back toward the skepticism of his earlier years. It may be no accident that one question that had bothered him ever since his year in Athens— the problem of the self-sufficiency of virtue as against the "external goods"—recurs with such agonizing frequency in the writings of his last years. In his predicament during those years, that of the virtuous man suffering from an accumulation of external

86. N. 69 above.

evils, this problem was for him more than a mere matter of ethical theory.

But once he returned to his old Skeptical affiliation, he was as consistent as he could manage to be. Even his last work as a master of rhetoric, *Orator* of 46 B.C., ends on a note of clear Academic Skepticism which presages much of what we find in his later works. The Academy and Cicero's relation to it are not mentioned explicitly there. The Academy has, indeed, been mentioned before (12) as Cicero's training ground as an orator, and not just as a philosopher. Even the Platonic Ideas are mentioned in 9–10 to illustrate Cicero's conception of the ideal orator. But when we turn to 237, we cannot help being struck by expressions such as "nor shall I ever affirm that this opinion of mine is truer than yours," where "I shall affirm" (*affirmabo*) presages Cicero's frequent use of that verb in the Academic books in a "dogmatic" sense (e.g., *Acad.* 1.46; *Luc.* 8, 14); or the next sentence: "Not only may you and I differ in our opinion, but I myself may have different opinions at different times," which presages "we live from day to day" of the *Tusculans*.

There was, however, one corner which Cicero appears to have kept sealed off from this renewed Skepticism, albeit without pointing this out (as he might have done in the 50s). It is, I suspect, no mere accident that Carneades is totally absent from the first two books of the *Tusculans*, which deal with contemning death and enduring pain and suffering. It is, of course, no accident that the fragments of his *Consolatio* show no trace of Skepticism. They deal with life as a punishment and a migration (1–2); with the divine nature of the soul (4); with apotheosis and life after death (5–6); and with the blessings of consolation for Cicero and for some of his Roman forebears (7–10).[87] Tullia's

87. There is no modern critical edition of Cicero's *Consolatio* available to me. Since this is not a crucial matter for our argument, I have used vol. 4, part 2 of J. C. Orelli's great edition of Cicero (Zurich, 1828), 489–91, and I give his numbers for the fragments.

death and consecration were too close to Cicero's heart to be tampered with by Skepticism, not merely because (as Pliny, *NH Praef.* 22, tells us) he followed an earlier *Consolatio* by Crantor the "dogmatic" Academic (albeit Arcesilaus' bosom friend), which Panaetius had recommended to Aelius Tubero to learn by heart (*Luc.* 135). After all, in *De officiis* Cicero follows Panaetius himself, but this does not deter him from declaring his loyalty to the Skeptical Academy a few times in the course of that work.

There are two other works of Cicero's later period that show no trace of Skepticism. Again, it is no accident that both of them are of a somewhat private nature: for they are dedicated to Cicero's lifelong and closest friend, Atticus, and they deal with two issues shared by both of them: friendship and old age. This is not the place to enter into the intricate problem of the composition and sources of *Cato maior de senectute* and *Laelius de amicitia*, both written in 44 B.C. But one common characteristic makes them stand out against all other extant works of the same period. In both, Cicero has abandoned the milieu of the other works of this period—that of Cicero himself and his friends—and has returned to earlier generations and to the great departed, as he did in *De republica* and *De oratore*. He himself tells us that this is no accident: "Besides, discourses of this kind seem in some way to acquire greater dignity when founded on the authority of men of old, especially such as are renowned; and hence, in reading my own work [*sc. On Old Age*], I am at times so affected that I think the speaker is Cato and not myself."

More dignity? More than what—or whose? As to "authority," is this a proper expression for a Skeptical Academic to use? After all, if the Skeptic does not disclose his opinion, it is "in order that the listeners may be guided by reason rather than authority" (*Luc.* 60). But the passage we have just quoted from *De amicitia* 4 is reminiscent of Cotta's words in *ND* 3.5: "But on any question of religion I am guided by the high priests Titus Coruncanius, Publius Scipio, and Publius Scaevola, not Zeno or Cleanthes or Chrysippus; and I have Gaius Laelius, augur and philosopher in one, whom I would rather hear discoursing on religion . . . than any leading Stoic." This in contrast to Cotta's own earlier statement: "For I am in no small way moved by your authority, Balbus." "Authority" again—and here again the authority of those ancient and illustrious men—and Romans—as against that of any philosopher, including Carneades, whose refutation of the Stoics is about to be expounded by Cotta himself, Cicero's mouthpiece in this work. The arguments of the Academics cannot easily be refuted (1.13), but in matters of religion, the authority of our Roman ancestors is far greater.

There is one issue in *Laelius de amicitia* about which I have always felt somewhat perturbed. The work is dedicated to Atticus; and when Cicero comes to define friendship, it is (20) "complete agreement on all matters human and divine, accompanied by goodwill and affection." That there existed between Cicero and Atticus "goodwill and affection," this goes without saying. But "complete agreement on all matters human and divine" between an Epicurean and one of the most thorough critics of Epicurean philosophy in the whole of extant literature?

Old age and suffering may have helped Cicero turn back to Academic Skepticism in matters philosophical. He may not have made up his mind to his dying day concerning the sufficiency of virtue to happiness and the importance of external goods. He may have found the various philosophical proofs for the existence of the gods and arguments about their nature inadequate, contradictory, and sufficiently refuted by Carneades. But for the consolations of religion, with its promise of life after death, and for the consolations of old age and friendship, he reserved a corner which was not to be invaded by his skepticism.

JAAP MANSFELD

3

Philosophy in the service of Scripture

Philo's exegetical strategies

INTRODUCTION

Whatever one may think of the terms *eclecticism* and *eclectic* as used in a general sense, they continue to be useful and applicable in the case of Philo's philosophical interpretations of Scripture and of his scriptural interpretations of Greek philosophy.

In this chapter I shall try to describe the different levels on which Philo's eclectic strategies work and to provide the necessary qualifications so far as the idea of eclecticism itself is concerned. In Part 1, I shall attempt to account for the two ways of

For Philo, I have used the Loeb edition and the volumes that have been published of *Les oeuvres de Philon d'Alexandrie* (1961–), abbreviated here as *Oeuv. PhA*. Other editions used are indicated in the footnotes. Translations of Philonic texts are from the Loeb edition, with occasional modifications. Indispensable instruments for research included G. Mayer, *Index Philoneus* (Berlin, 1974) (does not include the fragments); *Biblia patristica: Supplément. Philon d'Alexandrie* (Paris, 1982) (index of all the biblical passages quoted or alluded to); and R. Radice, *Filone d'Alessandria: bibliografia generale 1937–1982* (Naples, 1983) (*bibliographie raisonnée*).

interpreting Scripture that are valid according to Philo: the literal way, and the allegorical way. Some of the interpretations called literal by Philo may strike us as being allegorical, for instance the one concerned with the Platonic cosmology, which he finds in the first chapters of Genesis. For Philo, however, the allegorical or, as he often calls it, the deeper interpretation pertains to the inner, not the outer, world. It follows that philosophical theories that are useful at the literal level need not be so at the allegorical, and conversely. The application of this distinction throws some light on the vexed problem of the place of the so-called philosophical treatises within the Philonic *corpus*.

In Part 2, I shall deal with Philo's use of the Skeptic technique of constructing a "disagreement" (*diaphōnia*) by arranging the theories of the philosophers in polar opposition. Philo exploits this technique in order to neutralize and overcome these conflicting views. Yet a responsible choice among the more important of the warring doctrines is feasible, because for Philo what Moses says is decisive. Philo feels he has a right to adduce the philosophical views of the Greeks because he is convinced that Greek philosophy itself derives from the interpretation of the books of Moses.

1. REZEPTION AND LEVELS OF EXEGESIS

Exegesis of the Torah by means of concepts and terms derived from Greek philosophy did not begin with Philo. Fragments of the writings of his predecessor and fellow-Alexandrian Aristobulus (perhaps ca. 100 B.C.) survive. In his books, Philo often enough refers to other Jewish exegetes who had proposed a philosophical interpretation of Scripture. For example, at *QG* 1.8 he attributes to *others* the important (Middle) Platonizing exegesis of Genesis 1:27 as referring to an intelligible, and of 2:7 as referring to a sensible, Man ("some . . . have said").[1] Aristobulus had already stated that Pythagoras, Plato, and Socrates, as well as Orpheus, Linus, Hesiod, Homer, and even Aratus, are dependent on Moses (*ap.* Euseb. *PE* 13.12 = Aristob. frr. 3–5). As is well known, this is also Philo's view. According to the fragment *De deo* 6–7 (partly printed at *SVF* 2.422),[2] Moses spoke of the "technical fire" which informs the world long before the (Stoic) philosophers did, and much more clearly. Plato's account of the formation of the world and of man in the *Timaeus* had been anticipated in a superior way in the first chapters of Genesis.[3] The paradoxical view of the Stoic Zeno that only the wise man is free (*Prob.* 53) and his ethical principle that one should live in agreement with nature (160) have been derived from the lawgiver of the Jews (57, 160). Heraclitus's view that as long as we are in the body we live the death of the soul[4] has been derived (*LA* 1.107) or even stolen (*QG* 4.152) from Moses, and his theory that the opposites are "one" comes from the same source (*Her.* 214, *QG* 3.5). The "deeper meaning" of Genesis 15:18 is said to have been "praised by some of the philosophers who came afterward: Aristotle and the Peripatetics, . . . Pythagoras" (*QG* 3.16). In a remarkable passage (*Aet.* 76), Philo argues that the Stoics Boethus of Sidon and Panaetius, who abandoned the theory of the periodical conflagrations and regenerations of the world, did so under "divine inspiration" (*theoleptoi*; this is the only occurrence of the adjective listed in the *Index Philoneus*).

There is today a growing consensus that Philo was, first and foremost, a deeply religious Jewish person who lived according

---

1. Cf. below, p. 81, pp. 87ff.

2. Newly translated from the Armenian by F. Siegert, *Drei hellenistisch-jüdische Predigten*, Wiss. Unt. N.T. 20 (Tübingen, 1980), 84ff.

3. For the influence of *Tim.* see the exhaustive study by D. T. Runia, *Philo of Alexandria and the Timaeus of Plato*, Philosophia antiqua 44 (Leiden, 1986).

4. Cf. my paper "Heraclitus, Empedocles and Others in a Middle Platonist Cento in Philo of Alexandria," in *Vig Chr.* 39 (1985), 131ff.

to the Mosaic laws and whose primary objective as a writer and
scholar was the faithful interpretation of Scripture. This, it is
thought, explains what is often called his eclecticism,[5] or rather,
(as I would prefer to say) his preferences in the fields of Greek
philosophy. To attribute a naive sort of eclectic attitude to him
or to suggest that he was merely a constant dabbler in the com-
monplaces found in abundance in the philosophical and rhetorical circles of his day would be not only unfair but false. There
is more system in his interpretation of the sacred text than is
visible at first blush: there are themes, such as the creation of the
world by a provident God, or the "migration" of the soul, that
are overwhelmingly present in most of what survives. Furthermore, once it is acknowledged that some of the individual tracts
constituting the *Allegorical Commentary* are constructed as a series of questions and answers geared to the exegesis of the individual verses that form a biblical pericope, after the pattern of
the much more formal *Quaestiones et solutiones in Genesim* and
In Exodum, these treatises turn out to be far less rambling and
incoherent than they have often been assumed to be.[6] I would
like to add that in these more formal commentaries the individual
questions and answers dealing with separate lemmata tend to
group themselves in clusters which possess a definite thematic
unity; they are therefore comparable to the individual allegorical
tracts with their larger and more varied themes. Indeed, for all
their roots in the Sabbath liturgy of the synagogue and the study-
house which may have been connected therewith, and for all their

5. See V. Nikiprowetzky, *Le commentaire de l'Ecriture chez Philon d'Alexandrie*, ALGHJ 11 (Leiden, 1977), 191f.

6. P. Borgen and R. Skarsten, "Quaestiones et Solutiones: Some Ob-
servations on the Form of Philo's Exegesis," *Studia Philonica* 4 (1976–1977),
1ff; Nikiprowetzky (n. 5 above), passim, and his chapter in D. Winston and
J. Dillon, *Two Treatises of Philo of Alexandria*, Brown Univ. Jud. St. 25 (Chico,
California, 1983), 5ff. See now also D. T. Runia, "The Structure of Philo's
Allegorical Treatises," *Vig. Chr.* 38 (1984), 209ff., and R. Radice, "Filone
d'Allessandria nella interpretazione di V. Nikiprowetzky e della sua scuola,"
Rivista di Filosofia Neoscolastica 76 (1984), 15ff.

affinities with earlier Greek literary forms (the scientific *problē-mata*, or the "problems and solutions" literature dealing with the poets already mentioned by Aristotle in *Poet.* 25.1460b6), large sections of the *Quaestiones* are very much concerned with one dominant theme: the vicissitudes of the human soul. That, presumably, can be explained on the assumption that Philo was familiar with a Middle Platonist exegesis of the *Odyssey*[7] according to which Odysseus's arduous journey home symbolizes the labors of the soul attempting to return to its original abode. (But we do not know that this was a formal commentary of the "problems and solutions" type.)

However, a better understanding of Philo's exegetical aims and method of presentation is by no means equivalent to an explanation of his so-called eclecticism, that is to say, his important use of Greek philosophical ideas. The matter is much more complicated than that. Philo belongs to two different worlds and to two traditions, that of Greek philosophy and that of the Jewish exegesis of the Bible. Perhaps the German term *Reƶeption*, less ambiguous and more informative than *eclecticism*, should be preferred. In Philo's case, as in that of some of his Jewish predecessors, *Reƶeption*—for which "assimilation" is perhaps a better equivalent than the ugly "reception"—is concerned with two inherited historical complexities, each of which has its own definite and special character. Yet Philo endeavors to interpret each of these in terms of the other. Consequently, the attempt to unravel

7. Cf. P. Boyancé, "Echos des exégèses de la mythologie grecque chez Philon," in *Philon d'Alexandrie* (Lyon, 1967), 169ff.; U. Früchtel, "Die kosmologischen Vorstellungen bei Philon von Alexandrien," ALGHJ 2 (Leiden, 1968), 104–5; J. Dillon, "Ganymede as the Logos: Traces of a Forgotten Allegorization in Philo?" *CQ* 31 (1981), 183ff.; and esp. H. Tobin, *The Creation of Man: Philo and the History of Interpretation*, Cath. Bibl. Qu. Monogr. 14 (Washington, D.C., 1983), 150ff., with other references to the learned literature. F. Buffière, *Les mythes d'Homère et la pensée grecque* (Paris, 1956), 392ff., remains important for the allegorized *Odyssey*, although he failed to take account of the evidence in Philo.

the strands of his ingenious fabric is uphill work. His attitude toward Greek philosophy is dependent on his position as an exegete, and his attitude toward the Bible is to a large degree dependent on his philosophical beliefs. The student of Philo is therefore faced with an interpretive circle that threatens to be vicious rather than hermeneutical. Philo's attitude toward Greek philosophy may be eclectic, and his *Rezeption* be determined by his Jewish background. However, his attitude toward the exegesis of Scripture may also be eclectic, both because, from a philosophical point of view, he believed that certain things in Scripture are more important than other things, and insofar as concerns his evaluation of the works of his Jewish predecessors (some of whom were themselves interested in Greek philosophy).

But the history of pre-Philonic Alexandrian exegesis of the Torah (for a clear general reference to which see, for example, *Mos.* 1.4) must for the most part be extracted from Philo's own works.[8] Furthermore, as I shall argue, Philo is *both* capable of assimilating an existing "eclectic" doctrine—or, as I would prefer to say, of reinterpreting and integrating doctrines considered to be Classical (here names such as Posidonius, Antiochus, and Eudorus come to mind)—*and* of distinguishing between the main schools of Greek philosophy in a more historically responsible manner. He is, moreover, quite capable of aligning himself with a doctrine that does fall outside the scope of, say, the Middle Platonism of his day. He is even capable of an eclectic, or reinterpretive, attitude toward certain Middle Platonist doctrines.

There is another important point. Philo throughout distinguishes between what he calls the "literal" and what he calls the "allegorical" interpretation, the latter as a rule representing the core of his thought. This distinction is largely unheeded in the

8. See Tobin (n. 7 above), passim, and the unphilosophical B. L. Mack, "Philo Judaeus and the Exegetical Tradition in Alexandria," *ANRW* 21 (Berlin, 1984), 227ff.

scholarly literature,[9] and understandably so, because the "literal" interpretations presented (or cited from others) often look quite allegorical to us. One should, however, follow Philo's own indications, for these are relevant to the evaluation of his attitude toward Greek philosophy (his "eclecticism"). I shall argue presently that philosophical theories exist which can be adduced at the literal but not at the allegorical level, and conversely.

But I do not wish to argue against the growing modern consensus[10] that claims that much of Philo's philosophizing reflects the reinterpretive system of his so-called Middle Platonist contemporaries. For instance, although Philo read the *Timaeus* for himself, *De opificio mundi*, the first treatise of the *Exposition of the Law*, is much influenced by Middle Platonism, and its points of view can be paralleled from numerous passages elsewhere in Philo. This is important, since our sources for Middle Platonism (with the exception of *Timaeus Locrus* and a few fragments of Eudorus and Arius Didymus) are all rather later than Philo. We are therefore in a position to postulate that this reinterpretive system originated in Alexandria after, say, 50 B.C.[11]

However, there are other works which cannot, by any stretching of the term, be called Middle Platonist. For instance, if his

9. Tobin's pioneering and inspiring study (n. 7 above) is a notable exception.

10. Boyancé (n. 7 above), "Sur la théologie de Varron," *REA* 57 (1955), 57ff.; "Fulvius Nobilior et le Dieu ineffable," *RPh* 29 (1955), 172ff.; "Sur le discours d'Anchise," in *Homm. Duméʒil*, Coll. Latomus 45 (Brussels, 1960), 60ff.; "Etudes philoniennes," *REG* 76 (1963), 64ff.; "Sur l'exégèse hellénistique du Phèdre," in *Miscellanea Rostagni* (Turin, 1963), 45ff. Boyancé tends to overemphasize Antiochus's contribution. W. Theiler, "Philon von Alexandria und der Beginn des kaiserzeitlichen Platonismus" (1965), repr. in his *Untersuchungen ʒur antiken Literatur* (Berlin, 1970), 484ff.; "Philon von Alexandria und der hellenisierte Timaeus," in *Philomathes: Festschrift Merlan* (The Hague, 1971), 20ff. Früchtel (n. 7 above). J. Dillon, *The Middle Platonists* (London, 1977), 139ff. P. L. Donini, *Le scuole l'anima l'impero* (Turin, 1982), 100ff. Tobin (n. 7 above), 11ff. Interesting and useful critical remarks in Runia (n. 3 above), 483ff., 505ff.

11. For my discussion of this aspect of Philo's thought, cf. n. 4 above.

only surviving works were *Quod omnis probus liber* and *De animalibus*, would we not say that "if he had made a few little changes," Philo could be designated a "most genuine Stoic," even more so, perhaps, than Antiochus, for whom the sobriquet was coined by Cicero (*Acad.* 2.132)?[12] In Philo's day, the theories of the Stoics (unlike those of the Presocratics) lived on not only in books, but also in persons who saw themselves as Stoics. Indeed, not only does there exist the phenomenon known as Roman Stoicism, but there were even Stoics around in the days of Alexander of Aphrodisias and Plotinus. It may therefore be of some importance to point out that Philo's contemporary and fellow-Alexandrian, Chaeremon, who was a notorious enemy of the Jews, was a Stoic. Chaeremon interpreted Egyptian religion in the terms of Greek philosophy, just as Philo did for the Jewish religion; he appears to have been a member of the Egyptian embassy to Gaius in A.D. 40, just as Philo was one of the Jewish embassy.[13] Philo may have been familiar with Chaeremon's views, for (*Mos.* 1.23) he speaks of the Egyptian "philosophy conveyed in symbols, as displayed in the so-called holy letters" (the hieroglyphs), thus mentioning one of Chaeremon's favorite themes.[14] If even an Egyptian could be a Stoic in Alexandria, there must, of course, have been other Stoics in town.

Furthermore, in another philosophical work, *De aeternitate mundi*, Philo, rather than proceeding in a Middle Platonist way, displays a rather thorough knowledge of the various doctrines concerned with this topic as professed by the important schools

12. For *Prob.* cf. M. Petit, *Oeuv. PhA.* 28, 54ff., 78ff.; for *Anim.* see A. Terian, *Philonis Alexandrini De animalibus*, Stud. Hell. Jud. 1 (Chico, California, 1981), 49f., and "A Critical Introduction to Philo's Dialogues," *ANRW* 21 (1984), 277f. (also on Stoic arguments in *Prov.*).

13. See now P.W. van der Horst, *Chaeremon: Egyptian Priest and Stoic Philosopher*, EPRO 101 (Leiden, 1984).

14. Cf. fr. 12 van der Horst. On *Mos.* 1.23 see P.W. van der Horst, "The Secret Hieroglyphs in Classical Literature," *Actus: Festschrift Nelson* (Utrecht, 1982), 116, who, however, does not suggest that Philo may have known Chaeremon's work.

and is perfectly capable of distinguishing the Stoics from Plato and Aristotle, and Aristotle from the Stoics and Plato. He lists three views concerning the cosmos that have been put forward:[15] (1) that the world is eternal, uncreated and imperishable; (2) the opposite view, that it is created and will be destroyed; the third view (3) is a compromise, which "takes from"[16] (2) the idea that it is created and from (1) that it is imperishable (*Aet.* 7). This presentation is systematic, not historical.

The three main views are presented in the manner of a Skeptic "disagreement" followed by a compromise. In *Aet.* 7, the Aristotelian (and Pythagorean) view is cited first and that of (Democritus), Epicurus, and the Stoics second; in 8–12, this order is reversed. The view of Plato (and Hesiod) is cited last both at 7 and at 8–18. The suggestion at *Aet.* 7 that the third view is a compromise between the other two is of course only tenable from a systematic and not from a historical point of view (cf. n. 16 above). The "Succession" in the descriptive passage (8–18) is determined by both systematic and historical considerations. The important views, those of the Epicureans-and-Stoics/Aristotle/ Plato, are presented in an inverted historical sequence. Presumably, Philo believes that the history of Greek philosophy is one of decadence and that the farther one goes back, the nearer one gets to the truth, that is to say, to what Moses taught. The same

15. Cf. my paper "Providence and the Destruction of the Universe in Early Stoic Thought," in M. J. Vermaseren, ed., *Studies in Hellenistic Religion*, EPRO 78 (Leiden, 1979), 136ff.; D. T. Runia, "Philo's *De aeternitate mundi*," *Vig. Chr.* 35 (1981), 105ff.

16. John Dillon pointed out in the discussion of my paper that *Aet.* 7 surprisingly describes the third view as an *eclectic* combination of elements taken from both others (although chronologically it is the earliest): εἰσὶ δ' οἳ παρ' ἑκατέρων ἐκλαβόντες . . . μικτὴν δόξαν ἀπέλιπον. For the expression μικτὴν δόξαν, cf. *Comm. Lucani*, p. 290 Usener (*SVF* 2.817, 225, line 3) *mixtum dogma cum Platonico Stoicum*. Philo's scheme of two opposed views and a third, mixed one is anticipated at Aristotle *De an.* 1.2.404b30ff. (μίξαντες . . . ἀπ' ἀμφοῖν). A similar (though not unchronological) presentation of a "disagreement" and a compromise view is found at Cicero *Fat.* 39 (= *SVF* 2.974).

suggestion is entailed by the series of ancestors of the main views—Democritus/some Pythagoreans/Hesiod—the earliest of whom is again closest to Moses.

Philo, naturally, sides with Moses.[17] However, the text of *De aeternitate*, after an extensive presentation of Aristotle's case (taken up—as Philo shows—also by Theophrastus and other Peripatetics, and by some Stoics) against the orthodox Stoic view that the world will necessarily be destroyed and reborn again, breaks off with the announcement that the Aristotelian arguments will be met "point by point" (150).

The various doctrines, I would like to suggest, are here described in an order of validity. The theory of Democritus and Epicurus, cited first, is farthest from the truth, because these thinkers, when generating and destroying a plurality of worlds, only appeal to matter and chance. The Stoic theory is better, because it ascribes the generation of the one world to God and its destruction to Fire. It is curious that Philo has here chosen to present a very unorthodox Stoic view of the world-conflagration; possibly he could not resist the temptation to forget that the Stoic Fire is the same god as the god who generates the universe, in order to have the Stoic Fire resemble the elemental instrument used by his own god. He also argues that in a way the Stoics present the world as being eternal. Presumably, he emphasizes this aspect of genuine Stoic thought in order to expose it as a bastard form of Aristotelianism, or at any rate in order to bring it closer to Aristotle's view. Aristotle's theory, he argues, is better insofar as it is more God-fearing, since he does not want to credit God with creating something that would be less than perfect, i.e., destructible. Plato's theory however, is the best, because it comes closest to Moses'.

The best parallels for this presentation in the guise of an evaluative sequence are to be found in the later philosophical works

17. Cf. Runia (n. 15 above), 126f.

of Cicero, for which I may refer to W. Görler's discovery[18] of
what he calls a *Stufensystem*, a triadic pattern according to which
you first have a "low" view; next, an "elevated" view sharply
opposed to the low view; and, third, a "middle" view that is a
sort of compromise between the two others. In *ND* 1, for instance, the Epicurean view, the first to be discussed, is rejected
(cf. the position of the Epicurean view in *De aeternitate*). The
Stoic position, presented next (*ND* 2), is admired, but a more
moderate view is argued in book 3. According to Görler, Cicero
does not really choose between the more elevated and the middle
position; the latter is to be preferred from a rational point of view,
while the former is what he would really like to prefer. Görler
argues that this refusal to take sides in a definite way is characteristic of Cicero and in fact is what his philosophical position
amounts to, which may be right. What cannot be right, however,
is his claim that the pattern of presentation is Cicero's, for this is
ruled out by the parallel in Philo.[19] Philo, who has no affinities
with Skepticism so far as his own convictions are concerned, is
in a position to make a definite choice among possible options.[20]
Cicero and Philo each use the pattern in their own way, which I
think proves that the scheme is traditional.

However this may be, as one studies the way Philo presents
various philosophical doctrines in *De aeternitate mundi*, it grad-
ually becomes clear that he is not merely dependent on "eclectic"

18. W. Görler, *Untersuchungen zu Ciceros Philosophie* (Heidelberg, 1974),
esp. 20–62; there is a survey of "stages" (*Stufen*) at p. 61, and Cicero is
called "originator of this method" at p. 15. Cicero's Skepticism should be
freshly studied in the light of Behrends's argument that the legal experts of
Cicero's generation were all influenced by Skepticism; this, I think, helps to
explain Cicero's change (or rather return) to Skepticism in his later years
(O. Behrends, *Die Fraus Legis* [Göttingen, 1982]; cf. also the review by U.
Manthe, *Gnomon* 56 [1984], esp. 145–46, and Glucker's study in this
volume).

19. More instances from Philo are cited by Runia (n. 15 above), 147 n.
94.

20. See further below, part 2.

systems such as the (largely hypothetical) Alexandrian Platonism of his day, but is also familiar (as is Cicero), with a more historical approach to the great men and systems of the Greek past which enables him to state, compare, and judge their respective views. Actually, Philo's contemporary, the Neo-Pythagorean or Middle Platonist Eudorus, is also said to have written an extensive historical work in which he described the various doctrines of the schools, and Arius Didymus apparently did something similar.[21]

In another philosophical work, *De animalibus*, Philo in his reply to Alexander's array of arguments (73–100) defends the Stoic view that the animals do not possess reason; they have been created for the benefit of man. Although Philo does not say so, it is certain that the opposite view is unacceptable to him, not only because it conflicts with the prescriptions of the Mosaic cult but also because it cannot be squared with statements about man and the animals in Scripture; in this work, however, no biblical references are given.[22] At Genesis 2:19, man is said to have *given names* to the animals (this is Philo's *sensible* man, to be distinguished from the intelligible man at Genesis 1:27). At *Opif.* 148–49 and 1.18, 20, 21, Philo argues that man obtains this honor because he is the lord of the animals (cf. *Praem.* 9). Scriptural support for the latter idea is found elsewhere, at Genesis 1:26 (*archetōsan*) and 1:28 (*archete*), i.e., in the pericope which, according to Philo, deals with the *intelligible* man. There is only one quotation of Genesis 1:28 in Philo: at *QG* 2.56 (pp. 140–41 Marcus), where it serves to explain God's speech to Noah at Genesis 9:1–2 (which echoes 1:28). Noah is made "righteous king of earthly creatures" and is said to have "been equal in honor not to the molded and earthly Man [of Genesis 2:7] but to him who was made in the likeness and form, who is incorporeal" (p. 141 Marcus, whose partly hypothetical translation I

21. Cf. Dillon (n. 10 above), 116.
22. See Terian (n. 12 above), 46f.

have corrected; cf. also *Oeuvr. Ph. ad loc.*). According to Philo (p. 142 Marcus), this is the "literal" interpretation—which, one should note, he does not reject; the "deeper meaning" is concerned with the domination of mind over the body, the senses, and the passions. The theme of man's domination of the animals (in a literal sense) also occurs elsewhere (e.g., *Opif.* 83–84, 142, *Agric.* 8, *Prov.* 1.9, 2.105), where scriptural evidence is not quoted.

It appears to be the case that Genesis 1:26 and 28 were no favorites with Philo (and/or with the Jewish exegetical tradition he is following) and that he preferred to conflate the idea of domination from Genesis 1:26 and 29 with that of the giving of names at Genesis 2:19, which figures much more prominently in his oeuvre. That tralaticious material is used by Philo also appears from *QG* 2.66, where another tradition is followed (or another possibility is exploited) and Noah is made to represent the "first molded [i.e., sensible] man."

The lack of biblical references in *De animalibus* may therefore be explained by means of Philo's attitude toward Genesis 1:26 and 28 elsewhere. Furthermore, it does not seem to have been noticed that in a remote corner of the *QG* (1.94), where he comments on Genesis 6:7 (God will wipe out man and destroy the beasts), Philo argues as follows: "The literal meaning is this [N.B. what follows has also been preserved in Greek]: *it makes it clearly known that the beasts* [aloga] *were not primarily generated for their own sakes, but for the sake of men and for their service.* And when these were destroyed, the former were rightly destroyed together with them, since there no longer existed those for which they were made" (my italics). This "literal meaning" of Genesis 6:7 (for which cf. also *Abrah.* 45) not only agrees with the interpretation of Genesis 2:19 at *Opif.* 148–49 and *QG* 1.18, 20, 21 (where, as we have noticed, the idea of domination has been blended in from Genesis 1:26 and 28) but also with the point of view defended by Philo in *Anim.* 73–100. According to *QG* 1.94, the "allegorical meaning" is that "Man is the mind within us, and beast is sensation." The latter is very close to the view presented in the allegorical commentary (*LA* 2.9–18; exegesis of Genesis 2:19 again), where, however, the animals are said to represent the passions (for which cf. also the "deeper meaning" at *QG* 2.56).

Another parallel is at *QG* 2.9 (on Genesis 6:17, "whatever is on earth shall die." Question: "What sins did the beasts commit?"). Here the "literal meaning" is set out at much greater length, and an interesting and significant link with the *philosophical* views *rejected* in *De animalibus* is to be found in Philo's phrase, "the beasts were made, not for their own sake, *as wise men reason*, but for . . . men" (my italics). According to the "deeper meaning" as set out here, the animals represent the "earthly part of the body," i.e., the senses, which must die together with the body (cf. *QG* 1.94) when the latter is "deluged by streams of passion. . . . For a life of evil is death." (Cf. also *Conf.* 23–24.)

It follows that the philosophical view defended by Philo in *De animalibus*, which is that of the Stoics, is pertinent only at the *literal level of the interpretation* of the relevant texts in Scripture. According to Philo, the literal interpretation, if it provides a satisfactory sense, is fully acceptable; the symbolic or allegorical or deeper interpretation, however, is what his exegesis is really about. Apparently, it is important for Philo that the literal interpretation of man's naming of the animals, blended with the idea of his lordship over them, can be defended on purely philosophical grounds and that here Greek philosophy (in the guise of a Stoic doctrine) and Scripture meet. It should also be noted that the allegorical interpretation, i.e., the *domination* of mind over the body, the senses, the passions, is *derived from* (or, rather, geared to) the *domination* of the animals by man in the literal interpretation. The deeper meaning exploits themes familiar from both Stoic and Platonic philosophy: reason versus the passions or, more Platonically, reason versus the body. *De animalibus* itself only enters the outer orbit of Philo's thought, that connected with the literal interpretation.

From the passages studied above it appears that Philo's attitude toward Greek philosophy is a very complicated one indeed. He may draw on "eclectic" Middle Platonist theories for the literal interpretation of the creation story as well as on purely Stoic ideas for the literal interpretation of man's relation to the animals. But what is useful at the literal level need not be so at the allegorical. Furthermore, even at the literal level Philo may see fit to produce an interpretive blend of his own, as in the case of the world's possible end, described in terms both Platonic and Stoic. The demands of scriptural exegesis seem often to be decisive in respect to the option chosen. Some of Philo's literal interpretations seem to be an already traditional part of Jewish philosophical exegesis (e.g., the two types of man, *QG* 1.8). Doubtless, there are also unphilosophical Jewish motifs of an already traditional nature in Philo, which further influenced his selection among possible options; but this is a subject better left to the historians of Jewish thought.[23] Reading through Philo, however, one cannot help feeling that for all his Jewish piety and loyalty to Moses and for all his indebtedness to specifically Jewish exegetical themes, Greek philosophy really dominates the field,[24] and that Moses and the Jewish prophets are virtually converted into Greek philosophers. The attitude of Philo and his Alexandrian predecessors was not adopted by the rabbis who gave shape to the orthodox Judaism which was to develop after the destruction of the temple by Titus. This shows that in the interpretation of Scripture other options were open.

23. See P. Borgen, "Philo of Alexandria: A Critical and Synthetical Survey of Research since World War II," in *ANRW* 21 (Berlin, 1984), 124ff., 132ff.; P. Borgen in M.E. Stone, éd., *Jewish Writings of the Second Temple Period* [*Compendia rerum Iudaicarum ad Novum Testamentum*, Section 2] (Assen, 1984), 259ff., 264ff.; Mack (n. 8 above).

24. Cf. also Runia (n. 3 above), 535ff.

An important question, then, which I believe has not yet been answered in a fully satisfactory way, is: why did Philo and his Alexandrian predecessors choose to interpret Scripture as a (Greek) philosophy? The answer, I believe, is provided by Philo's (and his predecessors') view of the history of Mosaic philosophy. Moses came first, and the Greeks have taken over his ideas, or perhaps in individual cases been favored with a special revelation which made them talk in the manner of Moses. It follows that, for Philo, it is perfectly legitimate to adduce the views of the Greek philosophers for the interpretation of Scripture; for all practical purposes, they can be seen as *fellow-exegetes*. Without exception, Philo cites his Jewish predecessors without giving their names. A few times, he gives the names of his Greek predecessors, but their views, too, are usually cited (or even paraphrased) anonymously.[25] In this way, Greek philosophy, which by no means always provides a correct interpretation of Scripture, is as indispensable to exegesis as the not always correct views of the Jewish exegetes cited by Philo.

Furthermore, the history of Greek philosophy itself can be understood as one of (re-)interpretation: Aristotle's interpretation of Plato,[26] Zeno's interpretation of Plato and Aristotle (think of Antiochus). The Middle Platonists of Philo's Alexandria certainly belonged to such an interpretive tradition or school of thought, and it is only natural that Philo turned to these contemporaries and studied the most up-to-date interpretation of Plato that was available (indeed, his predecessors who introduced the two types of man seem already to have done so). The study of Greek philosophy, when viewed from this angle, is, ultimately, a study of the pagan interpretive tradition which itself, in the last

25. Why Greek names are (sometimes) given, but Jewish names never, remains a mystery; in the Talmud names are the rule. Perhaps the simple fact is that before, and in, Philo's time most Jewish exegetes preferred anonymity, whereas the Greek philosophers had after all signed their works and were persons of great prestige.

26. Note, however, that Philo, *Aet.* 16, is aware of important innovations on Aristotle's part.

resort, is nothing but an interpretation of Scripture, either directly or at one or more removes.

When placed in this perspective, Philo's so-called philosophical works are not as singular as they have often been thought to be. All of them deal with matters that are ultimately geared to the interpretation of Scripture. Philo must really have felt rather superior to his Greek colleagues, for they did not have the books of Moses. His willingness in the philosophical works to meet them, as it were, in their own field (cf. *Det.* 1ff.) shows his sense of security: only the follower of Moses (to whose authority a discreet reference is several times inserted at focal points of the argument) is in a position to adjudicate between the competing views of the Greek experts. On the other hand, Philo believes that the study of pagan philosophy (itself the sequel to the study of the "standard curriculum" [*enkuklia*]) is a necessary condition for the study and understanding of the true, i.e., the Mosaic philosophy.[27] This suggests that he believed the Greeks had often been better exegetes of Scripture than their Jewish colleagues, or at least not inferior to them. The philosophical works, among which *De animalibus* and *De providentia* 2 have been proved to be works of Philo's old age,[28] in this sense pave the way for the exegesis of Scripture.

Some of these writings (*Aet., Prov.* 1, and *Prob.*)[29] may have had as their intended public the pagan philosophical milieu, and others (*Prov.* 2, *Anim.*) the Jewish apostates. This does not entail, however, that no systematic position is reserved for them in the developing grand design of Philo's work. Philo's proof, presented to the Greeks, that their own philosophy in its most representative and valuable aspects is confirmed by and even derived from

27. See P. Borgen, *Bread from Heaven*, Suppl. n.s. 10 (Leiden, 1965), 99ff.; Nikiprowetzky (n. 5 above), 97ff.; A. Mendelson, *Secular Education in Philo of Alexandria*, Monogr. Hebr. Un. Coll. 7 (Cincinnati, 1982), 35ff.

28. Terian (n. 12 above) (1981), 28ff.; (1984), 289ff. Note that this proof is valid for the dialogues only, not for *Prov.* 1, *Prob.*, *Aet.*

29. The dates of *Aet.* and *Prov.* 1 are uncertain, but the old hypothesis of the "early writings" has lost its charm.

the Law implies that it would be useful for Greek philosophers to study the Torah. Jewish apostates who use Greek philosophy against the Torah, as Alexander did, are invited to return to the truth. Simultaneously, however, these works may serve as an introduction to the more important discussions of Greek philosophers about subjects that are dominant in the Torah, an introduction already doctored to suit the Jewish point of view, which those who want to interpret Scripture in a rational way may use with profit.

Because the Greek philosophers are Philo's predecessors, he can use them the way he uses his Jewish colleagues: he can read them with an open mind, reject what is wrong or one-sided, and adduce and use what is satisfactory and feasible. On the other hand, his use of Scripture is not as invariably decisive as a modern consensus would want us to believe. I have already referred[30] to the curious way Genesis 1:26 and 28 are treated, and I would like to add a related instance.

In Philo, we find *both* the view that Genesis 1:27 and 2:7 are about the creation of the same man *and* that they are about different types of man, i.e., the "*created* man" (*epoiēsen*) and the "molded man" (*eplastēsen*). The latter view, as we have noticed, is attributed by him to others (*QG* 1.8)[31] but not rejected (it is also the starting point of the allegory at *LA* 1.35ff.).[32] The other view is not rejected either. Tobin has argued that the "two types" interpretation is later than the "one man" interpretation.[33] There is an interesting complication which, to my knowledge, has not

30. Above, p. 82.

31. Above, p. 71.

32. Biblical scholarship attributes Genesis 1:27 to the *Priesterschrift*, 2:7 to the *Jahwist*. See, e.g., R. Smend, *Die Entstehung des Alten Testaments*, Theol. Wiss. 1 (Stuttgart³, 1984), 40. Philo and his predecessors were faced with a real exegetical problem, that of the double version of the same story which also inspired the modern *Quellenforschung*. The *LXX* introduces the word *Adam* only at Genesis 2:16; in parts, this translation is a *midrash*.

33. Tobin (n. 7 above), 102ff. Runia (n. 3 above), 556ff., with backward references, has bravely argued that according to Philo, Genesis 1:27 and 2:7 are about one and the same man.

been observed: Genesis 5:1b–2 does not enter into this discussion. Here, it would appear, the text of the Bible states beyond possible doubt that the "created" (intelligible) man, i.e., the man "in the image" of Genesis 1:27, and the "molded" (sensible) man of 2:7 are the same person:

> (1b) On the day on which God created [*epoiēsen*] Adam, he created [*epoiēsen*] him in the image of God. (2) Male and female he created [*epoiēsen*] them, and he praised them. And he called them by the name of Adam, on the day on which he created [*epoiēsen*] them. (3) And Adam lived for two hundred and thirty years and begat
> . . .

The (sensible) Adam (the "molded" man of 2:7) who begat Seth (5:3, cf. 4:25) is "male and female," just like the (intelligible) *anthrōpos* at 1:27, and the verb for *created* at 5:1b–2 is none other than the *epoiēsen* also found at 1:27. Yet Philo can be very dogmatic about the differences between the two types of man (as at *Opif.* 134–35).

Now, as long as Jewish exegetes believed that 1:27 and 2:7 refer to the same man, they were in a position to ignore 5:1b–2, which merely confirms this view. But it is certainly odd that those who believed that two types of man are involved ignored 5:1b–2, which contradicts this interpretation (they also virtually ignored Genesis 1:26 and 28, likewise hard to square with the two different types).[34] One may, of course, assume that they kept silent about this part of the evidence on purpose, but it is perhaps more to the point to assume that what they did was not so much interpret the Bible as reinterpret the view of their predecessors, who had only discussed 1:27 and 2:7. Philo *never* quotes or refers to Genesis 5:1b–2, although he quotes and comments on 5:1a, "this is the book of the generation of men."[35] Most remarkably, however, he connects this half-verse not with what follows but with what precedes, that is, with the brief genealogy of Adam

34. The point I am about to make corroborates Tobin's thesis that the "one man" interpretation is earlier.

35. αὕτη ἡ βίβλος γενέσεως ἀνθρώπων (*sefer toledoth adam*).

that concludes Genesis 4 (*QG* 1.79–80, *Det.* 138–39; cf. esp. *Abrah.* 9, *epilegei*). Yet he *knows* that Genesis 5 also contains the (full) "genealogy of Adam," for he cites and interprets the characterization of Seth at *QG* 1.81 from this chapter (Genesis 5:3). Thus the awkward, or unwelcome, verses 5:1b–2 were tactfully omitted. To repeat, we may perhaps assume that Philo, rather than willfully distorting the evidence, felt committed, without noticing what this entailed, to an exegetical tradition that had failed to take these verses into account. Yet in a person who is merely a loyal follower of Moses this procedure is most noteworthy. We are justified in concluding that his predecessors, and Philo himself, really *wanted* very much to produce a (Middle) Platonizing interpretation of the creation story in Genesis. In other words, they were prepared to be silent about scriptural evidence that could not find a place in their philosophy. And yet, at *QG* 3.3 (Greek fragment), Philo posits that one should not interpret Scripture by arguing from the part to the whole, but, conversely, should adduce all the evidence available.

2. DISSENSION AND DECISION

The Skeptical[36] technical term for disagreement, *diaphōnia* (*dissensio*),[37] occurs only once in the Philonic corpus, at *Her.* 248:

36. For Philo's Skepticism see, e.g., Früchtel (n. 7 above), 132ff., and especially Nikiprowetzky (n. 5 above), 183ff., who, however, overemphasizes Philo's pious indifference to the debates of physical science. Philo is not indifferent when the major issues of physics (including theology) are concerned, but only when lesser questions are at stake. Note that the *dissensio* in Cicero *Acad.* 2.117ff. first lists the major issues (118–21), then the minor ones (122–25).

37. An argument for *dissensio* is already attributed to the Skeptical Academy at Cicero *Acad.* 2.117f.; the word occurs at 117, and a plurality of discrepant philosophical views is listed at 118 (cf. also, e.g., *Lael.* 32, *dissentiunt*; *Tusc.* 5.83, *dissentientium*). One may further adduce the instance cited above in n. 16. That Arcesilaus already opposed conflicting theoretical views is argued by G. Striker, "Über den Unterschied zwischen den Pyrrhoneern und den Akademikern," *Phronesis* 26 (1981), 156ff., and by A. M. Ioppolo, "Doxa ed epoche in Arcesilao," *Elenchos* 5 (1984), 36, 41.

"Philosophy is full of *disagreement*, because truth flees from the credulous mind, which deals in conjecture. It is her nature to elude discovery and pursuit, and it is this which in my opinion produces these verbal feudings [*staseis*]." These sentences round off a description (246–47) of what Philo calls the "dogmatic [*dogmatikas*] wranglings of the sophists," of which he lists the following (246): (1) those who say the universe has not come to be versus those who say it has, and (2) those who say it will be destroyed versus those who say that "though by nature destructible, it will never be destroyed, since it is held together by a bond of superior strength, namely the will of its Maker." In a parallel passage (*Ebr.* 199), which derives from one of Aenesidemus's tropes,[38] Philo in a similar way opposes the anti-creationists to the creationists, and those who reject providence (the description recalls Democritus and the Epicureans) to those who believe in it.[39] We are of course immediately reminded of the debate reported by Philo in *De aeternitate mundi* and *De providentia* 1 and recall that in these philosophical works (as indeed also elsewhere) he each time adopted one of these opposed options: the world has been created, is therefore by nature destructible, but is held together by the will of its creator. At *Her.* 246, Philo next opposes (3) those who maintain that "nothing is but all things

38. As was discovered by von Arnim and has now been definitively proved by K. Janáček, "Philon von Alexandria und skeptische Tropen," *Eirene* 19 (1982), 83ff., esp. 84–85.

39. For providence, cf. Aenesidemus's last trope *ap.* Sextus *PH* 1.151: "we oppose dogmatic conceptions to one another when we say that some declare . . . that human affairs are controlled by the providence of the gods, and others without providence." See also *Eugnostos the Blessed*, *NHC* 3, 4.70.10–21: "But the speculation has not reached the truth. For the ordering is spoken of in three [different] opinions by all the philosophers, and hence they do not agree. For some say about the world that it was directed by itself. Some, that it is providence [that directs it]. Some, that it is fate" (trans. D. M. Parrott in J. M. Robinson, ed., *The Nag Hammadi Library in English* [Leiden, 1977], 208). I owe this parallel to R. van den Broek. The Greek original of *Eugnostos* appears to have been composed by an Alexandrian Jewish near-contemporary of Philo's.

become" to those who assume the opposite. Although these or similar issues are familiar (cf. Xenophon *Mem.* 1.1, 14, Plato *Tht.* 152E, Aristotle *Cael.* 3.1, 298b14–33 [although in a more intricate form], and ps.-Arist. *MXG* 1.974a2–4 and 975a14–15), the most plausible assumption is that Philo here reproduces a Skeptic "disagreement."

Next, Philo turns (4) to those who make man the criterion[40] (his actual words refer to those who say man is the measure of all things), whom he opposes to those who make havoc of the criteria of both sense-perception and mind; and (5) to those who maintain that all things are beyond comprehension, whom he opposes to those who hold that a good many things can be known. The Protagorean reference in (4) may be read as a caption for those who assign complete reliability to all sense-experience such as the Epicureans, they being opposed to thorough-going Skeptics such as the Pyrrhonists. At (5) he clearly has the Academic Skeptics and presumably their opponents, the Stoics, in mind. These neat "reversals" (*peritropai*), which reduce the Academics and the Pyrrhonists to mere parties in a "disagreement" (*diaphōnia*), may conceivably be Philo's own clever idea. He wants no truck with Skepticism, of whatever denomination, as a serious sect (cf. *QG* 3.33, which mentions "Academics" and "Skeptics" in one breath). One may compare the characterization of the Sophist as a Skeptic at *Fug.* 210: "He strikes all representatives of learning, opposing each individually and all in common, and is struck by all in return, since they naturally defend the doctrines [*dogmata*] to which their soul has given birth." (For this conflict between all the others and the Skeptics, cf. also Cicero *Acad.* 2.70.)

Finally, in *Her.* 247, Philo briefly lists the "disagreements"

40. For man as the criterion, cf. Sextus *PH* 2.22–42, G. Striker, "The Ten Tropes of Aenesidemus" in M. Burnyeat, ed., *The Skeptical Tradition* (Berkeley and Los Angeles, 1983), 106ff., and Long's study in this volume, pp. 188–91.

concerned with a plurality of natural phenomena, in a manner that anticipates the use of ps.-Plutarch by, say, Irenaeus and Eusebius, and of ps.-Plutarch and Aetius by Theodoretus.[41] According to Philo in *Her.* 247, these quarrels go on until the "male midwife who is also the judge observes the brood of each disputant's soul, throws away all that is not worth rearing, but saves what is worth saving and approves it for such careful treatment as is required." Colson *ad loc.* of course refers to Socrates (e.g., Plato *Tht.* 151), and Marguerite Harl *ad loc.* links the "judge" with Abraham, i.e., "the human intellect in its highest function, which assimilates it to the divine Logos" (my translation). One may also think of passages such as Plato *Phaedo* 96A–99E, and perhaps Xenophon *Mem.* 1.1.11–14, where Socrates, disappointed by the disagreement among the natural philosophers, goes his own way (note that the latter passage is quoted in a Skeptical context by Eusebius *PE* 15.62.7ff.). As far as the image of the judge is concerned, it is also interesting to recall Aristotle *Metaph. B* 1.995b2f.: "one who has heard all the conflicting theories, like one who has heard both sides in a lawsuit, is necessarily more competent to judge" (trans. Tredennick). One may also compare Cicero *Fat.* 39: "Chrysippus in the guise of a respected umpire" (*Chrysippus tamquam arbiter honorarius*).

41. Cf. R. M. Grant, *Miracle and Natural Law* (Amsterdam, 1952), 80f., on Irenaeus *Adv. haer.* 2.28.1–2; Grant, *After the New Testament* (Philadelphia, 1967), 158ff.; W. R. Schoedel, "Philosophy and Rhetoric in the *Adversus Haereses* of Irenaeus," *Vig. Chr.* 13 (1959), 22ff.; and W. C. van Unnik, "Theological Speculation and Its Limits," in W. R. Schoedel and R. L. Wilcken, eds., *Early Christian Literature and the Classical Intellectual Tradition*, Theol. Hist. 54 (Paris, 1979), 33ff., who emphasizes Irenaeus's theological inference. Cf. Eusebius *PE* 1.7.16 (διαφωνίας) and the chapter title of 1.8; also 14.13.9 (ἀντιδοξίας) and Theodoretus *Gr. aff. cur.* 4.31 (διαφωνίαν), and note that Theodoretus distinguishes between Aetius and ps.-Plut. See also R. van den Broek, "Eugnostos: Via Skepsis naar Gnosis," *Ned. Theol. Tijdschr.* 37 (1983), 104ff. Philo also knew "Aetius"; cf. on *Prov.* 1.22, P. Wendland, "Eine doxographische Quelle Philos," *Sitzb. Akad. Berl.* (1897), 1074ff., and my remarks in *The Pseudo-Hippocratic Tract ΠΕΡΙ ΈΒΔΟΜΑΔΩΝ* (Assen, 1971), 130f. n. 4.

In another passage, *Abr.* 162–64, the "disagreement" is presented in much less scathing terms, and indeed culminates in a list of issues that are of primary importance to Philo. He here explains why God spared one of the cities of the plain: the five cities symbolize the senses, the fifth representing sight. The eyes observe the heavens and draw the mind in the same direction so that it starts wondering and philosophizing (a Platonic theme, cf. *Tim.* 47a). This wondering is not open-minded, but follows the pattern of a "disagreement": are these phenomena created, or do they have a beginning? Are they infinitely many, or finitely many (cf. the related points of Aenesidemus *ap.* Sextus *PH* 1.151 and Philo *Ebr.* 199)? Are there four elements, or should one add a more divine substance as a fifth? The question that follows suggests an answer is possible and leads to further questions, thus showing what philosophy really is about: "If the world has indeed come into being, by whose agency did it come into being and who is the Demiurge as to his being and quality, what was his purpose in making it, and what does he do now, and what is his occupation and way of life?"

Briefly commenting on the former passage (*Her.* 246–48), Nikiprowetzky points out: "The disagreements which abound in philosophy are brought about by the fact that the mind—without doubt for lack of an unerring criterion—has let go of the truth in favor of conjectures and probabilities."[42] This is not entirely correct; as long as no definite and objective decision regarding warring views is feasible, the mind cannot reach the truth on its own. However, Philo suggests that such a decision is, after all, within reach; the passage on the "male midwife and judge" may of course be read as an exhortation to proceed in an eclectic way, but there is more to it. Truth, which flees the conjecturing soul, may reveal itself to the right sort of person, who is then able to decide which philosophical views are incorrect and which are correct, and to what extent. As Seneca said, "The truth is mine"

42. Nikiprowetzky (n. 5 above), 98 (my translation).

(*quod verum est, meum est, Ep.* 12.11). The question as to the manner in which, according to Philo, such a decision is brought about or rendered possible is therefore a legitimate one. The answer, as will appear from the passage to be studied now, is: because God takes the decision for us and makes it known to us, either immediately or through the books of his prophets, especially Moses.

As Janáček has shown,[43] Philo, when speaking of dilemmas in a Skeptical manner (or of Skeptical dilemmas) introduces a vocabulary for "to be in doubt" that is his own: *endoiazein, epamphoterizein*, etc. Several times Philo tells us that God is not one who does not know the answer (*QG* 1.21, "God does not doubt [*endoiazei*]"; 1.55, "there is neither doubt [*endoiasmos*] nor jealousy about God"; cf., e.g., *Opif.* 149). Man, however, is a "natural doubter" (*epamphoteristēn tēi phusei, QG* 1.55). Man's natural propensity to doubt is presented here in terms that are a fascinating distortion of the very familiar Stoic theory of perception. Whereas Stoics supposed that certain sense-impressions, by their sheer clarity, naturally induce the mind's assent, Philo suggests that man's natural response to all impressions is ambivalent. I quote this text after the Greek (the Armenian is confused): "Whenever the impression of an object occurs [to us], three things immediately result: disinclination away from what appears, inclination toward what appears, and, third, doubt [*endoiasmos*] inclined toward both these directions, because the soul is drawn both ways as to whether [the impression] should be accepted or not."[44] Time and again, Philo in such contexts uses the metaphor of the scales of the balance.

Several passages in the biography of Moses repay further study in this context. At *Mos.* 1.21–24, we are informed about

43. Janáček (n. 38 above).
44. ὅταν γὰρ προσπέσῃ τινὸς φαντασία, τρία εὐθὺς ἐπιγίνεται· ἀφορμὴ ἐκ τοῦ φανέντος, ὁρμὴ πρὸς τὸ φανέν, τρίτον ἐνδοιασμὸς ἀμφικλινής, ἀντισπωμένης τῆς ψυχῆς εἴθ᾽ αἱρετέον εἴτε μή. Cf. also *QG* 3.58.

the education of the young prince. He has Egyptians instructing him in a number of subjects, and "Greeks to teach him the other standard disciplines" (23), who have been summoned from Greece at great expense (21). Chaldaean scholars teach him their native "science of the heavenly bodies," which he acquires from the Egyptians as well, who further instruct him in the "philosophy conveyed in symbols as displayed in their so-called holy letters" (23–24).[45] Moses was a prodigious pupil (21–22), forestalling the instruction of his teachers and advancing beyond their capacities, "so that his seemed a case rather of recollection [*anamnēsis*] than of learning, and indeed he himself devised and propounded problems that are difficult to solve. For great natures carve out much that is new in the way of knowledge [*epistēmē*]. . . . The gifted soul [*euphuēs psuchē*] takes the lead in meeting the lessons given by itself [cf. above, "recollection"] rather than by the teacher[46] . . . and as soon as it has a grasp of some scientific principle presses forward."

The amusing anachronisms need not bother us. What is at issue is that Philo improvises an explanation for Moses' development toward his outstanding role as *the* prophet of God. He cannot, of course, have the Greeks teach him philosophy, since all such philosophy, according to Philo, is later than and derived from Moses. He cannot have him study the books of Moses either. Therefore, recourse is had to a Platonizing suggestion: in going beyond his teachers, i.e., toward philosophy, Moses seems to remember what his soul would have known before entering his body. It is, by the way, rather astonishing that Philo is silent about possible Jewish teachers; presumably, he believed that one could not speak of these in the context of the education of an Egyptian prince. Nothing is said about the influence upon young Moses of the stories about the "living laws" (*sc.* the Patriarchs) either.

45. Cf. nn. 13 and 14 above.
46. D. T. Runia points out that *Aet.* 16, on Aristotle's originality, provides a sort of parallel to me.

Now, Moses' attitude toward his teacher much resembles that toward the teachings of Greek philosophy recommended by Philo elsewhere: "When he had mastered the lore of *both groups* of teachers, *both where they agreed and where they differed* [*en hois te sumphōnousi kai diapherousi*], he rose above their quarrels [*eridas*] without infatuation with victory [*aphiloneikōs*; cf. below] and sought for the *truth*. His mind was incapable of accepting any falsehood, as is the way with the *aggressive sectarians* [*hairesiomachois*], who defend the doctrines [*dogmata*] they have propounded without examining whether they can stand scrutiny, and thus put themselves on a par with hired lawyers who have no thought or care for justice" (24; my italics). Apparently, such sectarians argue that "the truth is mine." The term *hairesiomachos* is unique not only in the Philonic corpus but, it appears, in the whole of Greek literature (cf., however, *Prov.* 2.85, "in the manner of those who indulge in sectarian strife").

One cannot help feeling that Philo somewhat overplays his hand; his description of Moses' attitude toward the aggressive sectarians would be rather more apt as an analysis of the recommended attitude toward dissenting philosophers. The term *erides*, "quarrels," is also found in the "disagreement" of the philosophers at *Her.* 247. (Cf. *Mos.* 1.24, "without infatuation with victory eschewing the quarrels" [*aphiloneikōs tas eridas huperbas*]; *Her.* 247 "quarrels and infatuations with victory" [*eridas kai philoneikeias*]). Moses is "without infatuation with victory" in contrast to the *haeresiomachoi*,[47] and *haeresis* is a term denoting a

47. For φιλονεικία as characteristic of the diehard sectarian see Galen *De plac. Hipp. et Plat.* 2, p. 102, lines 12f. De Lacy: "all such notions have been boldly advanced by men who were ambitious [φιλονεικούντων] to overthrow all the excellent teachings of the ancients, in order to found a newer sect [*hairesis*] of their own"; cf. also 3, pp. 194, line 20, and 198, line 28; 3, p. 288, line 14; 5, p. 294, lines 11 and 17. It may be doubted whether Proclus *ap.* Philop. *Aet. mund.*, p. 32, 8 Rabe, διὰ φιλονικίαν ἀντιλέγειν (= Aristotle, *De Philos.*, fr. 10 Ross), reflects Aristotle's own usage. The Stoics defined φιλονεικία as ἐπιθυμία τις περὶ αἱρέσεως (Diogenes Laertius 7.113 = *SVF* 3.396).

philosophical sect (or school of thought). The division of the teachers in the opposite camps required by a Skeptic "disagreement" is labored, since no information is provided as to the point where the Egyptians and the Chaldaeans (and presumably the Greeks) differed. The only philosophical studies hinted at are in the field of astronomy (Chaldaeans and Egyptians), insofar as the theory of the heavenly bodies is part of physics (cf. *Her.* 247; *Abrah.* 162f.), and an Egyptian type of mystery is hinted at. In the concluding sentence, the warring parties are described as what Philo elsewhere calls "sophists" (cf., e.g., *Mos.* 2.212, "the word-catchers and sophists who *sell* their tenets and arguments [*dogmata kai logous*] . . . , who forever use philosophy against philosophy without a blush"). Philo suggests that Moses is capable of determining which, among the opposed views, is true (cf. the interesting parallel about the element of truth in the "standard curriculum" at *QG* 3.32), just like the "male midwife and judge" at *Her.* 247; and it is interesting to note that he is credited with an understanding not only of the disagreement, but also of the agreement (*Mos.* 1.24, *sumphōnousi*) among the sectarians, a point which reminds us of Antiochus and others. But Moses, as Philo says—and had to say in view of what he saw as Moses' contribution to human thought—not only took from his teachers what was true, but went much farther.

A later stage in his development is described at *Mos.* 1.47f.: he has left Egypt and lives in Arabia. Already he has a special relationship with God (46). He now pursues the exercise of virtue (*aretē*), trained by his own wise reason (*en heautōi logismon asteion*; cf. above on his gifted nature and *anamnēsis*), and under this management he "labored to fit himself for the best forms of life, the theoretical and practical. *He was forever opening the scroll of philosophical doctrines* [*philosophias aei anelittōn dogmata*], digested them inwardly, *committed them to memory* and brought his personal conduct into conformity with them; for he desired *truth* rather than seeming" (48; my italics). Here the anachronism is flagrant even from Philo's own point of view; momentarily forgetting his conviction that all philosophy derives from Moses, i.e., from the books later composed by Moses himself, he has him make a thorough study of the philosophical *literature* (on his own, to be sure). Consequently, Moses follows the educational course prescribed by Philo elsewhere: first the "standard curriculum" (*Mos.* 1.21–24), then the philosophical theories (47). According to Philo, the good philosopher is one whose life agrees with his doctrine (and he believes this can best be realized in a Jewish context; cf. two important passages, *Mos.* 2.48 and *Prob.* 160). Moses is such a philosopher; he pursues the *truth*, so we may presume his attitude toward the philosophical doctrines anachronistically studied by him resembled that toward the "standard curriculum."

The reconstruction provided by Philo of Moses' educational career is most revealing. Perhaps better than any other passage it tells us how important a Greek education (including philosophy) really was in his view, for he cannot imagine the development of his greatest hero in any other terms.

We should now turn to some passages, dealing with important points of law, where even Moses himself is (uncharacteristically) in doubt. His first problem, involving the conflict between a divine rule and a reasonable human claim, is described at *Mos.* 2.225–28. Moses "wavered in his judgment, and oscillated as on a balance. . . . So, vacillating between refusal and assent, he besought God to act as a judge [cf. *Her.* 247] and give an oracle declaring his decision. And God hearkened to him and vouchsafed an answer."[48] God, it will be recalled, is not a doubter. His

---

48. ἐπαμφοτερίζων δὲ τὴν γνώμην καὶ ὥσπερ ἐπὶ πλάστιγγος ἀντιρρέπων . . . ἀρνήσεως καὶ συγκαταθέσεως μεταξὺ φορούμενος ἱκετεύει τὸν θεὸν δικαστὴν γενέσθαι καὶ χρησμῷ τὴν κρίσιν ἀποφῆναι, *Mos.* 2.228. For an interesting parallel showing in what way a rationalist may escape from the Skeptic trap see Galen *De plac. Hipp. et Plat.* 5, pp. 314, line 25–316, line 3 De Lacy. Galen here surveys the attitudes that are possible when two judgments are in conflict: "If the judgments should be of equal credibility, we must suspend judgment [*epechein*] about the reality of the state

"oracle"—in Philo, *chrēsmos* usually denotes a verse, or set of verses, from Scripture—is a sort of compromise providing a rider to the rule that allows for the reasonable claim. The section *Mos.* 2.222–32 as a whole is based on Numbers 9:1–14; in the biblical text, when presented with the problem (9–10), Moses says: "Stand here, and I shall hear whether God utters a command about you." The text continues: "And God spoke to Moses, saying . . ." The important epistemological interlude has therefore been interpolated by Philo.

Moses' second problem is described at *Mos.* 2.234–45 and is based on Numbers 27:1–11. Here he is presented with a petition of orphaned girls which similarly entails a conflict between an established rule and a reasonable claim. "Naturally, therefore, in this wavering and undecided state of mind, he referred the difficulty to God, who alone, as he knew, can distinguish by infallible and absolutely unerring criteria the finest differences and thereby show his truth and justice."[49] This time, God's answer is not an amendment of the rule, but a decision between the rival claims, and he comes down in favor of the girls' case. Again, Moses' doubt is not found in the biblical passage, which merely says (Numbers 27:5–6): "And Moses brought the judgment about them before God. And the Lord said . . ."

With these passages in *De vita Moysis*, D. Daube[50] has inter-

---

of affairs; but if one of them should appear far more convincing, we must assent to it." A person who makes a supposition "may have yet another supposition that pulls against it [*antispōmenēs*]; or someone may, like Pyrrho, assign equal value to both and suspend judgment as to assertion and assent" (trans. De Lacy, modified). The text is not included by F. Decleva Caizzi, although it agrees with T67 and T68 in her *Pirrone, Testimonianze*, Elenchos 5 (Naples, 1981).

49. τῆς διανοίας ἀμφικλινῶς ἐχούσης καὶ ἀντισπωμένης, ἀναφέρει τῷ θεῷ τὴν διαπόρησιν, ὃν ᾔδει μόνον ἀψευδέσι καὶ ἀπλανεστάτοις κριτηρίοις τὰς κατὰ μικρὸν διαφορὰς διαστέλλοντα πρὸς ἐπίδειξιν ἀληθείας καὶ δικαιοσύνης, *Mos.* 2.237. The "finest differences" recall the Stoic argument against the Skeptics at Cicero *Acad.* 2.56–58 (not in *SVF*).

50. D. Daube, "Alexandrian Methods of Interpretation and the Rabbis," repr. in H. A. Fischel, ed., *Essays in Greco-Roman and Related Talmudic Literature* (New York, 1977), 174–75.

estingly compared the thirteenth interpretive rule (*Middah*) attributed to Rabbi Ishmael (new compared with those of Hillel):[51] "Two scriptural passages may contradict one another until a third one comes and *tips the balance* between them" (my italics). Note that at *QG* 3.3 (Greek fragment) Philo, against the extreme literalists, emphasizes the unity of Scripture: one should judge the part from the whole. It is not clear whether Ishmael's rule derives from Philo,[52] or whether, perhaps, both Philo and Ishmael reflect an established rule of *midrash* which Philo would project into the distant past, in order to show God actually delivering an "oracle." We may compare Eusebius's characterization of the activities of the Jewish exegetes: "the logical method [*logikos tropos*] of the philosophy of the Hebrews," "a logic which pursues the truth, unlike the clever sophistries of the Greeks" (*PE* 11.5.1).

However this may be, if we adduce the Philonic passages about the conflicting ideas of the philosophers that are adjudicated by the true judge, a sort of methodology appears. Man is uncertain, a doubter by nature; one may, in the Skeptic way, describe how opinions differ and clash. But the *epochē* of Skepticism is not acceptable, because a decision is needed. Such a decision is provided by God, either directly (as when the sage— e.g., Moses—is in doubt) or through his oracles as taken down by Moses. The teachings of Scripture are decisive for the adjudication of the conflicts among the Greek philosophers, who, themselves, have borrowed some of Moses' ideas and interpreted them more or less correctly, but who have never taken the whole of the teachings contained in Scripture seriously enough.[53] Diversity and disagreement could arise precisely because Scripture was not adduced the way it should be.

51. See [H.L. Strack–]G. Stemberger, *Einleitung in Talmud und Midrasch*[7] (Munich, 1982), 31.

52. S. Lieberman, *Hellenism in Jewish Palestine*, Texts and Stud. Jew. Theol. Sem. Amer. 18 (New York, 1950, 1962²), 54f.

53. Cf. the examples in Runia (n. 3 above), 528ff.

A *midrashic* origin for Philo's rule of adjudication is, as we have seen, not certain. What is at any rate certain is that the metaphor of the balance in relation to human ratiocinative processes is not his own idea. We may assume he borrowed it from Stoicizing sources, or from the common philosophical jargon of his time.[54] It occurs in passages where Sextus discusses Stoic epistemology (*M*. 7.37 = *SVF* 2.107; *M*. 7.440 = *SVF* 2.158, p. 36, lines 8–9), and, in a Stoic context, in Philo himself, *Prob.* 61 = *SVF* 3.363, p. 89, line 3 (typical Philonic terminology: "The mind is poised [*isorropei*] as on a balance [*plastingi*]"). These three texts were discussed some years ago by K.-H. Rolke in a study dealing with the metaphors in the Stoic fragments;[55] because the evidence is late and couched in general language, he can only suggest that it is not incompatible with Chrysippus's epistemology. However, he has missed the most important text, Plutarch *St. Rep.* 1045B–D (= *SVF* 2.973): this proves that Chrysippus here refutes the Epicureans[56] who—Chrysippus implies—had argued that when it is necessary to choose one of two equivalent and equally pressing alternatives, the "adventitious motion" in the soul "takes an inclination [*epiklisis*] of itself and resolves the perplexity." "In many places," however, Chrysippus cited as evidence dice and "the balance" (*zugon;*[57] cf. *SVF* 2.107, 158, cited above) and many other things "that cannot fall or incline now one way now another without some cause."

54. Note that the "scales" listed by Th. H. Billings, *The Platonism of Philo Judaeus* (Chicago, 1919; repr. New York, 1979), 101, is a different figure.

55. K.-H. Rolke, *Die bildhaften Vergleiche in den Fragmenten der Stoiker von Zenon bis Panaitios*, Spudasmata 32 (Hildesheim, 1971), 208–14.

56. Cf. Cherniss *ad loc.* I cannot enter here into the implications of this neglected text (not printed by Usener, not translated by M. Isnardi Parente, *Opere di Epicuro* [Turin, 1983²], and not, to my knowledge, adduced in the recent scholarly literature) for the study of the Epicurean arguments against determinism. For other evidence concerning Chrysippus's objections to "uncaused motion" see M. Isnardi Parente, "Stoici, Epicurei, e il 'motus sine causa,'" *RSF* 35 (1980), 23ff.

57. Philo uses πλάστιγξ, presumably because this is a Platonic word.

To conclude, I would like to point out that Philo really needed the Skeptic aloofness from the theories of the dogmatists, because in this way (strategically adopting the Skeptics' technique of organization) he could begin by, so to speak, neutralizing them and reducing them to one side in a "disagreement." Unlike the Skeptics, however, he believed that the scales could be, and should be, tipped, at least where the more important perplexities are at issue. God takes the decision for us—not, however, without an enduring effort on our own side (cf. *Sacrif.* 8off.). Even Moses only received his revelations after a preparatory period. In Philo's day, God's decisions are represented by the collected oracles of Moses (and his fellow-prophets) and their correct exegesis, and Philo seems to assume that God assists and inspires[58] the studious and humble interpreter (cf. esp. *Sacrif.* 77–79). With the backing of the books of Moses and supported by the religious traditions of his people which are grounded in these books, the studious exegete is in a position to lord it over the Greek philosophers. The other side of this coin,[59] of course, is that it is the body of divergent opinions among the Greek philosophers that is adjudicated by Scripture and its correct interpretation. Inevitably, the male midwife and judge will make an eclectic impression. However, to the extent that—as we noticed in the first part of this chapter—Philo's exegesis operates on different levels, his eclecticism may be said to be free of syncretistic taints.[60]

58. On inspiration (also of exegetes) according to Philo see Billings (n. 54 above), 67.

59. Cf. the detailed analysis of the Greekness of the arguments against the Greeks in *C. Ap.* by C. Schaublin, "Josephus und die Griechen," *Hermes* 110 (1982), 316ff.

60. I wish to thank the members of the Dublin colloquium, as well as R. van den Broek, P.W. van der Horst, J.C.M. van Winden, and especially D.T. Runia, for their comments, and C.W. Hudson for looking at my English.

JOHN M. DILLON

4

"Orthodoxy" and "Eclecticism"
Middle Platonists and Neo-Pythagoreans

The disappearance from the philosophic scene, after 88 B.C., of the Platonic Academy as an institution is now, I think, following on the researches of John Lynch and John Glucker, an accepted fact, and one that raises a number of interesting issues.[1] Chief among these is a question that is central to this book, to wit, what criteria can be established for estimating orthodoxy and heterodoxy in Platonism during the period commonly known as Middle Platonic, that is, from Antiochus of Ascalon in the 80s and 70s B.C. to Plotinus in the mid-third century A.D.?

I do not propose to conduct a slow march through the period in question in search of material for my theme. I want instead to focus on a number of revealing instances where the issue of orthodoxy or eclecticism—being part of, or outside of, a consensus or a mainstream—becomes a vital matter, since such instances will suffice very well to illustrate the dimensions of the problem.

1. John Lynch, *Aristotle's School* (Berkeley and Los Angeles, 1972), 177–89; John Glucker, *Antiochus and the Late Academy* (Göttingen, 1978).

I

First, let us consider Antiochus of Ascalon and his claims of a return to the Old Academy, since it is with Antiochus that the issue of eclecticism begins to raise its head seriously in the history of later Platonism (Panaetius and Posidonius could be seen, I suppose, as "eclectic" Stoics)—indeed, in many older works Antiochus is presented as inaugurating a long period of "eclectic philosophy."[2] I am on record as protesting against the use of this word as a label for the Platonist (and other) philosophers of this period,[3] but my protest is only valid if the term be used in a dismissive or pejorative sense, with the implication that the philosophers concerned were too muddleheaded or light-minded to stick to the principles of any one of the four main Hellenistic schools. In fact, there is nothing at all wrong with being "eclectic," if that means simply that one is prepared to adopt a good formulation, or a valid line of argument, from a rival school or individual and adjust one's philosophical position accordingly.[4] In this sense, most of the great philosophers are eclectics, and eclecticism is a mark of acuteness and originality, as opposed to narrow-minded sectarianism.[5]

---

2. Those of Zeller and Praechter in particular. See the excellent discussion of this by P. L. Donini in Chapter 1 above, pp. 22–29.

3. *The Middle Platonists* (London, 1977) (henceforth referred to as *Middle Platonists*), xiv–xv. Daniel Babut, in *Plutarque et le Stoïcisme* (Paris, 1969), 6, discussing the question of Plutarch's "eclecticism," produces a good definition of the term in its objectionable sense: "la tendence au compromis . . . l'habitude d'associer sans discrimination des thèmes empruntés à plusieurs doctrines, sans être conscient ou sans tenir compte des frontières qui les séparent." A "supermarket" approach to philosophy, one might term it (I owe the phrase to Jacques Brunschwig).

4. Pierre Thévenaz, in *L'âme du monde: le devenir et la matière chez Plutarque* (Neuchâtel, 1938), while characterizing Plutarch as eclectic, makes the reasonable remark, "L'eclectisme n'est pas toujours le signe d'une impuissance créatrice" (p. 125).

5. It was this, of course, which made it such a positive value word for

On that interpretation of the term, there can be no dispute, I think, that Antiochus was eclectic, offensive as the term would have seemed to him. His striving—and that is what makes him interesting in the present context—was all for orthodoxy and a return to purity of doctrine.

Despite the strong polemical context of his move (his distancing of himself from Philo of Larissa and the Fourth Academy), there is no need to doubt that Antiochus genuinely felt himself to be returning to the true Platonic tradition of the Old Academy by rejecting the (excessive) skepticism of the New. If his epistemology, with its criterion of certainty in *katalēptikē phantasia*, and his ethics, with its basis in *oikeiōsis*, and his physics, with its *logos*-theory, sound suspiciously like Stoicism to us, he has a coherent explanation: Zeno was a pupil of Polemo, the last head of the Old Academy, and he learned his lessons there better than his fellow-pupil Arcesilaus, who took over the Academy from Polemo (cf. Cicero *Fin.* 4.3.25). As for the Peripatos, Aristotle and Theophrastus are part of the Old Academic consensus (cf. Cicero *Acad.* 2.15ff.). Such disagreements as they had were matters of terminology, not substance (*Acad.* 1.18).

The accuracy of Antiochus's view of the history of philosophy is not our concern in the present context.[6] All that is relevant is his striving for orthodoxy, with his simultaneous belief that he was justified in appropriating such Stoic doctrines and formulations as he could find any adumbrations of in Plato or the Old Academics. He is not uncritical of the Stoics, in fact. He feels that they went too far, in the sphere of ethics, in denying any role in happiness to bodily and external goods, and he sharply criticizes Chrysippus (*ap.* Cicero *Fin.* 5.28) for treating man, for theoretical purposes, not as a mind in a body, but as mind and nothing else. In this respect Zeno deviated from the Academic consensus

---

Enlightenment figures such as Brucker and Diderot (cf. Donini, Chapter 1 above, pp. 18–22).

6. Cf. *Middle Platonists*, 55–59.

(which, for Antiochus, incorporates Aristotle's teaching in the *Ethics*, which he had learned from Polemo), and Antiochus condemns him for that.

In fact, Antiochus appears to have fooled nobody—not his contemporary and admirer, Cicero, nor later commentators, such as Plutarch or Numenius,[7] but he did perhaps start something, and that is a controversy about orthodoxy within the Platonist tradition. The controversy, strictly speaking, began with the attempt by Philo of Larissa to argue for the unity of the Academic tradition, trying to show, on the one hand, that the Skepticism of the New Academy could claim support from the procedures of both Socrates and Plato, and, on the other, that the New Academicians—in particular, Carneades—did not absolutely withhold assent to impressions, but only denied the Stoic criterion of certainty. Philo stated a position, but it was Antiochus's violent reaction to this[8] that really started the controversy, one carried on by the author of the *Anonymous Theaetetus Commentary*—whoever and whenever he was; Plutarch, in his lost work, *On the Unity of the Academy since Plato*, Lamprias Cat. 63; and Numenius, in his work *On the Divergence of the Academics from Plato*, of which we have a number of entertaining fragments. What side one took in this controversy inevitably had some bearing on one's own attitude to Skepticism. Plutarch, for instance, is quite hospitable to it, though chiefly as a weapon to use against the Stoics. I cannot see Plutarch as a genuine Skeptic, but he does cherish the Skeptical tradition,[9] as did Cicero before him, and as Numenius does not.

---

7. Cf. Plutarch *Cicero* 4: Numenius, fr. 28 Des Places.

8. Cf. Cicero *Acad.* 2.11, where Lucullus is made to recount Antiochus's reaction to hearing a reading of Philo's work. Antiochus's reaction was recorded in his dialogue *Sosus*.

9. Besides his work on the unity of the Academy, at least four other titles of lost works indicate sympathy with the New Academic tradition: Lamprias Cat. 64, *On the difference between the Pyrrhonians and the Academics*; 146 *That there is no such thing as understanding* (συνιέναι); 158, *On Pyrrho's*

II

It is not this aspect of Plutarch, however, that I want to discuss next (our evidence on it has, unfortunately, largely vanished), but, rather, his place in the spectrum of contemporary Platonism between the poles of Stoicism and Peripateticism, on which all Platonists are inevitably situated (even if they choose to take up a "Pythagorean" stance, they cannot entirely sidestep this situation).

Plutarch's position within the Platonist tradition cannot be properly evaluated, it seems to me, so long as the notion of an "orthodox" Platonism is maintained—propounded, necessarily, by an official Platonic Academy. Heinrich Dörrie's study "Die Stellung Plutarchs im Platonismus seiner Zeit,"[10] for instance,

---

Ten Tropes; 210, *Whether he who suspends judgment* (ὁ ἐπέχων) *on everything is condemned to inaction.* We may also note the reproach of the Stoic Pharnaces in *De facie* (922F): "Here we are faced again with that stock maneuver (τὸ περίακτον) of the Academy on each occasion that they engage in discourse with others. They will not offer any accounting of their own assertions, but must keep their interlocutors on the defensive lest they become the prosecutors." Lamprias has just been satirizing the Stoic theory of the moon's substance (see Donini, Chapter 5, p. 134). This is a good indication that Plutarch recognizes New Academic methods of argument as a proper part of a Platonist's armory, but we must also bear in mind that Lamprias goes on to present a positive theory as to the moon's composition. The Skeptical tradition, then, is drawn on by Plutarch primarily in connection with inter-school controversy.

Secondarily, also, as in the case of Cicero before him, he employs it to save himself the trouble of going any deeper into questions of *physical* philosophy than he wants to. Cf., e.g., his remarks at the end of his short essay on *The Principle of Cold* (955A)—significantly enough, addressed to Favorinus, who professed Academic Skepticism: "Compare these statements, Favorinus, with the pronouncements of others; and if these notions of mine are neither deficient nor much superior in plausibility (πιθανότης) to those of others, say farewell to dogma (δόξαι), being convinced as you are that it is more philosophical to suspend judgment (ἐπέχειν) when the truth is obscure than to come to conclusions (συνκατατίθεσθαι)" (trans. Helmbold, emended).

10. In R. Palmer and R. Hamerton-Kelly, eds., *Philomathes: Studies and*

while presenting Plutarch's philosophical position fairly enough, misrepresents the situation, it seems to me, by postulating something he terms *school-Platonism* (represented by such figures as Albinus and Taurus), and setting Plutarch over against this, as if it were an official orthodoxy.

The only place where we find Plutarch setting himself explicitly against what could be regarded as the orthodox Platonist position is in his treatise *On the Creation of the Soul in the Timaeus*, and it is interesting to observe how he phrases his opposition. *Pace* Dörrie (p. 48), he does not present himself as taking on a Platonist "establishment." He recognizes that he is going against the views of all, or at least "the most highly regarded" (1012D), of previous commentators, but he does not view those commentators as a homogeneous group. Though all choose to deny that the world was created at a point in time (1013A), some are followers of Xenocrates' view, and others of that of Crantor, while still others, like Eudorus, seek to reconcile the two views and Plutarch deals with each of them in turn. Nor does he speak here as an outsider attacking the establishment, but as the true interpreter of Plato's doctrine correcting the mistakes of predecessors: "Such being the whole of what they say . . . to me they both seem to be utterly mistaken about Plato's opinion, if a standard of plausibility is to be used, not in promotion of one's own doctrines, but with a desire to say something that agrees with Plato" (1013B, trans. Cherniss).

It may seem to us that promoting his own doctrines in the guise of an exegesis of the *Timaeus* is precisely what Plutarch himself is doing, but that is not, plainly, how he sees it. Elsewhere, in his treatise *On Moral Virtue*, though his position of hospitality to Aristotelian ethical doctrine might be considered

---

Essays in Memory of Philip Merlan (The Hague, 1971), 36–56. Dörrie does, however, reject the idea of applying the epithet *eclecticism* to Plutarch's position (52).

almost as controversial, we find no suggestion that he has any consciousness of this. His polemic is all with outsiders, chiefly the Stoics. And yet there is much that is peculiar in his doctrine here.

One of Plutarch's most distinctive doctrines, apart from his well-known dualism (though closely involved with it), is his view of the soul as essentially nonrational (*hautē kath'heautēn*) (*Proc. an.* 1014D–E) and distinct from intellect. It is this essential soul that he sees in the "nature divided about bodies" of *Timaeus* 35A and in the "maleficent soul" of *Laws* 10, and it is the cornerstone of his theory in *On the Creation of the Soul.* It also figures in the treatise *On Moral Virtue.*[11]

At the outset (440D), Plutarch raises the question of

> what the essential nature [*ousia*] of moral virtue is, and how it arises; and whether that part of the soul which receives it is equipped with its own reason [*logos*], or merely shares in one alien to it; and if the latter, whether it does this after the manner of things which are mingled with something better, or, rather, whether it is said to participate in the potency [*dunamis*] of the ruling element through submitting to its administration and governance.

Here, admittedly, he speaks of a part [*morion*] of the soul, rather than of soul in general, but it presently becomes plain that what he has in mind is not really the lower or "passionate" soul in the traditional Platonic sense, so much as soul distinct from intellect. A little further on (441D), in the course of his introductory survey of previous opinion, he criticizes those, particularly the Stoics, who assume intellect and soul to be a unity: "It seems to have eluded all these philosophers in what way each of us is truly twofold and composite. For that other twofold nature

11. Plutarch's doctrine of the soul has recently been excellently set out in the most useful study by Werner Deuse, *Untersuchungen zur mittelplatonische und neuplatonische Seelenlehre* (Wiesbaden, 1983), 12–47, though Deuse does not pay as much attention to the *Virt. mor.* as he should have, but confines himself largely to *Proc. an.* and *De Is. et Os.*

of ours they have not discerned, but merely the more obvious one, the blend of soul and body."

Pythagoras, however, and, above all, Plato recognized "that there is some element of composition, some twofold nature and dissimilarity of the very soul within itself, since the irrational, like an alien body, is mingled and joined with reason [*logos*] by some compulsion of nature."[12] Here he speaks, rather misleadingly, of the twofold nature of "the very soul within itself," but we can take it, I think, that he is using *soul* in a loose sense, as those who have not discerned the true situation would use it. The truth, as we see, is that there are three entities, body, soul, and *nous* (intellect), and this trichotomy leaves soul as essentially and of itself *alogos*, nonrational, though having a part that is receptive to reason (441F ff.).

In *On Moral Virtue*, it must be admitted, Plutarch obscures the doctrine which he presents very plainly in *On the Creation of the Soul*, by speaking, for the most part, of the "nonrational part" (*alogon meros*) of the soul, rather than soul itself, as opposed to *nous*, and it is possible that he has not yet fully clarified his position in his own mind (if, as I assume, *On Moral Virtue* is earlier than *On the Creation of the Soul*), but he says enough, I think, to show that this remarkable doctrine was already in his mind.[13] What is interesting for our present purpose is that he shows no consciousness of unorthodoxy on this point, as he does on the matter of the temporal creation of the world (though, as I have said earlier, *unorthodoxy* is not quite the right word).

The other notable aspect of the treatise *On Moral Virtue*, of course, is its wholehearted adoption of Aristotelian doctrine, derived directly from the *Nicomachean Ethics*, chiefly Books 2.5–7

---

12. Helmbold's Loeb trans., slightly emended.

13. Even in the midst of his exposition of the doctrine in the *De facie* (943D) he refers, using traditional terminology, to those who have made τῆς ψυχῆς τὸ ἄλογον καὶ τὸ παθητικόν orderly and amenable to their λόγος.

(on the mean) and 7 (on *akrasia*), with some influence also from the *De anima*.[14] This can be labeled eclecticism, but I do not see that the term is very useful. It is clear from his presentation of Aristotle's position at 442B–C that Plutarch regards him as substantially adopting Plato's doctrine of the soul (except that he "later" assigned the "spirited" part [*thumoeides*] unequivocally to the irrational part of the soul—a development Plutarch does not quarrel with). This enables Plutarch to present, for instance, the theory of the mean (in 444C–445A) unhesitatingly as Platonic doctrine.

Although the chief source for his doctrine here, as I have said, is *Nicomachean Ethics* 2.5–7, there are some elements observable, modifying the Aristotelian position, which, once again, might misleadingly be termed eclectic. First of all, Aristotle describes virtue as a *hexis* or state (1106b36), but Plutarch, at 444F, describes it as a "movement" (*kinēsis*) and "power" (*dunamis*) concerned with the management of the irrational, and doing this by fine-tuning and harmonizing its discordant excesses (cf. 444E, 445C). This seems a Pythagorizing turn of phrase, and that, together with the laudatory mention of Pythagoras in the doxography (441E), points to a Pythagorean element in the mix that Plutarch is presenting to us. This Pythagoreanism can be shown with fair certainty to be mediated through Posidonius, by a comparison with Galen *De plac. Hipp. et Plat.* 4.7.39 (p. 290 De Lacy) and 5.6.43 (p. 334 De Lacy),[15] but Plutarch's interest in Pythagoras and Pythagoreanism is well enough attested apart

14. See on this the useful discussion of D. Babut, pp. 44–46 of the Introduction to his edition of the work, *Plutarque, De la vertu éthique* (Paris, 1969). He satisfactorily refutes earlier attempts to postulate Posidonius or Andronicus of Rhodes as intermediary for the doctrine of this part of the work, though the anti-Stoic polemic of the second part (from 446E on) does show dependence on Posidonius (as reported in Galen, *De plac. Hipp. et Plat.* 4). His view, with which I concur, is that Plutarch read Aristotle for himself, though he was doubtless acquainted with later Peripatetic works as well.

15. Quoted by Babut in his notes *ad loc.*

from this[16] to make it probable that he is not simply dependent on Posidonius here. Further, the activity of virtue is described as a "harmonizing" (*sunharmoga*) of the irrational by the rational soul in a variety of Pythagorean pseudepigrapha,[17] which indicates a tendency in many of these works to claim Aristotelian ethical theory for Pythagoras. Metopos's treatise *On Virtue* (pp. 116–21 Thesleff) is a good example of this (he also produces the formulation, found at *Virt. mor.* 440D, that the passions are the "matter" [*hulē*] of ethical virtue, 119, line 8). While not being necessarily *dependent* on any of these intermediate sources for his interpretation of Aristotle, therefore, Plutarch was doubtless aware of most of them.

If this is eclecticism, it is certainly not mindless eclecticism. It is based on a view of the history of philosophy, mistaken perhaps, but perfectly coherent, which sees Plato as a follower of Pythagoras, Aristotle as essentially still a Platonist, and a consistent ethical position being held by all three. As to the doctrine of the distinctness of soul and intellect, which does not, as I say, receive clear articulation in this treatise but comes out clearly in the dialogues *On the Face in the Moon* (943A ff.) and *On the Daemon of Socrates* (591D ff.), as well as in *On the Creation of the Soul*, that is a piece of "unorthodoxy," on the origins of which I have speculated elsewhere, though without definite conclusions,[18] but it is one for which Plutarch is at pains to find Platonic antecedents (e.g., *Tim.* 30B, 90A, *Phaedr.* 247C, *Laws* 12.961D,

---

16. E.g., *De Is. et Os.* 360D, 384A, *Proc. an.* 1027F, 1020E ff., *Quaest. conv.* 8.7 and 8, *De E* 388C.

17. Archytas Π. νόμου καὶ δικαιοσύνης, 33, line 17 Thesleff (*Pythagorean Texts*); Metopos Π. ἀρετῆς, 119, line 27; Theages Π. ἀρετῆς, 190, lines 1ff.

18. *Middle Platonists*, 211–14. A similar distinction is made in some treatises of the *Corpus Hermeticum* (notably 1 and 10), and it is analogous to the distinction in Gnostic thought between *psuchē* and *pneuma*, soul and spirit, but I am uncertain what to conclude from this. Attributing the doctrine to Posidonius, in default of any hard evidence, is a once-easy option no longer open, I think.

966D–E), and which, as I have said, he does not regard as setting him in opposition to any official Platonic tradition.[19] In summary, Plutarch may be a bit of a maverick, but he does not view himself as such (except perhaps in the matter of a temporal creation), and I can see no evidence of any contemporary "school-Platonism" from which he can be said to deviate.

III

Plutarch did not, however, escape criticism, at least in a later generation. The situation in Athenian Platonism during the rest of the second century A.D. is in fact interestingly complex. We know of no Platonist in Athens, after Ammonius's death, during Plutarch's lifetime (unless perhaps Gaius or the shadowy figure of Nicostratus was based there), but in the decades after his death the dominant Platonist in Athens, Calvenus Taurus, regards Plutarch with affection and likes to quote him (cf. Aulus Gellius *NA* 1.26). Taurus's position in ethics accords with Plutarch's (*NA* 1.26) and so does his propensity for attacking the Stoics (he wrote, like Plutarch, a work exposing their inconsistencies [*NA* 12.5]), but on the question of the temporal creation of the world (which resolves itself into the question of the true meaning of Plato's *gegonen*, at *Tim.* 28B), he reverts to the more traditional line that it is not to be taken literally, and he indeed produces an elaborate list of four possible nonliteral meanings (*ap.* Philoponus *De aet. mundi*, p. 145, lines 13ff. Rabe). He refers to "certain others" who have held that the world according to Plato is created, but without any particular rancor or any suggestion that they should be excommunicated. He is simply concerned to defend the opposite point of view.

19. At *De facie* 943A, he criticizes "the many" for wrongly believing man to be composed of just two parts, but these need not be regarded as any set of philosophers, let alone Platonist philosophers.

IV

Rather more rancor appears a generation later, in the treatise of Atticus, the dominant Athenian Platonist of the next generation (fl. A.D. 175—possibly because he was then appointed Regius Professor of Platonism by Marcus Aurelius), entitled, belligerently, *Against those who claim to interpret the doctrine of Plato through that of Aristotle.*[20] I have suggested elsewhere[21] that Atticus was not necessarily always as bad-tempered as this but was provoked by the attempt of a contemporary Peripatetic—perhaps Aristocles, in his *History of Philosophy* (quoted by Eusebius just before his quotations from Atticus)—to subsume Plato under Aristotle by arguing for their essential agreement, but with Aristotle presented as the perfecter of Plato's doctrines. In fact, in launching this attack Atticus is out of line with the majority of Platonist opinion. Antiochus, Plutarch, Taurus, and Albinus all accepted the broad agreement of Plato and Aristotle, though with Aristotle properly subordinated to Plato; any of them would probably have bristled at a complementary move toward annexation on the part of an Aristotelian, though none of them, perhaps, would have gone as far as Atticus.[22]

Atticus's name is regularly linked by later Neoplatonists with that of Plutarch, since they both maintained the doctrine of the creation of the world, but in fact on most questions they were far apart. Atticus's attack on Aristotelian ethical theory is also an attack on previous Platonists, such as Plutarch and Taurus. He

20. Fragments preserved in Eusebius's *Praeparatio evangelica* and collected now in a new Budé edition by E. Des Places (1977) (previous Budé ed. by J. Baudry, 1931). Atticus's position is well discussed by M. Baltes, in *Die Weltentstehung des Platonischen Timaios nach den antiken Interpreten*, vol. 1 (Leiden, 1976), 45–63.

21. *Middle Platonists*, 249–50.

22. Taurus did actually write a treatise on *The Difference between the Teachings of Plato and Aristotle*, attested by the *Suda* s.v. Ταῦρος. We know nothing of its contents, but it must inevitably have been critical of Aristotle.

takes a strong line on the issue of the self-sufficiency of virtue for happiness, excoriating Aristotle for making happiness dependent on bodily and external goods, as well as spiritual ones (fr. 2 Des Places, 894C ff.):

> His first disagreement with Plato is in a most general, vast and essential matter: he does not preserve the condition of happiness nor allow that virtue is sufficient for its attainment, but he abases the power of virtue and considers it to be in need of the advantage accruing from chance, in order with their help to be able to attain happiness; left to itself, he alleges, it would be quite incapable of attaining happiness.

Now Plutarch does not actually take a position on this in *On Moral Virtue*, since the question does not come up, but in the course of a polemic against Chrysippus, in *Comm. not.* 1060C ff., he attacks him for not admitting bodily and external goods as forming an essential part (*sumplērōtika*) of happiness, although nature commends them to us. So his attitude is not in doubt, and Atticus is in direct conflict with it.

Taurus, too, was critical of the Stoic position in ethics. We have a most interesting passage in Aulus Gellius (*NA* 12.5), where Taurus, after reminding his hearers of his disagreement with the Stoa, gives an account of Stoic ethical theory. He does not, however, give his own view, apart from criticizing the Stoic ideal of freedom from passion (*apatheia*, 10); but I think it is safe to assume that he agreed with Plutarch, since preference for moderation in passions (*metriopatheia*) over *apatheia* seems to go together with acceptance of the role in happiness of bodily and external goods.

Even on the question of the interpretation of *Timaeus* 35A ff. (the description of the creation of the World Soul, which is bound up with their doctrine on the creation of the world), Atticus is not entirely at one with Plutarch, as has been well shown recently by Werner Deuse.[23] They both believe in a pre-cosmic maleficent

23. (N. 11 above), 51–61.

soul, but Atticus appears to retreat from Plutarch's radical distinction between soul and intellect into a more orthodox position. Plutarch had taken the "undivided essence" of *Tim.* 35A to be *nous*, but the evidence of Proclus (via Porphyry) is that Atticus took it to be "divine soul" (*theia psuchē*).[24] This might seem to be a slender foundation on which to build a difference of opinion, but, as Deuse shows, the interpretation of this passage by Galen in his *Compendium of the Timaeus*,[25] chap. 4, shows that, while interpreting it as a literal creation in agreement with Plutarch and Atticus, he takes the "undivided essence" to be, not *nous*, but "that soul which is of the nature of that which always remains in one and the same state," which is plainly not intellect itself but, rather, rational divine soul; while the "divided essence" he interprets as a disorderly soul immanent in matter. The inference is reasonable, I think, that Galen is influenced here by Atticus's *Commentary on the Timaeus*, rather than by Plutarch.

If this difference between Plutarch and Atticus is not a mirage, what is the significance of it? Presumably Atticus disliked Plutarch's theory that soul *in its essence* is nonrational, a doctrine harder to justify Platonically than that of the existence of a maleficent soul as well as a rational one. But if Atticus did make this alteration, he seems to have made it without much fanfare. On the general question of the creation of the world, however, he is just as defensive as Plutarch (fr. 4, 801C):

> At this point, we would ask not to be harassed by those from our own hearth [*sc.* fellow-Platonists], who hold the view that the world is uncreated according to Plato. They must pardon us if, in interpreting the doctrines of Plato, we rely on what he, as a Greek, is saying to us as Greeks, in clear and straightforward idiom.

24. *In Tim.* 2.153, lines 25ff. = fr. 35 Des Places.
25. Available only in Arabic translation (*Compendium Timaei Platonis*, ed. P. Kraus and R. Walzer [London, 1951]), *Corpus Platonicum Medii Aevi, Plato Arabus I.*

He then goes on to quote *Tim.* 30A3–6. We must remember that in the interval between himself and Plutarch, Taurus in his *Commentary* had come to the defense of the nonliteral interpretation of the *Timaeus* account, in particular with the subtle distinction of various possible meanings of *generated* (*genētos*). Atticus's emphasis on "we Greeks" sounds rather like a sneer at over-subtle Levantines like Taurus (who came from Beirut), whose Greek may not be of the purest.[26]

Atticus's reason for postulating the creation of the world is actually rather different from Plutarch's. He is concerned with the preservation of divine providence, which he sees Aristotle as undermining, not least by his postulation of the uncreatedness of the world (fr. 4, 801C), on the ground that that which never came into being would not be in need of providential care to maintain itself in being. This forms no part of Plutarch's argument in *On the Creation of the Soul*, though he would doubtless not have dissented from it.

The question must now be asked, does Atticus's strong opposition to Peripateticism qualify him for the epithet *orthodox*? For some historians of philosophy, Atticus is a paradigm of orthodoxy. Philip Merlan, for instance, in *The Cambridge History of Later Greek and Early Medieval Philosophy* (p. 73) says, correctly: "Atticus is opposed not only to any kind of eclecticism or syncretism. He objects even to what in later Platonism will become standard, viz. treating Aristotle's philosophy as a kind of introduction to Plato." Karl Mras, in an article in *Glotta*,[27] rejects the epithet *eclectic* applied to Atticus by his earlier Budé editor, Baudry, in his Introduction (pp. viii–xxxii). I agree with Mras in

26. The suggestions of C. Moreschini ("La posizione di Apuleio e della scuola di Gaio nell' ambito del medioplatonismo," *Ann. d. Scuola Norm. Sup. di Pisa* 33 [1964], 35) that the School of Gaius is being referred to, and of K. Mras (n. 27 below), 188, that Numenius is the villain are to my mind less likely. In fact, Numenius seems, on the evidence of Calcidius *In Tim.* chap. 295, to hold to a theory of the creation of the world.

27. "Zu Attikos, Porphyrios und Eusebios," *Glotta* 25 (1936), 183–88.

rejecting the epithet, but I agree with Baudry in his presentation of Atticus's position. Baudry shows very well how Atticus's opposition to Peripateticism again and again involves him in taking up positions that are frankly Stoic.

In ethics, although he could find some justification in a tendentious interpretation of certain passages of Plato (e.g., *Meno* 87E–88E, *Rep.* 9.580D–583A, or *Laws* 1.631B–D, all of which, however, could be equally well adduced in support of the opposite position) for his doctrine of the self-sufficiency of virtue, Atticus can only attack Aristotle by going over wholeheartedly to Chrysippus.

Again, in the area of metaphysics, we get a passage like this (fr. 8, 814A ff.):

> Further, Plato says that the soul organizes the universe, penetrating through all of it, . . . and that nature is nothing else but soul—and obviously rational soul—and he concludes from this that everything happens according to providence, as it happens according to nature.

Now, this passage uses terminology found in the *Cratylus* (*diakosmein*, cf. 400A9) and the *Phaedrus* (*dioikeisthai*, cf. 246C2), but the overall tone is Stoic, the rational soul filling the role of the *logos*, or indeed of god himself (cf., e.g., *SVF* 2.1029 [from Hippolytus], 1035 [from Clement], 1042 [from Proclus]).

In the area of logic, again, the game of attacking Aristotle's *Categories*, in which we know from Simplicius that Atticus joined with a will, involved one almost inevitably in adopting principles and formulations of Stoic logic.

The truth is, of course, that no later Platonist, starting from Speusippus and Xenocrates, could be strictly "orthodox," since Plato did not leave a body of doctrine which could simply be adopted, but, rather, a series of guiding ideas, replete with loose ends and even contradictions, which required interpretation.[28] By

28. On this see the excellent discussion of Harold Cherniss in *The Riddle of the Early Academy* (Berkeley and Los Angeles, 1945), chap. 3, "The Academy: Orthodoxy, Heresy, or Philosophical Interpretation?"

the second century A.D., one in effect had the choice of adopting Aristotelian or Stoic terminology and concepts to give formal structure to one's interpretation of what Plato meant, and there was no central authority such as a Platonic Academy to make *ex cathedra* pronouncements on how far one could go. Nor, I think, was Platonism any the worse for that.

V

A rather different, and most interesting, situation is that of the Neo-Pythagoreans, and specifically such men as Moderatus of Gades (late first century A.D.), Nicomachus of Gerasa (ca. A.D. 70–150), and Numenius of Apamea (fl. ca. A.D. 150). Here the problem is one not so much of orthodoxy, but of how seriously to take heresy, in the original sense of *hairesis*.[29] In *The Middle Platonists* (chap. 7) I firmly included these men, and the Neo-Pythagorean movement as a whole, as a subdivision of Platonism, and in that I am unrepentant, but I would not wish to deny that there are complications.

Neo-Pythagoreanism (or "Pythagoreanism," as its partisans would certainly prefer!) is a rather special state of mind. It may, of course, be more than that. It may even go so far as to enjoin upon its partisans a distinct *bios*, or way of life, involving vegetarianism, periods of silence, and the observance of sundry taboos and practices, though it need not. At the least, however, it issues in a general attitude of one-upmanship in relation to all "later" philosophies (except, of course, Epicureanism, to which one had no desire to claim an ancestry). The various pseudo-Pythagoric texts (now conveniently collected by Holger Thesleff)[30] exemplify this very well. These Hellenistic productions, in

29. See Glucker's excellent discussion of the term: (n. 1 above), 166–93.
30. *The Pythagorean Texts of the Hellenistic Period* (Åbo, 1965). The contributions both of Thesleff and of Walter Burkert to the 1972 Entretiens of the Fondation Hardt on *Pseudo-Pythagorica* are also most useful.

their bogus Doric, are cleverly composed to prefigure various salient aspects of Platonic, Aristotelian, or Stoic ethics, physics, or even (as in the case of "Archytas" *On the Categories*) logic. Primarily, however, the target is Plato, since he is the man considered to have had personal contacts with Pythagoreans, and when identifiable Pythagoreans arise, from the first century B.C. on, it is as adherents (albeit of varying degrees of dissidence) of the Platonic *hairesis* that they appear.

It is this dissidence of theirs, both from the general run of Platonists and to some extent from each other, that I wish to consider now. In its extreme form it can be quite belligerent. Consider Moderatus's complaint against the Platonists, preserved for us by Porphyry in his *Life of Pythagoras* (53). Moderatus has just explained that Pythagorean philosophy proper became extinct because of its difficult and enigmatic form, and because it was written in Doric:

> And in addition Plato and Aristotle and Speusippus and Aristoxenus and Xenocrates appropriated for themselves what was fruitful with only minor touching up, while what was superficial or frivolous, and whatever could be put forward by way of refutation and mockery of the School by those who later were concerned to slander it, they collected and set apart as the distinctive teaching of the movement.

These are strong words, and put Moderatus in an interesting position. All Pythagoreans professed to regard Plato as no more than a brilliant follower of Pythagoras, but no one else, I think, is recorded as grumbling that the whole movement was hijacked by *arriviste* Platonists (and Aristotelians). Numenius is prepared to be censorious about the New Academy (and about Antiochus of Ascalon's new dogmatism) in his treatise *On the Divergence of the Academics from Plato,*[31] but that is quite another matter: Numenius is presenting himself as the defender of Platonic (though

31. Substantial passages preserved by Eusebius in his *Praeparatio evangelica* (Numenius, frr. 24–28 Des Places).

also, of course, Pythagorean) "orthodoxy." All he is doing is rejecting the "Socratic" element in Platonism in favor of the dogmatic *autos epha* tradition of Pythagoras. His treatise *On the Secret Doctrines of Plato* (of which we know almost nothing) was presumably in support of the same line. As for Nicomachus, he is quite content to expound a mathematical Platonism in his *Introduction to Arithmetic* and *Manual of Harmonics*, though he asserts his Pythagoreanism through his *Life of Pythagoras* (which forms an important source for those of Porphyry and Iamblichus) and by his quoting of numerous Pythagorean pseudepigrapha.[32] His *Theology of Arithmetic* is also inspired by Pythagorean number-mysticism, though expounding doctrines that fit within the Platonic spectrum.[33]

Nicomachus is not (in his surviving works) a controversialist, but he almost inevitably inserts himself into a distinctively Pythagorean controversy, on a question no less basic than that of the first principles. Which way true orthodoxy lies in this matter is not entirely clear, but on the whole it seems that the Old Pythagorean doctrine envisaged a pair of principles, the monad and the dyad, both equally primordial, though the monad was naturally dominant.[34] Later speculation, however, as represented by the sources behind Alexander Polyhistor (*ap.* Diogenes Laertius 8.24–33) and Sextus Empiricus (*M* 10.248–84), and, most spectacularly, Eudorus of Alexandria (*ap.* Simplicius *In phys.*, 181, lines 10ff. Diels), proposed the monad, or the One, as the supreme principle, from which the dyad derived. Eudorus, indeed, goes further (perhaps trying to reconcile the two traditions) and declares: "It must be said that the Pythagoreans postulated

---

32. Philolaus, Archytas, and Androcydes in *Intro. Arith.* 1.3.3; Philolaus in *Man. Harm.*, chap. 9; Androcydes, Eubulides, Aristaeus, and Prorus in *Theol. Ar.*, 52, line 11, 54, line 9, 57, line 15 De Falco.

33. See on this *Middle Platonists*, 355–59.

34. See W. Burkert, *Lore and Science in Early Pythagoreanism* (Cambridge, Mass., 1972), chaps. 1 and 2; J. E. Raven, *Pythagoreans and Eleatics* (Cambridge, England, 1948), chap. 9.

on the highest level the One as a first principle, and then on a secondary level two principles of existent things, the One and the nature opposed to this." This secondary One he goes on to term the monad, and its opposite number the indefinite dyad.

This rather daring innovation Eudorus may have derived from reflection on the "limit" (*peras*), "unlimited" (*apeiron*), and "cause of the mixture" of *Philebus* 26E–30E; certainly it puts him beyond the pale of Pythagorean orthodoxy. Indeed, he does not count in the tradition as a Pythagorean but, rather, as an "Academic,"[35] so that he ranks more as a fellow-traveler, a Pythagorizing Platonist, than as a Pythagorean. There are considerable subtleties here, within the spectrum.

It is this question of first principles, though, that is the subject of the clearest intra-school controversy between Pythagoreans of which we have evidence. Calcidius, in chap. 295 of his *Timaeus Commentary*, reports Numenius's views on this question, apparently almost verbatim. It is worth, I think, quoting the passage *in extenso*,[36] since it gives a good idea not only of Numenius's relation to his immediate Pythagorean predecessors, but also of his stance within Platonism as a whole:

> Now the doctrine of Pythagoras must be discussed. The Pythagorean Numenius attacks this Stoic doctrine of the principles on the basis of the doctrine of Pythagoras (with which, in his opinion, Plato's doctrine is in complete accordance), and he says that Pythagoras calls the Godhead the monad, matter the dyad. Now, according to Pythagoras, in as far as this dyad is undetermined it did not originate, but in so far as it is determined it has an origin. In other words: before it was adorned with form and order, it was without beginning or origin, but its generation was the adornment and embellishment by the Godhead who regulated it. Since, therefore, this generation is a later event, the unadorned and unborn substance should be held to be as old as God by whom it was regulated. But some Pythagoreans misunderstood this theory

35. Stobaeus *Ecl.* 2, p. 42, line 7 Wachsmuth.
36. In J. C. M. van Winden's translation, in *Calcidius on Matter: His Doctrine and Sources* (Leiden, 1965), 103 (slightly emended).

and came to think that also this unqualified and limitless dyad was produced by the utterly unique monad and that, thus, the monad abandoning its own nature assumed the appearance of the dyad. But this is wrong, because in this case that which was, the monad, would cease to exist and that which was not, the dyad, would come into being, and God would be changed into matter and the monad into the unqualified and limitless dyad. Even to people of mediocre education this is obviously impossible.

What Numenius is in fact doing here is undertaking an interpretation of the doctrine of the *Timaeus* not unlike that of Plutarch, but presented as the teaching of Pythagoras. The Demiurge is the monad, the primitive chaos of *Tim.* 30A is the dyad, which then is adorned and receives ordering by the Demiurge, and as such may be said to be "created," but is otherwise uncreated, and coeval with the monad.

His attack on those Pythagoreans who "misunderstood this theory," a class which certainly includes both Moderatus and Nicomachus,[37] as well as the tradition represented by Alexander Polyhistor, is interestingly comparable to that of Plutarch on his Platonic predecessors in *On the Creation of the Soul.* In each case, the prevailing orthodoxy is being condemned from the perspective of a "truer" orthodoxy, which goes back to the roots of the tradition.

This is not, of course, to imply that Numenius is really a "conservative" Pythagorean. He is simply using the tradition to serve his philosophic purposes, as was Plutarch. In fact, he ranged widely, as we know, over the field of Eastern wisdom, picking up reinforcement for his ideas from Jewish, Iranian,

---

37. Moderatus, as we can see from the fragment of his treatise *On Matter* preserved by Simplicius (*In phys.*, 181, lines 17ff. Diels), held matter to be derivative from the One (at every level), while Nicomachus's denomination of the monad as male-female (ἀρσενόθηλυς) in the *Theologoumena Arithmeticae* (4, lines 1 and 17ff. De Falco) marks it out as a supreme principle. It generates the dyad, or matter, he tells us below (5, lines 3–4), by a process of self-doubling (διφορηθεῖσα).

Egyptian, and even Indian religion. Eusebius quotes a significant extract from book 1 of his dialogue *On the Good*:[38]

> On this question, after having cited, and sealed ourselves with, the evidences of Plato, we should go back further and gird ourselves with[39] the teachings of Pythagoras, and then call in the aid of peoples of renown, adducing their rites of initiation, their doctrines, and their established traditions, performed in conformity with Plato's precepts, such as are ordained by the Brahmans, the Jews, the Magi, and the Egyptians.

Not only the content, but the terminology of this passage is significant. Numenius proposes to take his start from Plato, and signed with the sign of Plato—his use of *sēmainomai* here introduces a mildly hieratic note—then gird himself about with the doctrines of Pythagoras, before taking on the inherited wisdom of "peoples of renown" (*ta ethnē ta eudokimounta*). The order of progression is significant: Pythagoras and *ta ethnē* are highly honored, but they must conform to the doctrines of Plato.

Now all this is distinctly eccentric, but who will dare to call it eclectic? Numenius is not just browsing in the supermarket of philosophy and comparative religion. He has a coherent system, a rather dualistic form of Platonism, and he is embellishing and enriching it by the application of a further principle—the same that for the Neoplatonists brought Homer, Hesiod, Orpheus, and the gods of Chaldaea into the fold—that Plato is divinely inspired and thus will be found to be in accord with all other divinely inspired individuals and traditions.

This theory may not commend itself very strongly to us, but it has to be acknowledged as a theory, and following it does not, it seems to me, make one an eclectic, at least in the pejorative sense in which this word is generally used. Numenius's innova-

38. *Praep. ev.* 9.7.1 = fr. 1a Des Places.
39. Des Places (*ad loc.*) renders this "les rattacher aux enseignements de Pythagore," referring to the evidences of Plato, which is possible, but the middle of συνδέω seems to me to carry, rather, the connotation "gird oneself about."

tions in doctrine, such as the distinction between the Father and the Creator (frr. 11, 21), the splitting of the Demiurge (fr. 11), or the theory of two souls (frr. 44, 52), are developments explicable from within Platonism, not importations from without (though the possibility of influence from Persia or from the Gnostics cannot be excluded). He is, I have said, sealed with the seal of Plato, and this is his talisman or phylactery when plunging into the maze of Oriental religion.

VI

This investigation has proceeded far enough to make its point. We have looked at two groups within later Platonism, the second-century Athenians (I will not call them a school), and a succession of distinguished "Pythagoreans." The study of each group is instructive in its way and demonstrates sufficiently, I think, the limitations of any interpretation that employs the concepts of *orthodoxy* and *eclecticism*.

To end where we began: any living philosophical movement, composed of independent minds unfettered by an official establishment of Guardians of the Faith, is going to be "eclectic" in a positive sense. Are Peter Geach and Elizabeth Anscombe "orthodox" or "eclectic" Wittgensteinians? Is A. J. Ayer an eclectic Humean? Are Sartre and Merleau-Ponty to be seen as eclectic phenomenologists? Is it a sin or a virtue to be an eclectic Hegelian, Marxist, or Freudian? *Eclecticism* has for too long been used as a term of contempt in the area of later Greek philosophy. As such, let us have done with it.

PIERLUIGI DONINI

5

Science and metaphysics
Platonism, Aristotelianism, and Stoicism in Plutarch's On the Face in the Moon

The treatise *De facie in orbe lunae* is certainly one of the least studied among Plutarch's philosophical writings. The difficult and technical nature of some scientific discussions in the treatise probably explains its lack of popularity, but its extremely composite nature must also have contributed. Indeed, the *De facie* may be considered composite in two ways and for two different reasons.

First, there is an obvious problem in the plan of the work, which consists of two sections widely divergent in nature. The first part is a scientific discussion, and according to the experts it is a high-quality account for the man in the street.[1] Physics, astronomy, and geometrical optics are here used to explain the

I would like to thank F. E. Brenk, S. J., for his helpful suggestions.

1. A collection of opinions is found in H. Görgemanns, *Untersuchungen zu Plutarchs Dialog de facie in orbe lunae* (Heidelberg, 1970), 13f. The praise given by S. Sambursky, *The Physical World of the Greeks* (London, 1956), chap. 9, is particularly emphatic. The text and translation I use in this paper are those of H. Cherniss, *Plutarch's Moralia*, vol. 12 (Cambridge, Mass., 1957).

nature of the moon and its spots, and the explanation proposed is the closest to scientific truth that we know from antiquity. The second part is as different from this as one could imagine: it is a fanciful eschatological myth, filled with souls and demons, where the moon and the sun, which are held to be the soul's origin and destination, serve to explain its life away from the earth. Current interpretations of the *De facie* either totally ignore the existence of one of the two parts,[2] or disregard one of them by subordinating its meaning and function to the revelation or demonstration of a "truth" which is held to be fully expressed only in the other.[3] The only useful starting point for understanding the work is the suggestion that the question of the final cause is the theme connecting its two parts.[4]

The *De facie*, however, has a composite character in a second sense too. Its contents are enormously varied and heterogeneous; not only are data of ancient science assembled, but also themes whose origin is philosophical and which derive from Plato, Aristotle, and the Stoics. It does not seem reasonable to seek to explain the presence of these different scientific and philosophical themes without trying to solve the problem of the unity and of

2. This is very clearly the case in Sambursky (n. 1 above), who does not even mention the existence of the myth at the end of the work.

3. Thus, according to Cherniss (n. 1 above), 18, "there cannot be any doubt that the purpose of the whole is to establish and defend the position that the moon is entirely earthy in its constitution and that on this hypothesis alone can the astronomical phenomena and the existence of the moon itself be accounted for." But in this way the myth is disregarded and one forgets that in the second part Plutarch explicitly states that the moon *is not* entirely earthy. Y. Vernière, *Symboles et mythes dans la pensée du Plutarque* (Paris, 1977), acts in the opposite way and completely gives up the scientific section in favor of the myth, which alone, in her opinion, enables one to solve all the difficulties.

4. Put forward by Görgemanns (n. 1 above), 79–81, 84–86. The reasons for my partial disagreement with Görgemanns will become clear in the rest of my discussion: basically, Görgemanns does not make a serious attempt to interpret the myth and the relationship between myth and science and refuses to acknowledge that there are in Plutarch and in the *De facie* the essential marks of Middle Platonism (cf. especially 116ff.).

the whole meaning of the dialogue—unless one resorts to traditional philological explanations (mechanical contamination of
sources and double versions), with which current Plutarch scholars are (rightly, in my opinion) increasingly dissatisfied.

Let us then ask ourselves to what extent and how the different
philosophical streams found in the *De facie* contribute to a possible general plan. It is obvious, and has never been doubted, that
Plato more than anyone else influenced Plutarch.[5] Themes of
Platonic origin are concentrated in two sections, which are the
most important for the philosophical meaning of the dialogue.
The first (chapters 12–15) is also the high point of a fierce quarrel
with Stoicism. The emphasis on the teleology underlying the
organization of the universe and the corporeal structure of living
beings, and the stress on the superiority of "what is better" over
necessity, both recall well-known Platonic texts, from the *Phaedo*
to the *Timaeus*, and also Platonic writings closer in time to Plutarch (for example, Galen's *De usu partium*). The other important·
topic showing Platonic inspiration is the eschatological myth.[6]
The scenery with imaginary geographical elements calls to mind
the *Timaeus* and the Atlantis myth; the experiences undergone
away from the earth by the souls look back to the myths in the
Phaedrus and *Republic*; and the presence of the demons reminds
one of the *Symposium*, but even more of the demonological theories of Xenocrates, a Platonist who is explicitly named in 943F.
However, in the *De facie* there are also some themes that are not
only foreign but perhaps even hostile to Plato's philosophy (at
least apparently so).

In the final myth Plato alone would not suffice to explain the

5. Cherniss's notes have abundant references to Platonic texts. For the
dependence on the *Timaeus* particularly, cf. Görgemanns (n. 1 above), 57,
and Vernière (n. 3 above), 96f., and for an earlier view, R. Hirzel, *Der Dialog*
(Leipzig, 1895), vol. 2, 183.

6. For its dependence on Plato cf. W. Hamilton, "The Myth in Plutarch's
De facie," *CQ* 28 (1934), 24–30; also R. M. Jones, *The Platonism of Plutarch*
(Menasha, Wisc., 1916; reprinted New York, 1980), 51–56.

hypothesis of the "double death," together with all the elements connected with it; and whereas it is perhaps right to consider such details as the connection of the souls with the moon and the sun relatively insignificant (for these may be mere fancies justified by the myth but without any real philosophical importance), we are certainly worried by the bodily nature with which the souls suddenly seem endowed when they reach the moon, and in which, sooner or later, they are fated to dissolve.[7] Therefore at least in this case the hypothesis of Stoic influence, which in the past has often been put forward, seems somewhat plausible; for it cannot be denied that the role of Stoicism in the *De facie* is very important. Stoicism is the chief focus of the dispute in the first part. The earthy nature of the moon is demonstrated by confuting different theses, and of these the one that receives most attention is indeed the Stoic theory (according to which the moon is a mixture of air and fire); it is also demonstrated by confuting the theory of natural places, which is attributed only to the Stoics. (The speakers opposed to it do not involve Aristotle in the quarrel.) Besides this, in accordance with a good method commonly used by Plutarch in philosophical disputes, the Stoic theses serve also to inspire those who criticize them.[8] When they are turned against their supporters and carried to absurdity or placed in contradiction among themselves, they help to demonstrate the opposite argument, which Plutarch favors. The disputes are not always well founded,[9] but as a general rule it is always possible to say that Plutarch's intention was to use his opponents' arguments to destroy Stoicism from inside and with its own weapons. This clear and strong interest in his opponents' theses may have facilitated his assimilation of Stoic elements.

7. *De facie* 943D–E, 945A–B. Cf. below.
8. Cf. D. Babut, *Plutarque et le Stoicisme* (Paris, 1969), 124ff., and also Görgemanns (n. 1 above), 70ff., 75. The method is obviously derived from the Skeptical Academy.
9. See the analysis of chapters 6–15 in Görgemanns (n. 1 above), 90–120.

But we can go further. The scientific core of the *De facie*, or essentially the whole of the first part with the exception of the philosophical quarrel in chapters 12–15, certainly cannot be derived from Plato. First, the theory of the earthy nature of the moon is not at all Platonic;[10] second, it is impossible to find in Plato a similar example of a serious discussion of a problem in physics (even though Plutarch is dealing with celestial physics), let alone such a discussion carried on with the aid of other special sciences such as astronomy and optics. Both the scientific content and the method of the discussion cannot, then, be explained in terms of a precise Platonic model. However, this conclusion is perhaps not very important; in other words, one should not make the mistake of identifying the area of Platonism in Plutarch only with that of the coincidences with the *Dialogues* of Plato. Sometimes one forgets that there were nearly five centuries of changes (including changes within the schools that followed Plato) between Plutarch and his distant master. But once this is remembered, Plutarch can be allowed to find some Platonic doctrine which is not to be found explicitly in the *Dialogues* but had by then become part of the tradition of the school. In explaining the situation of the *De facie*, we can usefully invoke the doctrines current in Platonism in the early imperial period, which by now had appropriated the Aristotelian threefold division of theoretical sciences. As the *Didaskalikos* shows,[11] physics, together with

10. According to Görgemanns' accurate discussion (n. 1 above), 34–37, it goes back to the Presocratic period (Anaxagoras, Democritus, and Philolaus). However, no philosophical school accepted it and the theory survived only in some fantastic descriptions. As for Plato, it is impossible to find in him any specific statement on the substance of the moon (ibid., 35 n. 62); at most, by distorting the sense of *Tim.* 31B–32C, the view that the stars are made of a mixture of earth and fire could be ascribed to him. This is just what Plutarch attempts to do in *De facie* 943F, but even with this distortion the view ascribed to Plato remains different from the one upheld in the first part of the dialogue.

11. *Didaskalikos* 153.36–154.4H. The position of astronomy was, however, uncertain; in this passage of the *Didaskalikos* it is considered part of physics, but in 161.22 it is part of mathematics. Cf. also G. Invernizzi, *Il Didaskalikos di Albino e il medioplatonismo* (Rome, 1976), vol. 2, 85 n. 23.

mathematics, was accepted as one of the speculative sciences of lower rank than theology. In the framework of such Platonism even the first part of the *De facie* could be considered perfectly Platonic. In any case it is well known that Plutarch elsewhere shows important contacts with contemporary Platonism, which had absorbed many Aristotelian doctrines.[12]

The *De facie* includes passages[13] which could suggest that Plutarch, in his very tendentious attempt to present Stoicism as a modern materialism that denied divine providence, considered Aristotle and Aristotelians as valuable allies. But it is even more important to note that Plutarch knew the threefold Aristotelian division of theoretical sciences and used it in the *De facie*, though in the disguised form of myth. Thus the information (942B) about the activities of the stranger in the island of Cronos (and the stranger is the source from which the myth appears to have come) can hardly be anything but a metaphorical hint of this doctrine. The stranger, we are told, "while he served the god became at his leisure acquainted with astronomy, in which he made as much progress as one can by practicing geometry, and with the rest of philosophy by dealing with so much of it as is possible for the natural philosopher." The choice of the sciences and activities necessary for the servants of Cronos is obviously

12. See the discussion by Ph. Merlan in A. H. Armstrong, ed., *The Cambridge History of Later Greek and Early Medieval Philosophy* (Cambridge, England, 1967), 59 (on the question of what Plutarch actually knew of Aristotelian texts Merlan is, however, certainly refuted by F. Sandbach, "Plutarch and Aristotle," *Illinois Class. Stud.* 7, 2 [1982]) and my paper "Lo scetticismo academico: Aristotele e l'unità della tradizione platonica secondo Plutarco," in G. Cambiano, ed., *Storiografia e dossografia nella filosofia antica* (Turin, 1986), 203–26. On the *De genio Socratis*, cf. the essay cited below in n. 24.

13. Above all, the entire criticism of the theory of natural places in chapters 7–15, which are entirely aimed against Stoicism, without the slightest reference to Aristotle. (However, the *De def. orac.* 424B–C shows that Plutarch knew that the theory was also Aristotelian.) See also 928F–29A, which contain a mild and courteous criticism of the theory of ether, and 932B–C, where there is an artificial contrast between Aristotle and Posidonius which is entirely to the former's advantage.

deliberate. We find astronomy and geometry joined together to form the bulk of mathematics (this is one of the possible positions of astronomy in Middle Platonism, though according to another interpretation it belonged to physics);[14] and we find the remainder of philosophy, which belongs to physics. But everything is at the god's service and designed for his worship. Here we see the obvious preeminence of theology over all the theoretical sciences.

The island of Cronos thus seems to be a metaphor for a Platonic school of the first or second century A.D.; and the program of activities of the god's servants seems to coincide with the conceptual framework of the *De facie* itself. But what consequences derive from this as far as the composition of the dialogue and the relationship between myth and science are concerned? Some form of subordination or inferiority of the other two theoretical sciences to theology is clearly implicit in Plutarch's exposition.[15] For Aristotle, too, first philosophy, i.e., theology, was superior to the other sciences. But is myth simply identical with theology? And precisely in what sense are the results of the scientific section of the *De facie* inferior or subordinate to the truths of theology?

It is possible to answer the first question immediately. Myth cannot be considered as the literal expression of supreme theological science. It is at most a foreshadowing or metaphor of a

14. Cf. n. 11 above.

15. The supremacy of theology and the subordination of all other sciences to it are convictions Plutarch often expresses: cf. Babut (n. 8 above), 283 and n. 5, where there is a list of relevant passages. Of these, *De def. orac.* 410B is the most explicit, but since it represents the position of Cleombrotus one may hesitate before seeing in it Plutarch's own position: on this question cf. F. E. Brenk, *In Mist Apparelled: Religious Themes in Plutarch's Moralia and Lives* (Leiden, 1977), 85–112; R. Flacelière, "La théologie selon Plutarque," *Mélanges Boyancé* (Rome, 1974), 273–80; H. Dörrie, "Der Weise vom Roten Meer. Eine okkulte Offenbarung durch Plutarch als Plagiat entlarvt," *Festschrift R. Muth.* (Innsbruck, 1983), 95ff., esp. 96–97.

truth, which must still be interpreted in its entirety.[16] Because of this it is impossible that wherever the data of science and the information given by mythical characters conflict, such information should definitely be considered a literal truth that corrects the errors of science or extends its objective limits. But what are these limits, and wherein lies the inferiority of science to the theology foreshadowed in the myth?

Even though Platonists accepted physical science and astronomy within the realm of recognized theoretical sciences, they undoubtedly set limits to the cognitive value of these subjects. If they adopted from Aristotle the threefold division of the sciences, they could not endorse the theory it implied, the idea that the inferiority of physics to first philosophy was only axiological and the defense—which in Aristotle was doubtless inspired by the quarrel with Plato—of the independence and self-sufficiency of the special sciences, each of which was organized around principles that were proper to it and could not be deduced from any supposedly supreme science. Besides, such a theory of science coexists in Aristotle with the idea of an eternal world, which had neither been built originally by divine providence nor was governed by it. But if the world was formed by divine power (which for Plutarch is literally true) and is constantly watched over by god's providence, then physics cannot be based only on physical principles: it must at some point yield to theology, or at least it should draw its fundamental principles from this discipline. One can see, then, what difficulties were caused when a cosmology based on divine craftsmanship and providence, such as Middle Platonism and in particular Plutarch's philosophy, took over Aristotle's threefold division. Plutarch clearly shows what his position is when he briefly outlines the history of Greek thought in *Life of Nicias* 23, where Plato is praised precisely because "he had made the necessity of nature subordinate to divine and truer

16. Cf. above all *De Is. et Os.*, 359A and 374E (with the remarks of Brenk [n. 15 above], 103) and also *De gloria Athen.* 348A and *De genio Socr.* 589F.

principles."[17] According to Plutarch, then, physics looked back to metaphysical principles.

Many details in the scientific section of the *De facie* which may have seemed insignificant now become important, and some which could be explained only with difficulty now become transparent. We can, for example, better understand why the speakers who uphold the earthy nature of the moon and who have always been held to present the position of Plutarch himself never completely identify themselves with the thesis for which they argue. Lamprias and Lucius, even though they sometimes speak as if the argument about the earthy nature were their own (e.g., 921F, 926B, 935C), elsewhere speak as if the same argument had been stated by other persons, with whom they do not wish to identify themselves. The most disturbing instance is in 923A: "We express no opinion of our own now; but those who suppose that the moon is earth, why do they turn things upside down any more than you [Stoics]?" It is surely imprudent to suggest that these incongruities show traces of a double version of the *De facie*, one being more dogmatic and the other more skeptical.[18] The detachment with which, in 923A and elsewhere,[19] the theory of the earthy nature of the moon is presented reflects the proper caution of a Platonist—one who knows he is treating the question from an absolutely partial point of view, discussing as a

17. A passage which Brenk (n. 15 above), 42–44, explains well. There has been controversy on Plutarch's concept of the divine: H. Dörrie denied that Plutarch held the idea of a real transcendence, above all in his essay "Die Stellung Plutarchs im Platonismus seiner Zeit," in *Philomathes: Studies in Memory of Ph. Merlan* (The Hague, 1971), 36–56; but see now the remarks by C. J. De Vogel, "Der sog. Mittelplatonismus: Überwiegend eine Philosophie der Diesseitigkeit?" in *Platonismus und Christentum, Festschrift H. Dörrie* (Münster, 1983), 277–302, esp. 283–87, and by F. E. Brenk, *An Imperial Heritage: The Religious Spirit of Plutarch of Chaironeia,* under *Plutarch's Idea of God* (forthcoming; by the author's kindness, I have been enabled to read the typewritten text).

18. This opinion was put forward by Görgemanns (n. 1 above), 86–89.

19. E.g., 922E, 924F, 936E where Lamprias (or Lucius) uses the third person plural to speak of upholders of the earthy nature of the moon.

physicist and astronomer a matter which is not simply physical and astronomical. The scientific section of the *De facie* argues for the earthy nature of the moon as if the planet were only a body in a world containing bodies, which is clearly not the case: the moon is a *living* and *divine* body, as the advocates of its earthy nature do not themselves fail to note in 935C. The point of view expressed in the first part of the work must therefore seem limited and partial to Plutarch himself, and this explains his caution. We find this same caution in the question concerning the final cause of the moon, when the problem is posed in 928C. Here we learn that the moon transmits downward the heat of the upper regions and, inversely, serves as a filter to purify the exhalations which the earth sends upward. This could well be true, but it is certainly partial. Such an explanation considers the moon and the entire universe only from their material perspective and establishes their functions only for this aspect. If, however, the moon, the heavenly bodies, and the whole world are not merely material objects, there should be some other function for all of them, and this is suggested by the remark immediately added to the physical explanation already mentioned: "It is not clear to us whether her earthiness and solidity have any use suitable to other ends also" (928C). Plutarch has done all he could to be understood.

Now, the "other ends" which could be served by the planets, the moon and the sun in particular, are hinted at in the final myth. Of course, since this is a myth, only some of its elements are for Plutarch "truths" to be understood in an absolutely literal sense. They are relatively few, however, and restricted to those which agree with doctrines commonly accepted by Middle Platonism: that there is an intelligible divine element, whatever its structure may be; that the world and the heavenly bodies are visible and living divinities; that man's being has not a corporeal nature alone, but consists of the union of a body and a soul, of which at least a part must be immortal. Apart from these few fixed points of Platonic philosophy, everything cannot be understood simply in a literal sense, but needs to be interpreted. Now it is fairly difficult to try to guess the truth of which the myth could give a hint, but a good criterion of judgment could be the presupposition that there is a consistent connection between the two sections of the *De facie*, and that therefore what is said in the myth derives its meaning from the theses in the first section. I shall try to follow this criterion and discuss some details of the myth that are relevant to the total meaning of the dialogue.

In the first place, in some cases the myth expresses an opinion on the problems already discussed in the first section from a scientific point of view. The existence of islands in the ocean and of a great continent on the other side of the ocean, which is stated in the myth (941A–B), runs the risk of directly contradicting the thesis put forward in the first part of Lamprias's account, which declares with certainty that the idea of the outer ocean being not continuous but broken up by mainlands is "absurd and false" (921C). The chief subject of the discussion, the material nature of the moon, is explained differently in the two sections, though not with complete contradiction: by the earthy nature in the first part, and in the second by the suggestion that the moon is a mixture of the earth's and the stars' natures.

But precisely in the passage in which the myth suggests this new explanation, we find another potential contradiction to the arguments of science expressed in the first part. Sulla reports that the moon, insofar as it is a mixture of earth and of star or ether (by this he surely means the purest form of fire: cf. 943E–F), "is at once animated and fertile and at the same time has the proportion of lightness to heaviness in equipoise." It is not said explicitly but is suggested here that this balance between forces is the reason why the moon occupies in the universe the place that is proper to it; but in the scientific exposition in chapter 6 (923C–D), the speed of revolution is said to prevent the moon (in this case understood as being endowed with an earthy nature and hence heavy) from falling back on the earth.

It seems, then, that Plutarch is not at all worried by his contradiction in the myth of the scientific theories previously advanced. But there is even a case that leaves no doubt that Plutarch *wants* to stress in the myth that he is contradicting the science he had used in the first part. In 944A, after a digression on the nature of the heavenly bodies, Sulla continues as follows: "So much for the moon's substance. As to her breadth and magnitude, it is not what the geometers say, but many times greater. She measures off the earth's shadow with few of her own magnitudes not because it is small but she more ardently hastens her motion in order that she may quickly pass through the gloomy place bearing away the souls of the good which cry out and urge her . . ." Here we seem to have a completely deliberate and hostile reference to the arguments in 923B on the crossing of the earth's shadow in eclipses and to those in 932B, where there is a respectful citation of the calculations of Aristarchus proving that the moon's diameter is much shorter than the earth's. However, a few lines below we are astonished again, but in a very different manner. After speaking of the souls of the good, which hasten to come out of the shadow, Sulla describes the moaning procession of the souls of the evil, who press upon the moon from behind and are terrified by it: "The souls . . . are frightened off also by the so-called face when they get near it, for it has a grim and horrible aspect. It is no such thing, however, but just as our earth contains gulfs that are deep and extensive . . . so those features are depths and hollows of the moon" (944B–C).

This is indeed a remarkable passage; the explanation of the face of the moon is here exactly the same as the one proposed in the scientific section in 935C;[20] indeed, the confirmation science obtains here from the mythical account is even strengthened by the detail that Plutarch here stresses—that the souls of the *evil* see in the moon's face what is not there. It is implied that the souls of the good do not deceive themselves on the planet's

---

20. Even the text of the two passages is almost exactly the same: 935C ὥσπερ ἡ παρ᾽ ἡμῖν ἔχει γῆ κόλπους τινὰς μεγάλους; 944B ὥσπερ ἡ παρ᾽ ἡμῖν ἔχει γῆ κόλπους βαθεῖς καὶ μεγάλους.

true nature. (One should, rather, say that it is not simply implied, for Sulla relates an explanation which ultimately comes from the servants of Cronos, who belong indeed to the better souls; cf. 944D. These show themselves here, then, as no less than scientist demons rather than wise demons. Besides, are not physics and astronomy studied in the island of Cronos?)

As one can see, the picture resulting from a comparison between the answers given by the two parts of the *De facie* to some problems raised in both of them is full of contrasts: there are cases where myth deliberately contradicts science, others where myth corrects it, and others still where it confirms it fully. What could be the sense of such unequal correspondences? In fact it is not difficult to understand why Plutarch wanted to insert in the myth elements which contradicted the scientific theory. Even if it were true that they contain vestiges of Platonic irony,[21] the fact remains that they are concerned precisely with physical and mathematical-astronomical science. The contradictions must therefore have exactly the same sense as the somewhat skeptical reservation in the first part of the work; they have the purpose of insisting on the nondefinitive, not fully certain, nonabsolute nature of scientific explanations. The Platonic philosopher suggests that when one engages in the science of nature or of the heavens, one must always remember that in a wider vision (as should always be the case, since sciences are neither autonomous nor self-sufficient) the explanations could be different, involving metaphysical forces or entities which are not even exactly perceptible by science. Yet the explanations of the myth are not literally true: they are only an example and a suggestion of how matters could otherwise stand. At the end of the tale (945D) Sulla significantly invites his listeners not to "believe" it but to "make what they will" of it, that is, to interpret it in the manner in which

---

21. So H. von Arnim, "Plutarch über Dämonen und Mantik," *Verhand. der kon. Akad. van Wetensch.* (Amsterdam, 1921), 56, according to whom the "truth" of the *De facie* lay, however, only in the scientific part.

it may best be interpreted. Besides, just where the myth more explicitly contradicts science it does so in such a way, and with such enormously false reasoning,[22] that surely Plutarch's aim was not to advocate acceptance of the myth, least of all in this case, as pure truth: he probably wanted to suggest the exact opposite, that it cannot be true in the actual terms stated by Sulla, but must simply be understood as a hint of another truth, different from physical truth. What Plutarch means to produce with regard to scientific matters is, however, a sense of watchful reservation and not of corrosive mistrust; an irrationalist critic of science could never have written the first part of the *De facie*. For this reason, after having belied science in the most astonishing manner, he has inserted in the myth the explanation in 944B–C on the face of the moon, where the scientific theory is proposed again and confirmed.

Clearly, therefore, the effective and important subject of the *De facie* is not really the nature and functions of the moon. This question serves only to exemplify, through the discussion of a specific problem, the difficulties inherent in a more general question belonging to the speculative philosophy of Middle Platonism: the relationship between physics and metaphysics, and between special sciences and theology. This is the real problem, and it may be suggested that in Plutarch's oeuvre this question is not presented by the *De facie* alone.[23] If Plutarch has there discussed the implications for Platonism of certain key Aristotelian principles, that is not an unimportant point. The *De virtute*

22. Explained by H. Cherniss, "Notes on Plutarch's *De facie in orbe lunae*," *CPh* 46 (1951), 152 ff.

23. One thinks immediately of the *De def. orac.*, which begins with Cleombrotus's famous proposition on the subordination of scientific inquiry to a philosophy which reaches its highest point in theology. The analogies between the *De facie* and the *De defectu* have always seized the attention of scholars: cf., e.g., Hirzel (n. 5 above), vol. 2, 196; Görgemanns (n. 1 above), 67 and 111f.; Vernière (n. 3 above), 57f., 102f.; Brenk (n. 17 above). (There is, however, still uncertainty on the relative chronology.)

morali will no longer seem unique in his work; and if we also bear in mind the interpretation recently put forward for the *De genio Socratis*[24] (a well-constructed work on the contrast between an active and a speculative life), we shall have to admit that the presence of Aristotelianism in Plutarch is much greater than we had been accustomed to think.

Another problem raised by the myth in the *De facie* is the corporeality of the soul. This thesis is implicit in the passage (943D–E) where Sulla describes the second period of the souls' stay in the moon: "second, in appearance resembling a ray of light, but in respect of their nature, which in the upper region is buoyant as it is here in ours, resembling the ether about the moon, they get from it both tension and strength as edged instruments get a temper; for what laxness and diffuseness they still have is strengthened and becomes firm and translucent. In consequence they are nourished by any exhalation that reaches them, and Heraclitus was right in saying: 'Souls employ the sense of smell in Hades.'" Not only is the soul's corporeality here clearly stated, but the language is clearly that of the Stoics.[25] The same thesis is again confirmed in 945A–B, where the death of the souls is mentioned: "Of these, as has been said, the moon is the element, for they are resolved into it as the bodies of the dead are resolved into earth." If we admitted that Plutarch followed a

24. By D. Babut, "Le dialogue de Plutarque 'Sur le démon de Socrate,' essai d'interpretation," *Bull. de l'Ass. G. Budé*, no. 1 (1984), 51–75. It is also remarkable that the fundamental problem presented by the *De genio* to interpreters is absolutely similar to that of the *De facie*: in both cases the problem is finding *one* meaning for *two* parts and two subjects which seem to be completely heterogeneous.

25. Cherniss (n. 1 above), 203, classifies as Stoic the concept of *tonos*, the idea that the soul is nourished by exhalations, and the use of a quotation from Heraclitus. On the other hand, the idea that the soul is made of ether alone (or pure fire) does not coincide with Stoicism; nevertheless, the soul is corporeal as in the Stoic doctrine, even though its nature is conceived in a different manner.

Stoic source here,[26] we would also exacerbate the incongruity of which he would have been guilty. After having fought against the Stoics in most of his work, he would have derived from them a doctrine that is contrary to everything we would expect from a Platonist, and just in a context where the argument should by now be exclusively metaphysical and theological. If, however, we do not consider the myth a self-contained account but examine it in the light of the problems raised by the entire work and of the hypothesis that everything has *one* meaning, the difficulty appears to be far less serious: we may conclude that Plutarch was in a certain sense compelled to accept a kind of materialization of the soul.

Let us indeed consider once again the specific problem tackled in both parts of the *De facie*. It deals with the nature and function of the moon, i.e., the material and the final cause. The first part of the work goes some way toward specifying the material cause and, in connection with this, the final cause too: if the moon has an earthy nature, its function is compatible with such a nature, i.e., the reflection of the sun's rays and the transmission and purification of the earth's exhalations. But this same first part, as we have seen, leads one to understand that such accounts are inad-

26. This hypothesis was first put forward by R. Heinze, *Xenokrates* (Leipzig, 1892) 125 ff., and M. Adler, "Quibus ex fontibus Plutarchus libellum de facie in orbe lunae hauserit," diss. Vienna, 1910, 177. K. Reinhardt attributed precisely to Posidonius the myth in the *De facie* (cf. his latest views in the article "Poseidonios," *RE* 23, 1 (1953), 558ff., esp. 782–85). After the criticism presented by R. M. Jones, "Posidonius and Solar Eschatology," *CPh* 27 (1932), 113ff. (now also an appendix to the new edition of *The Platonism of Plutarch* [n. 6 above]) and M. Laffranque, *Poseidonios d'Apamée* (Paris, 1964), appendix, 519–27, this thesis may be considered almost completely demolished. It does not, however, seem to me reasonable to exclude all possibility that Plutarch made use of Stoic concepts, but the matter has no longer, in my opinion, any particular relevance; cf. below. In his posthumous edition of the fragments of Posidonius (*Poseidonios, Die Fragmente* [Berlin, 1982]), W. Theiler accepted the text of *De facie* 943A–B, 944E–945D as fr. 398. The commentary (vol. 2, 334f.) does not, however, adduce any significant argument.

equate, since they consider the moon solely as a physical and inanimate body. The myth has exactly the task of correcting these limitations of science; and it starts by correcting the account of the material cause. But it is important to note *how* it corrects it. At 943E we are told that the moon has not a simple and unmixed nature (in other words, it has not the same nature as the earth, as was argued in the first part) but is "a blend as it were of star and earth," and "because it has been permeated through and through by ether is animated and fertile." One must inevitably conclude from this that it is the addition of starry substance (ether or fire) that makes the moon animated; the moon's soul has therefore an ethereal nature. But this result has in turn some unavoidable consequences, which Plutarch draws with great coherence: according to the new explanation of the material nature, the account of final causality will also have to be corrected; the new specification of this will have to take the new nature into account, and since the nature is now animated, the final cause of the moon in the new account will deal with the soul, its vicissitudes, its origin, and its destination. At this point the identification of the soul's nature with the moon's ether (which is in fact clearly expressed in 943D), and hence the materialization of the soul, is imposed by the very logic of the construction. The final cause of the moon therefore becomes clear. It consists in the task of producing (945C) and receiving for a certain period of time the souls that have come back from their first death (the separation from the body) and finally dissolving them into the lunar substance itself.

Obviously, Plutarch does not at all intend to abandon the Platonic doctrine of the immortality of the soul. For in addition to a body and a mortal soul, man has *nous* or intelligence (943A). Fifty years ago Hamilton persuasively argued that Plutarch's distinction between soul and intelligence (even if it was certainly influenced by Aristotle) was meant to reproduce the *Timaeus*'s distinction between the mortal and the immortal part of the soul.[27] Further, there cannot be any doubt whatsoever that *nous* in Plutarch is immortal and immaterial. It is defined as *apathēs*, "impassible," nor is there ever any mention of a "third death" or of a dissolution of the intelligence into the sun. Finally, in the passage that indicates the separation of intelligence from the soul, we are clearly meant to understand that it yearns to be joined not to the sun as a heavenly body (besides, of what material substance or element could one still imagine intelligence to be made, seeing that ether has already been used in order to explain the mortal nature of the soul?). The aim of *nous* is instead the supreme and ideal goal that reveals itself in the sun, namely, the Good found in the *Republic*, or the first god found in Middle Platonism: "It is separated by love for the image in the sun through which shines forth manifest the desirable and fair and divine and blessed, toward which all nature in one way or another yearns."[28]

In conclusion, the materialization of the soul in the *De facie* is perfectly connected with the fundamental subjects of the treatise and is cleverly incorporated in an anthropology, psychology, and metaphysics which can be presented as an interpretation of the *Timaeus*. Given this situation, even the possible use of a Stoic source by Plutarch, which in fact is made at least probable by some passages in the myth,[29] is no longer at all alarming, incongruous, or scandalous. That Plutarch could put his wide reading to good use in composing the *De facie* is exactly what we should expect of him, but his total conception remains firmly Platonic-Aristotelian.

27. (N. 6 above), 26f.

28. *De facie* 944E. It is certainly wise to stress the presence in this passage of echoes of Aristotelian conceptions, as does Cherniss (n. 1 above), 213 n. g. Cf. also J. Dillon, *The Middle Platonists* (London, 1977), 213.

29. Cf. n. 25 above; the traits noticed by Cherniss in 943D–E. An equally clear case is in 943F, αὐτὸν οὕτως τὸν κόσμον κτλ.: this is pure Stoic doctrine, as was noted by Arnim (n. 21 above), 67.

If this is so, the *De facie* hardly justifies the old prejudice that makes Plutarch an eclectic, or at least an eclectic of lower quality.[30] Its Platonic-Aristotelian philosophical structure acts as a filter and criterion not only for conceptions of a different philosophical origin (Stoic elements and "skeptical" reservations), but also for the scientific problems discussed in the treatise. Therefore, if one really wanted to speak of eclecticism, one would have to say that the *De facie* is eclectic in one of the most positive senses that could be given to the term: for its wealth of philosophical knowledge and scientific information and for the solidity with which such knowledge and information is organized according to a precise philosophical position.

Still, it could be objected, this philosophical position has a composite character; it is not simply Platonism but a possible version of Platonism, such as Plutarch and other philosophers of those times conceived it, an interpretation of Platonism strongly exposed to Aristotelian influences. The criterion itself which Plutarch used could thus be considered "eclectic" in one of the current meanings of the term. I do not think that this objection can be sustained. Mutual influences between Platonism and Aristotelianism have existed since the time of the ancient Academy: should we then say that Platonic-Aristotelian eclecticism was born there and at that time? Many absurdities could result from this statement. It would perhaps be wiser to admit once and for all that the dialogue between the philosophies of Plato and Aristotle is something essential for all those who, at any time in the history of ancient thought, have looked back to the one or the other philosophy. Eclecticism is quite inadequate to describe this situation.

30. This prejudice was shared also by distinguished scholars such as Arnim (n. 21 above), 66 ("Eklektiker der geringeren Art"), and K. Praechter, *Die Philosophie des Altertums* (13th ed. Graz, 1953), 535. According to E. Zeller, who includes Plutarch among the forerunners of Neoplatonism, there is at least a resemblance ("Verwandtschaft"), (*Phil. d. Griechen*, vol. 3, 2 [4th ed. Leipzig, 1903], 179–80) between Plutarch and the eclectics of his time.

6

Sextus Empiricus on the *kritērion*
The Skeptic as conceptual legatee

Skepticism, as is well known, is a therapy for philosophical ill-nesses. But it does not spend much time in classifying those illnesses: the disease to fight against, in spite of its manifold forms, is always dogmatism. To the Skeptic, all non-Skeptical schools are dogmatic, whether "properly speaking" (*idiōs, PH* 1.3) or in a particular way: the Academy itself professes a kind of upside-down dogmatism (*PH* 1.226). Eclecticism is never mentioned by Sextus, although the thing is not unknown in an-cient philosophy, nor is the word unemployed (see Donini, Chapter 1 above). The reason for this silence is perhaps that eclecticism is less a philosophical illness than an alternative med-icine, aiming at curing the same ills as Skepticism does (namely,

This is a revised, somewhat enlarged, and as far as possible anglicized ver-sion of the paper read in French at the Dublin Congress. I benefited from observations made there, in particular by Pierluigi Donini, Tony Long, Jaap Mansfeld, and Reimar Müller; I am most grateful to them all. Another, more general version was read at the Freie Universität, Berlin, in January 1985; I received a number of useful suggestions from my audience there. I first tried to translate the French draft myself; but if it reads as tolerable English, this is entirely due to Jonathan Barnes's generous and careful help. I am afraid there are still many traces in this paper of its French descent; if such a doctor did not cure them, certainly they are incurable.

conflicts among the dogmatists), but in an opposite way and on the basis of a different diagnosis. To the eclectic, doctrinal conflicts are superficial conflicts; philosophical doctrines are compatible at bottom, at least piecemeal, and perhaps even globally they converge. When looking at the philosophical stage, the Skeptic sees quite a different play: to him, the disagreement between systems is irreducible. An eclectic philosopher might actually accuse the Skeptic of being himself a kind of metaphilosophical dogmatist, in the sense that he admits not only that philosophers *seem* to contradict each other, but also that they actually *do* so; one might remind him of his *zētētic* disposition and invite him to be more careful before asserting the objective reality of those conflicts. But the Skeptic would not be embarrassed by this objection: he could answer that in this context, there was no difference between saying and doing; if philosophers say that they contradict each other (and they say so rather loudly), this means that they do contradict each other. It would be a piece of real dogmatism to claim that deep-level agreement hides beneath surface-level disagreement.

By virtue of his initial decisions, the Skeptic is so immune to eclectic temptations that he does not even feel the need to speak about them. On the other hand, he is never tired of exhibiting the antagonisms between dogmatists, and he sharpens them by all the means at his disposal. He is so little prone to gloss over differences that he takes great pains to demarcate himself from those philosophical schools which for some reason have been taken as "close neighbors" to Skepticism (*PH* 1.210–41).[1]

---

1. This section of *PH* was perhaps paralleled in a lost part of *M*: in this case *M* 7.1 would allude to this parallel section in *M*, not to *PH*. This suggestion is convincingly put forward by Karel Janáček, "Die Hauptschrift des Sextus Empiricus als Torso erhalten," *Philologus* 107 (1963), 271–77. To his arguments I would add the following one: the verb ἐκτυπωθείς, which occurs in *M* 7.1, would be quite inappropriate as a reference to the Ὑπο-τυπώσεις: it does not mean "to sketch," but, on the contrary, "to describe accurately, reproducing all the details of what is described" (cf. συγκεχυ-

This fundamental opposition between eclecticism and Skepticism has certain consequences. Dogmatists contradict each other *in their statements*; those contradictions make dogmatism a weak position (and eclecticism a fundamentally meaningless one), *only if they are real contradictions*. The eclectic game will thus be to mitigate the contradictions, by showing that dogmatists do not speak about the same things, do not consider them in the same respects, do not designate them with the same words; their dissensions are merely verbal, since they use the same words for different concepts and different words for the same concepts; because they disagree on the conceptual level, they are able to agree at the level of dogma, to a greater extent than they themselves believe.[2] On the other hand, the Skeptic must assume that dogmatists, when quarreling about their opposite dogmas, all have *the same notions* and use *the same words* to express them: only on this condition can he claim that he understands what their debates are all about and attack their dogmas from a position of knowledge.

Let us notice, however, that this strategy is likely to come into conflict with another tendency, equally natural to the Skeptic. Accustomed as he is to point out the disagreements between dogmatic *doctrines*, when he notices that dogmatists give different definitions of the same terms he will inevitably be tempted to expose those *conceptual* disagreements; the reader will thus be presented with the broadest possible "disagreement" (*diaphōnia*) between dogmatists. But this is a dangerous game: if he tries to win on this ground too, he weakens his position elsewhere, since

μένως καὶ οὐκ ἐκτύπως, *M* 7.171; ἐξεργασία, used by Sextus *M* 7.1 as a description of the style in which what came before *M* 7 was written, is contrasted with ὑποτύπωσις in Plotinus 6.3.7).

2. Emphasis on the merely verbal character of disagreements among philosophers is a recurring feature in the Antiochean tradition: cf. Cicero *Fin.* 4.72 (*re consentire, verbis discrepare*), 5.22 (*nominibus aliis easdem res*), etc. The *locus classicus* of this conception of error and controversy is Spinoza *Eth.* II.47, schol.

he jeopardizes the identity of the conceptual legacy shared by the different schools. We may well expect that he will vacillate over what to do when it is clear that a given concept is differently construed by different schools: he has equally good reasons for pointing out this difference and for saying nothing about it, or even for denying it; but clearly he cannot do all these things at the same time.

We can see this vacillation, I believe, in more than one passage in Sextus. I shall content myself with one example, in which it is especially conspicuous. In *M* 8, Sextus devotes a lengthy section (300–336) to an analysis of the notion (*epinoia*) of proof (*apodeixis*). He barely mentions the disagreements between schools concerning certain aspects of this notion (336); everywhere else in this section, he offers as an investigation of a unitary concept of proof what is in fact (if I am not mistaken in what I said elsewhere about this section)[3] a patchwork of several palpably different definitions of this notion. After this analysis, the implicit meaning of which is that all philosophers have an almost completely identical notion of proof, Sextus takes up a new problem, namely, the problem of the existence (*huparxis*) of proof (336–37). He first asks if the concept (*epinoia kai prolēpsis*) implies the existence of its object. This is a vital question to Skepticism as a whole, and it has a relevance far beyond the particular case of the notion of proof, for if the "ontological" implication holds (i.e., if we may infer from essence to existence), the Skeptic finds himself in a very awkward position. How could he both claim that he has the *notion* of a proof and suspend judgment about the *existence* of proof? His enemies, particularly the Epicureans,[4] as

3. Cf. Jacques Brunschwig, "Proof Defined," in M. Schofield et al., eds., *Doubt and Dogmatism* (Oxford, 1980), 125–60.

4. It is no wonder that the Epicureans are specifically mentioned in this context: they notoriously insisted that any inquiry, discussion, or research necessarily presupposes a πρόληψις of its subject matter (cf. Epicurus *Ep. Hdt.* 37–38, Cicero *ND* 1.43, Sextus *M* 1.57, 11.21, Diogenes Laertius 10.33). Diotimus (in Sextus *M* 7.140) attributes the same doctrine to De-

Sextus says here, will try to catch him in the following trap: if you understand what a proof is, if you have a notion of it, then proof does exist; and if you do not understand it, then how can you inquire about something you have no notion of? Answering this objection, Sextus grants one of the premises: it is indeed impossible to conduct any inquiry without having a notion of what it bears on. But in order to get round the objection allegedly involved in this premise, he successively adopts two completely different tactics.

First (332A–33A), his reply is somewhat ironical. Far from saying that we have no notion of what the inquiry is about, we would say, on the contrary, that we have more than we need, for the dogmatists supply us with a quantity of such notions, and divergent ones at that; we are threatened not with conceptual vacuity but, rather, with conceptual surplus. Lacking any criterion to decide among the competing definitions, we should rather take refuge in suspension of judgment (*epochē*) once again. This answer presupposes that the definitions given of the same term by the different dogmatisms are different and indeed incompatible.[5] It seems to imply, moreover, that the Skeptic accepts the ontological implication: if, by counterfactual hypothesis, the dogmatists were presenting a unified front at the conceptual level, the Skeptic would have no other choice than to admit the existence of the object captured by their common concept. Sextus says so explicitly: "If [by counterfactual hypothesis][6] we had a single preconception of what the inquiry is about, we would

---

mocritus, with the rather unexpected support of a Platonic quotation (*Phaedr.* 237B) which, like the famous problem in Plato's *Meno*, 80E, seems to have played some part in the fortune of this idea (cf. Cicero *Fin.* 2.4).

5. Cf. 333a πολλὰς ἔχομεν τοῦ ἑνὸς ἐννοίας καὶ πολυτρόπους μαχομένας καὶ ἐπ' ἴσης πιστάς κτλ.

6. The counterfactual force of the εἰ μέν clause is made clear by νῦν δέ in the next one. I take ὑπάρχειν in this sentence as existential, *pace* Bury: the whole section is about the existence (ὕπαρξις) of proof; and τοιοῦτο is not normally coupled with ὁποῖον.

believe, under guidance of this preconception, that an object indeed exists, exactly as it would have been given to us in this unitary notion" (333a).

Second, in 334a–336a Sextus's tactics shift completely. He then quite clearly rejects the ontological implication, and he makes a sharp distinction between (a) conception (*ennoia, epinoia*), "mere motion of the intellect" which involves no judgment at all, no assertion whatsoever as to whether its object exists or not, and (b) grasping or understanding (*katalēpsis*), which has a propositional content and involves the assertion of this content.[7] Now the Skeptic can claim that he has notions of things, "in the way we mentioned" (334a),[8] without being thereby committed to admit that the thing understood exists. Turning the objection back on his opponents, he shows that unless this distinction is made, even a dogmatist like Epicurus could not himself reject, say, a physical doctrine that he disapproved of: if you wish to reject, e.g., the four-elements theory, you must have the preconception (*prolēpsis*) of the four elements; but this *prolēpsis* must not imply the *katalēpsis* that the elements are indeed four.

I think this passage shows clearly that two different and, indeed, incompatible answers to the same objection are put side by side. The first one accepts the ontological inference and is based on a supposed fact of conceptual *diaphōnia*; the second one rejects the "ontological" inference and admits that the different dogmatists, and the Skeptic himself, have the same concept in mind. The difference is great enough, I think, to prevent us from construing them as *alternative* strategies, to be adopted as occasion requires. For they do indeed presuppose philosophical as-

7. Cf. 335a κατείληφε τὸ τέσσαρα εἶναι στοιχεῖα, as opposed to 336a ἐπινοεῖ . . . τὰ τέσσαρα στοιχεῖα. To invert κατάληψις and ὕπαρξις in 334a, as was suggested by Werner Heintz, *Studien zu Sextus Empiricus* (Halle, 1932), 186, looks quite plausible.

8. I take this to refer to the possession of a single concept, as described *before* the first answer based on conceptual διαφωνία. On the connecting particle ἀλλὰ γάρ between the two sections, cf. n. 9 below.

sumptions, and those assumptions are at the same time heavy, contradictory, and crucial ones for the determination of the proper Skeptical attitude.

It is probably worthwhile to remark that this problem of a common language among philosophers, which is raised in *M* 8, as we have just seen, apropos of the particular case of the notion of proof, is also dealt with at the beginning of *PH* 2, but in quite general terms and in a place which marks it as a vital preliminary question. The problem is set in slightly different terms from those of *M* 8. Before beginning the detailed criticism of dogmatic philosophies, Sextus asks whether the Skeptic can legitimately conduct inquiries about whatever the dogmatists say unless he grasps it (*katalambanein*). Now if he grasps it, how can he remain perplexed (*aporein*) about what he is grasping? The problem is thus put in terms of *katalēpsis*; here it is solved via a distinction between two meanings of this word, only one of which matches the use made of it in the *M* 8 passage. In the weak sense, *katalēpsis* is equivalent to the mere conception (*noein haplōs* = *epinoia* in *M* 8), which does not involve any assertion of existence concerning the object conceived. In the strong sense (which is the Stoic sense of *katalēpsis*, and also the sense which in *M* 8 is opposed to *epinoia*), *katalēpsis* involves the assertion that its object exists. Those terminological differences apart, the solution to the problem in *PH* is the same as the second solution in the *M* 8 text. Sextus shows that if a *katalēpsis* in the strong sense was required for inquiries, the dogmatists would be unable to criticize each other; but since only *katalēpsis* in the weak sense is a prerequisite of research, nothing prevents the Skeptic from having a *noēsis* of what his inquiries are about, and this *noēsis* does not imply the existence of its object (*PH* 2.10). In this general treatment of the question in *PH*, the "ontological" implication is thus firmly rejected, and there is no mention whatsoever of conceptual *diaphōnia*; the first solution of the *M* 8 passage is not to be found in *PH*. Although the vexed question of the chronological relationships between *M* and *PH* lies outside the scope of this paper, I may remark in passing that on this point the *PH* version is clearer and more decided than the *M* version.[9]

These few general considerations do not claim to be anything more than a sketchy analysis of the problems Skepticism is faced with when trying to deal with the conceptual legacy it has inherited. I hope they will not prove useless when studying the particular notion with which the rest of this paper will deal, namely, the notion of a *kritērion*.[10] It goes without saying that this notion is supremely important in Sextus's inquiry, as it is central in the philosophical tenets of the Hellenistic period. When Sextus comes to grips with it, it already has a very long history; and this history has been further extended, in its earlier part, by the fact that earlier philosophical doctrines (of the classical and even the Archaic period) have been reinterpreted by the Skeptics and retrospectively construed as so many answers to the *kritērion* question. During this long history, the word *kritērion* was applied to different entities, construed in different meanings, subdivided along different lines. These intricate developments have been ex-

9. *PH* is generally supposed to be earlier than the parallel sections in *M*, since Janáček's studies (particularly Karel Janáček, *Prolegomena to Sextus Empiricus* [Olomouc, 1948]); on the same lines, cf. A. A. Long, "Sextus Empiricus on the Criterion of Truth," *BICS* 25 (1978), 35–49. However, there are some dissenting voices: David Glidden, "Skeptic Semiotics," *Phronesis* 28 (1983), 246 n. 24, says that "his [*sc.* Janáček's] stylistic considerations are consistent with *PH* I–II being a cleaned-up version of *M* VII–VIII." I must say I have the same impression, when reading Janáček as well as when comparing *PH* and *M* on some particular point I happen to come across. Some more examples will be given below. It is perhaps relevant to point out that the connecting particle between the two different answers in *M* 8.334a is ἀλλὰ γάρ: "the sense conveyed is that what precedes is irrelevant, unimportant, or subsidiary, and is consequently to be ruled out of discussion, or at least put in the shade" (J. D. Denniston, *The Greek Particles*, 2d ed. [Oxford, 1959], 101). One could not put it better.

10. In order to prevent the reader from automatically understanding this word in its modern sense, I keep it untranslated.

cellently analyzed not long ago.[11] I shall rely on this and try, by examining the regularities and irregularities in Sextus's own works, to uncover some traces of this past history, of the problems he inherited from it, and of the labor he had to expend because of those problems.

The word *kritērion*, according to Sextus, is used in many senses; he devotes two roughly parallel sections (*M* 7.29–37 and *PH* 2.14–17) to their orderly enumeration. Before looking at this classification, however, it may be of some interest to point out something peculiar to the *M* version. In *M* 7.25—i.e., even before giving any account of the several meanings of the word *kritērion*—Sextus makes use of this word; and the sense in which he uses it is at the same time (1) defined precisely and univocally, (2) determinative of the overall structure of books 7–8, (3) missing in the classification given later of the different meanings of this word in 7.29–37, and (4) inconsistent with the sense that, in this later classification, will be marked out as the proper object of Skeptical inquiry. Here indeed are a lot of anomalies. Let us look at them in a little more detail.

In the context of the passage I have in mind (7.24–25), Sextus is giving justifications for the plan he will follow in his "specific" examination of the three main parts of dogmatic philosophy (logic, physics, ethics).[12] He first explains why he begins with logic: all parts of philosophy employ "the principles and procedures" (*tas archas kai tous tropous*) of the discovery of truth; but only logic, inasmuch as it involves the theory of *kritēria* and *apodeixeis*, takes them as its explicit topics. The distinction thus

---

11. By Gisela Striker, *Kriterion tes aletheias. Nachrichten der Akademie der Wissenschaften in Göttingen*, Phil.-Hist. Kl. 2 (1974), 51–110. To give a full idea of my indebtedness to this book I should have to quote it on every page. (See also Long, Chapter 7 below, pp. 180–92).

12. Cf. *PH* 1.5–6, 2.1, 12, 13, *M* 7.1–2.

sketched is then taken up again with more detail, so as to offer a methodical subdivision for the whole survey of logic:

> Since it is generally accepted [*dokei*] that what is evident [*enargē*] is known from itself [*autothen*] through some criterion [*dia kritēriou tinos*], whereas what is nonmanifest [*adēla*] has to be tracked down through signs and proofs [*dia sēmeiōn kai apodeixeōn*], by way of transfer [*kata metabasin*] from what is evident, we shall ask ourselves in order, *first*, whether there is a criterion for things that show up from themselves, either perceptually or intellectually [*ei esti ti kritērion tōn autothen kat'aisthēsin ē dianoian prospiptontōn*], and *then*, whether there is a semiotic or probative procedure concerning nonmanifest things [*ei esti sēmeiōtikos ē apodeiktikos tōn adēlōn tropos*].

In this first occurrence, the notion of *kritērion* seems to be a univocal notion, about which there is a consensus (*dokei*) among philosophers; from what is said here, we could not guess that the word that expresses this notion is "used in more than one way" (*pollachōs legomenon*), as we shall learn later on. The Skeptic himself is a part of this consensus; he is of course about to throw suspicion on the existence of anything satisfying the definition of *kritērion*, but he does not think of criticizing the definition itself as such. This is indeed a case where the Skeptic has an *ennoia* in common with his opponents, which makes him competent to examine and challenge the dogmatic positions, some of them affirming and some denying that the object of this *ennoia* exists.[13]

This concept of a *kritērion* is given its sense by being contrasted with the concepts of a *sign* and of a *proof*. This contrast is paralleled, *a parte objecti*, by that between things evident (*enargē*, and also *prophanē*, 7.26, and *prodēla*, 8.141) and things nonmanifest (*adēla*, and also *suneskiasmena*, 7.26). The former may be known directly and immediately; the latter can only be attained mediately and indirectly, on the basis of evidence which

---

13. Those who deny the κριτήριον are ranked among dogmatists: cf. *M* 7.46–47. Cf. also 443, where their position is marked off from the Skeptical one.

stands to them as a sign to the thing signified, or a proof to the thing proved. *Immediate* knowledge is called knowledge through a *kritērion*, so that to say that there is a *kritērion* is exactly the same as to say that we do have some immediate knowledge.

No doubt there is some paradox in using the same preposition, *dia*, which brings to mind mediation or instrumentality or a middle term, to describe both the role of the *kritērion* in immediate knowledge (*dia kritēriou tinos*) and the function of signs and proofs in indirect knowledge (*dia sēmeiōn kai apodeixeōn*); this parallelism could suggest, misleadingly, that the *kritērion* acts as a middle term between the knower and the known, exactly like signs and proofs; in fact, what is known "through a *kritērion*" is known spontaneously (*autothen*), and thus without any middle term. To explain this paradox, we might well suppose that the theory which here comes into play implies not only that we do have some immediate knowledge, but also that it comes in various kinds. There are immediate truths which are perceptual and there are immediate truths which are intellectual (*kat'aisthēsin ē dianoian*). In order to distinguish them without suppressing what they have in common, it is tempting to say that perception and intellection are two different ways of grasping immediate truths. If they were not different from one another, it would probably be pointless to distinguish both of them (under the name of *kritēria*) from the knower himself, who grasps these immediate truths "through them," or, perhaps more exactly, by way of their specific tonality: *dia kritēriou tinos*, let us say, because *dia kritēriou tinos*.

The conception of a *kritērion*, which identifies knowledge through a *kritērion* with immediate knowledge, I shall christen *prodelic*. It is hardly necessary to point out that the prodelic conception of a *kritērion* is completely different from our own notion of a criterion in ordinary language. We make use of what we call a criterion when we are unable to answer some question immediately. For instance, when we cannot easily see whether some object *a* is F or not, we try to find a criterion for F-ness.

If there is a property G, other than F, such that (1) (x) Fx iff Gx, and (2) it is possible to decide immediately whether Ga or not, then we say that there is a criterion available. In a similar case, the prodelic conception of the *kritērion* would commit us to saying that here is a case of knowledge through a sign; only if we had been able to find immediately that Fa (or not-Fa) could we say that here is a case of knowledge through a *kritērion*.

The prodelic conception of the *kritērion* and the mediate/immediate distinction in knowledge with which it is linked constitute the very basis of the overall structure of *M* 7–8—with this qualification, that since the notion of a *kritērion* is specified as a *kritērion* of truth,[14] the first part of the books will fall into two sections, corresponding to the two halves of the phrase. We thus get the following scheme, as Sextus will work it out: (1.1) the *kritērion* (*M* 7.27–446); (1.2) the true and truth (*M* 8.1–140); (2.1) signs (*M* 8.141–299); (2.2) proofs (*M* 8.300–481). In *PH* the scheme is roughly the same.[15] Some interesting differences may be pointed out.

First, as I said earlier, *PH* gives no clue as to what is meant by *kritērion* before it distinguishes the several meanings of the word (*PH* 2.13–14).

Second, we can see that the prodelic conception of the *kritērion* still determines the structure of the account, if we look at the end of the section devoted to the *kritērion* of truth (*PH* 2.95–96). This is the way Sextus sums up what is to be learned from this section:

14. This is rather surreptitiously done in *M* 7.28 (ἐπεὶ δύο μέρη ἐμφέρεται τῇ προτάσει, τό τε κριτήριον καὶ ἡ ἀλήθεια). The phrase κριτήριον ἀληθείας occurs nowhere before this sentence, except in the lemma prefixed to 27–28 in the mss. (εἰ ἔστι κριτήριον ἀληθείας); one might suspect, from this state of affairs, that this lemma comes from Sextus's own hand and that he calls it a πρότασις. (I am grateful to my friend and colleague Jean-Marie Beyssade for this nice observation.)

15. Κριτήριον: *PH* 2.14–79. Truth and the true: 80–96. Signs: 97–133. Proofs: 134–203.

The *kritērion* of truth proved shaky [*aporou*]; so it is no more possible to be positive, either about things which seem to be evident [*peri tōn enargōn einai dokountōn*], to the extent that we rely on [*hoson epi*] what the dogmatists say, or about nonmanifest things [*peri tōn adēlōn*]; for since the dogmatists think that they can grasp the latter on the evidence of the former, if we are obliged to suspend [judgment] about things said to be evident [*peri tōn enargōn kaloumenōn*],[16] how could we dare to make pronouncements about nonmanifest things?

Here we can see that the *enargē*/*adēla* distinction is still predominant, but that nonetheless Sextus shows with clarity how greatly altered the *enargē* are after the theories of the *kritērion* have been subjected to criticism. Now the evident things are nothing more than "so-called evidences"; and this is because *kritērion* and *enargeia* are conceptually linked together, so that once the existence of anything satisfying the definition of a *kritērion* is made doubtful, the existence of anything *enarges* at once becomes questionable. No similar indication can be found in the corresponding passage of *M* 8, where Sextus sums up the results of his inquiry about the *kritērion* of truth (140).

Third, we may notice a similar contrast between the two versions on the following point. The *PH* version makes perfectly clear, as may be seen from the quotation above, that criticizing the *kritērion* leads to two different results: its first upshot, a direct one, is to make impossible any grasping of *enargē*, since these are the proper objects of knowledge through a *kritērion*; its second upshot, a consequential one, is to make impossible any access to *adēla*, by removing any basis on which signs and proofs might be grounded. It is thus theoretically superfluous to submit these latter procedures to a specific criticism; later on, the text makes clear that this criticism will be given "just as a makeweight" (*ek pollou tou periontos*, 2.96). In the *M* version, Sextus is far from showing such an awareness about this situation. True,

---

16. Bury's translation omits the word καλουμένων.

he describes signs and proofs as procedures "which start from the *kritērion* [*apo tou kritēriou*] to arrive at a grasp of those truths which do not show up from themselves" (8.40); but he also declares that once the criticism of the *kritērion* is brought to an end, "one still has to deal with the class of nonmanifest things" [*leipomenēs de eti tēs tōn adēlōn diaphoras*, 8.142]. In this he seems to have completely forgotten what he himself had said about the crucial role of *enargē* in the knowledge of *adēla* (7.25).

Now let us have a look at the division of the meanings of the term *kritērion*. In the *M* version, a preamble (7.27–28) comes before this division, the effect of which is to insert it into the overall frame of the discussion about the *kritērion* of truth. Sextus will deal separately, he says, with the notion of a *kritērion* and with the notion of truth. To each of these he will devote (1) an "exegetic" section, in which he will show (1.1) in how many senses it is said, and then (1.2) what nature the dogmatists have assigned to it; after that, (2) a "more aporetic" section will examine "whether anything of the kind can exist." The section about the *kritērion* is indeed articulated in this way.[17] This division is in principle clear and well formed. Section (1) corresponds to the analysis of *ennoia*, first as regards its various *meanings* (1.1), then as regards its various *references*, i.e., the various entities which, historically, have been identified as *kritēria* (1.2). Section (2) raises the problem of whether there exists some object matching the *ennoia* and conducts a critical inquiry into the doctrines that solve this problem in one way or another.

The comparative term *more aporetic* (*aporētikōteron*) suggests, however, that the division between exegesis and polemic is not totally watertight. As a matter of fact, we can see that the long historical review (7.46–262), which answers to section (2) and which supposedly is limited to a purely exegetical aim, is not without polemical bearings. There are two reasons for this. First,

17. (1.1) = 7.29–37. (1.2) = 46–262. (2) = 263–446.

when Sextus gives an account of various doctrines that made reason, or perception, or both, *kritēria* of truth, he cannot keep himself from pointing out delightedly that these views are not only different but also incompatible with one another, and hence rivals to one another (*staseis*, 7.47, 261–62). Second, in this section, which he claims will show that the dogmatists had different views about the "nature" of the *kritērion*, i.e., about the entity which is the *kritērion*, he lists not only those people who admit that there is a *kritērion* and locate it here or there, but also those who claim there is no *kritērion* at all; the latter, he thinks, are no less dogmatists than the former. This extensive "exegetical" account thus describes a fairly strenuous battle (*diastasis*, 7.46; *diaphōnia*, 7.261); to say the least, it prepares the way to the counterargument (*antirrhēsis*, 7.261) that is to follow, i.e., to section (2), the so-called more aporetic section.

All the more striking is the contrast between this section (1.2) and the previous one (1.1): here we find a table of the different meanings of the term *kritērion*, in which we cannot perceive the faintest hint that their differences are meant to be viewed as disagreements. True, the notion of a *kritērion* now appears as bereft of the univocal character it seemed to possess when it first occurred (7.25); but no philosophical conflicts are generated, on the face of it, by the plurality of its meanings.

On the one hand, it is not at all suggested that the dogmatic schools were unaware of this state of affairs, and that being unaware of it has involved them in artificial quarrels based on conceptual misunderstandings. (This is the way an eclectic would treat the matter.) On the other hand, it is not suggested either that the different meanings of the term *kritērion* are such that if you adopt one of them, you are committed to abandoning the others and to quarreling with those people who make a different choice. (This is the way a special kind of skeptic would treat the matter, namely, the champion of a conceptual skepticism, denying to philosophers any right to make use of the same vocabulary and to live in common on the same conceptual estate. Sextus does indeed sometimes apply this conceptual skepticism, as we have seen; but here he does not do anything of the kind.)

The table of the different meanings of *kritērion*, however, has some puzzles and a major surprise in store. Let us first recall its overall structure, which is roughly the same in *M* (7.29–37) as in *PH* (2.14–16); it descends in stages through three different levels of *diairesis*:

(A) 1. *Kritērion* of life or practical conduct.
  2. *Kritērion* of existence or truth.

(B) 2.1. General sense: "every measure of apprehension."
  2.2. Special sense: "every technical measure of apprehension."
  2.3. "Quite special" sense: "every [technical, *PH*] measure of apprehension of something nonmanifest [*adēlou pragmatos*]" = *kritērion logikon*.

(C) 2.3.1. As agent (*huph'ou*).
  2.3.2. As instrument (*di'hou*).
  2.3.3. As application or working out (*kath'ho, PH*; *hōs prosbolē kai schesis, M*).

Of course the surprise is that here the prodelic conception of a *kritērion* is supplanted by an adelic conception which is exactly its opposite. Before tackling this big knot, however, I shall make some remarks on other points.

It has been plausibly claimed that the three steps in Sextus's division came from different historical areas; he seems to have grafted initially independent divisions onto one another, and to have done so in a somewhat forced way.[18] The (A) distinction is at least as old as Epicurus,[19] and Skepticism made a constant and

18. Cf. Heintz (n. 6 above), 83–86; Striker (n. 11 above), 102–7.
19. Cf. Diogenes Laertius 10.31–34, and Democritus according to Diotimus, *M* 7.140.

central use of it.[20] The (B) division occurs in pseudo-Galen's *Historia philosopha*, which probably draws on the same source as does Sextus.[21] A somewhat different version of division (C) occurs in the criteriological considerations of the eclectic Potamo of Alexandria (Diogenes Laertius 1.21), who might have borrowed it from Posidonius, who wrote a *Peri kritēriou* (Diogenes Laertius 7.54).[22] From these historical parallels, let us here draw first of all the following conclusion: at every step of the *diairesis*, various meanings are put side by side, which are *not* there because Sextus himself, or his source, gathered them together in a critical or skeptical mood. Far from being various meanings some of which have been favored by one particular school and some by another, they are the result of conceptual distinctions worked out each time by the same philosopher or by the same school. Those different meanings are thus not viewed as exclusive of one another.

This may be seen most clearly in the case of division (C), which Sextus illustrates by means of a comparison with measuring. In order to weigh some object, for instance, an agent is needed, the weigher; an instrument, the scales; an application of the instrument to the object to be weighed, the using of the scales. Similarly, in order to make a judgment an agent is needed, man; an instrument, perception or intellection; an application of the instrument to the object to be judged, the using of mental impression (*prosbolē tēs phantasias*). This comparison makes perfectly clear that each of the three conditions is necessary and none is sufficient; hence it would be a mistake to describe man, perception, intellection, impression, as rival candidates to the title of *kritērion*. Some Skeptics, however, did so: they selected different philosophers as the supporters of these different candidates,

---

20. Cf. *PH* 1.21–24.
21. Cf. *Dox. Graeci*, 603–4, 606; Striker (n. 11 above), 106.
22. Cf. Striker (n. 11 above), 105. For Ptolemy's more elaborate version of (C) cf. Long, Chapter 7 below, p. 189.

and thus created an impression that there was a *diaphōnia* about the *kritērion* (Diogenes Laertius 9.95).[23]

Sextus ought to be free from this mistake. However, he once lapses into it (at least in the *M* version), namely in the transition from his exegetical to his aporetic section (*M* 7.261):

> As I have already said, (a) some people kept the *kritērion*, locating it within reason, some within irrational perceptions, and some within both; and (b) some have called this way the agent, e.g., man, some the instrument, e.g., perception and intellection, some the application, e.g., impression. Let us try to adjust, as far as possible, our objections to each of these parties [*staseis*].

This rather strange passage puts side by side (a) views about what is the *kritērion*, and (b) views about what a *kritērion* is, namely, those of division (C). The former are obviously incompatible; the latter are not so, and they are described by Sextus as being so, although he knows very well that they are not so. Understandably, some people have been tempted to emend the text, eliminating the (b) section as an interpolated gloss.[24] I believe we must resist this temptation, however, because the tripartite scheme of agent/instrument/application provides the very framework for the whole subsequent discussion:[25] it would be strange not to find it mentioned in the preamble which introduces this discussion. More generally, we already know that Sextus's strategy toward conceptual disagreements lacks continuity; here, as elsewhere, he might have allowed himself to introduce a *diaphōnia* in a context where it was quite out of place.

Something should also be said about division (B), which involves difficulties of another kind, in particular because *M* and *PH* differ textually. From a formal point of view, the meanings within this division are extensionally decreasing and intension-

23. Πρὸς τῷ καὶ διαφωνεῖσθαι τὸ κριτήριον, τῶν μὲν τὸν ἄνθρωπον κριτήριον εἶναι λεγόντων, τῶν δὲ τὰς αἰσθήσεις, ἄλλων τὸν λόγον, ἐνίων τὴν καταληπτικὴν φαντασίαν.

24. Cf. Heintz (n. 6 above), 122–24.

25. Respectively: *M* 7.263–342, 343–69, 370–446, *PH* 2.22–47, 48–69, 70–79.

ally increasing notions: there is a general sense of the *kritērion* (*koinōs*), a special sense (*idiōs*), and a "quite special" sense (*idiaitata*). In the general sense (2.1), "every measure of apprehension" (*pan metron katalēpseōs*) is a *kritērion*; in this first sense, we may call *kritēria* those "natural" *kritēria*, sight, hearing, taste, as well as others; they are explicitly mentioned here just because they will be eliminated in the next step of the division. In the special sense (2.2), indeed, only the "artificial measures of apprehension" (*pan metron katalēpseōs technikon*) are *kritēria*; in this sense, technical instruments of measure, such as rules, compasses, scales, are *kritēria*. Things get more complex with the "quite special" sense (2.3), which is defined, in the main manuscripts of *PH*, as "every artificial measure of apprehension of something nonmanifest" (*pan metron katalēpseōs technikon adēlou pragmatos*), and more briefly, in *M*, as "every measure of apprehension of something nonmanifest" (*pan metron katalēpseōs adēlou pragmatos*). Both versions agree in adding, in very similar terms, that this meaning excludes those *kritēria* which are of use in ordinary life (*biōtika*) and is satisfied only by those which are *logika* (rational, or, perhaps more accurately, discursive), namely, those which dogmatic philosophers introduced in order to discover or to discriminate what is true.

Let us put aside, for the moment, the question concerning the *adēlon* object. First, I should like to try to solve the problem concerning the variant readings. Moreover, as we shall see, the two questions are somehow connected. Almost everybody agrees in thinking that the *M* text and the *PH* text must be made to coincide;[26] but there are two ways of doing so, and each one has its champions.[27] By writing *technikon* in both texts (so W. Heintz and his followers), one admittedly gets a nicely articulated system

---

26. Except Bury, who gives different texts in both places.

27. Mutschmann in Hermann Mutschmann, ed., *Sexti Empirici Opera*, vol. 1, rev. J. Mau (Leipzig, 1958), 67, and in Hermann Mutschmann, ed., *Sexti Empirici Opera*, vol. 2 (Leipzig, 1914), 9, omits τεχνικόν in both places; Heintz (n. 6 above), 83–86, claims that τεχνικόν should be kept in both places; so Mau in Mutschmann-Mau, 215, and Striker (n. 11 above), 106.

of definitions that satisfactorily matches the *koinōs/idiōs/idiaitata* scheme:

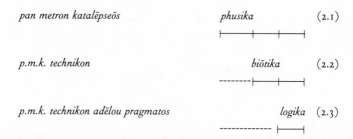

pan metron katalēpseōs	*phusika*	(2.1)
p.m.k. technikon	*biōtika*	(2.2)
p.m.k. technikon adēlou pragmatos	*logika*	(2.3)

A number of objections, however, can be raised against this scheme. (1) It is made suspect by its very formal perfection. The occurrence of *technikon* is what we might call a *lectio logice facilior*.

(2) In order to make this formal perfection complete, we have to reinterpret some elements in the text, in a somewhat forced way. When Sextus presents the (2.2) meaning, he says that it excludes *phusika*, and, when he presents the (2.3) meaning, that it excludes *biōtika*. In order to get matters quite in order, *biōtika* should form the exact surplus of (2.2) over (2.3), as *phusika* form the exact surplus of (2.1) over (2.2); that means that *biōtika* are just the artificial measuring instruments and that natural perceptive faculties are *not* covered by this word. Such a limitation of the concept of *kritēria biōtika* has found its champions;[28] but a sufficient reason for putting it aside is provided by *PH* 1.23–24, where Sextus enumerates the component parts of the "experience of life" (*biōtikē tērēsis*): the first one is "nature's guidance" (*huphēgēsis phuseōs*), which makes us "naturally apt at perceiving and intellegizing." Perceptive faculties are therefore covered by the term *biōtika*.[29]

---

28. So Heintz (n. 6 above), 84, following E. Pappenheim, *Erläuterungen zu des Sextus Empiricus Pyrrhoneischen Grundzügen* (Leipzig, 1881), 102.

29. The phrase περὶ ἑκάστου τῶν κατὰ τὸν βίον in *M* 7.34, too, is understandable only if βιωτικά covers two different classes, φυσικά and τεχνικά.

(3) In the *PH* version of the division, *kritēria logika* are a subset of *kritēria technika*. A proof that this is so is claimed to be found in Sextus's wording: in the (2.3) sense, he says, *biōtika* are not *kritēria* any longer (*ouketi*); only *logika* are. This word *ouketi* is supposed, it is claimed, to imply that *logika* clearly are *already* *kritēria* in the (2.2) sense.[30] This, I take it, is a non sequitur: from the fact that something is not the case any longer, it is not possible to infer that some other thing was already the case.[31]

(4) From the substantive point of view, it seems difficult to claim that *kritēria logika* are artificial *kritēria*. In fact, in the (C) division, Sextus distinguishes three meanings which are, he explicitly says, subdivisions of the *kritērion logikon* (*M* 7.35, *PH* 2.16); now these meanings are exemplified, respectively, by man, perception and intellection, and the application of the *phantasia*—i.e., by entities, faculties, or acts that are wholly natural.

In view of all these arguments, I think it better to abandon the idea of keeping the word *technikon* in *PH* and inserting it in *M*, within the definitions of the *kritērion* in the "quite special" meaning (2.3), i.e., of the *kritērion logikon*. I prefer to depict the (B) division along the following lines:

pan metron katalēpseōs	*phusika technika logika* (2.1)
	biōtika
	├──────┼──────┼──────┤
p.m.k. technikon	────────┼──────┤ ─────── (2.2)
p.m.k. adēlou pragmatos	───────────────── ├──────┤ (2.3)

This scheme is admittedly less satisfactory from a purely formal point of view, but it seems to fit better the ends at which this division is aiming; these are, I believe, to isolate and to specify that meaning of the word *kritērion* which is of interest only to

30. Heintz (n. 6 above), 84.
31. E.g., "there is no more milk, there is only bread." You cannot know if there was already bread when there was still milk.

philosophers, and which is the only one really of interest to them.[32]

Now, I think, we can finally come to grips with the main problem this division raises: namely, the abrupt substitution of *adēlon* for *prodēlon* as the specific object of knowledge through a *kritērion*. This is indeed a contradiction, since the different meanings of the word *kritērion* that occur in the relevant passages (*M* 7.25 and 33) are both supposed to be *the* meaning in which the word will be used throughout the whole inquiry in Book 7. Conceptual contradiction has been officially expelled through the door, in the meanings division; it seems to come back in through the window, in the unexpected form of a *diaphōnia* between Sextus and Sextus himself.

This anomaly has seldom been noticed, as far as I know; those commentators who have noticed it have tried to explain it away in two different fashions. One way (that of W. Heintz) is to make it sharper, but so as to lessen its importance. The other (that of G. Striker and also of J. Barnes, as we shall see), on the contrary, is to blunt it and reduce it to ambiguity. I shall say something about both attempts before suggesting a third way out of the puzzle.

As we have already seen, Heintz inserts the word *technikon* into the definition of *kritērion logikon* in *M* 7.33 (on the model

32. In this second scheme, the (2.3) meaning is admittedly not "still more special" than the (2.2) meaning. But the superlative ἰδιαίτατα can mean "in a quite special sense," i.e., special to philosophers (let us remember that κριτήριον λογικόν is this type of κριτήριον, which "philosophers repeatedly din into our ears," *M* 7.34). The progression from κοινῶς to ἰδίως and to ἰδιαίτατα is thus not necessarily rectilinear. We might also point out that in the *M* version, Sextus wavers between ἰδιαίτατα (7.31) and ἰδιαίτερον (7.33), whereas in the *PH* version, he keeps ἰδιαίτατα throughout (2.15, *bis*). The original version certainly gave ἰδιαίτατα (cf. ps.-Galen in *Dox. Graeci* 604, line 1, and 606, line 10). One might suppose that in the *M* version Sextus allowed himself, by way of the comparative ἰδιαίτερον, to introduce a more linear order into the series than was the case in the original source.

of the *PH* parallel). He knows very well that the later subdivision of this *kritērion*, which specifies it as perception, intellection, and impression (34–37), is not in favor of this suggestion: all those are *natural* faculties.[33] But he subtly turns the argument the other way around.[34] If *technikon* is read in 33, the contradiction between 33 and 34–37 is the same as that between 33 and 25; and he claims that 34–37 (in spite of what Sextus himself says) shows that when subdividing the *kritērion logikon*, Sextus no longer has any thought of the adelic conception of a *kritērion*, which he just described in 33; as a matter of fact, according to Heintz, what he has in mind is again the prodelic conception, which occurred in 25 and will be the single topic of everything which follows in Book 7. Some kind of momentary and unconscious aberration, caused by a laborious attempt to harmonize a number of different schemes, is thus supposed to be the reason why Sextus, if only briefly, attributes to the *kritērion* the task of knowing *adēla*. By the name of *kritēria logika*, in 33, he can only refer (contrary to his usual terminology) to sign and proof, i.e., dialectical (hence *technical*) procedures for grasping *adēla*; those will be studied

33. Cf. argument (4) above.

34. Here is the central passage in Heintz's argumentation, p. 85: "Sextus actually gives up in 34ff. the terminological scheme he has followed in 31–33, but without being aware of this. He *says* of course that he wants in what follows to treat only of the λογικὸν κριτήριον, that *this* is again to be understood in three senses, etc. But in fact the new threefold division shows that here he is no longer really thinking of the concept of the λογικὸν κριτήριον. The λογικὸν κριτήριον should refer to ἄδηλα πράγματα; the κριτήριον treated by Sextus in 34ff. and subsequently through the whole book has nothing to do with the ἄδηλα, but deals with the cognition of ἐναργῆ or φαινόμενα, the immediately sensible objects around us. Sextus first comes to the ἄδηλα in *M* 8, where σημεῖον and ἀπόδειξις, as routes to cognition of ἄδηλα, form his theme (cf. *M* 7.25, 8.140, 142, *PH* 2.95–96). It is these, σημεῖον and ἀπόδειξις, the appropriate cognitive means employed by dialectic in order to grasp ἄδηλα, that must be meant in 33 by κριτήρια λογικά, at least in the sense of the terminological scheme that Sextus uses there. He himself seems not to have been clear about this" (trans. A. A. Long).

only in Book 8, after the end of the inquiry concerning *kritērion* in the normal—i.e., prodelic—sense.

This interpretation is questionable in several ways. First, some terminological likenesses may be pointed out, which seem to show that (*pace* Heintz) the notion of a *kritērion logikon* has the same content in 33 (*ta logika kai haper hoi dogmatikoi tōn philosophōn pareisagousi*) as in 34 (*peri tou logikou kai para tois philosophois thruloumenou*). More generally, Heintz assigns to Sextus an implausible mixture of awareness and unawareness of what he is doing: he is supposed to try to harmonize different conceptual systems without clearly realizing their differences.

But the crucial point is to know whether Heintz is right in claiming that apart from its passing occurrence in 7.33 (and also in *PH* 2.15), the adelic concept of the *kritērion* plays no part in Sextus, and the prodelic concept is given pride of place in the whole inquiry concerning *kritērion*. It is perfectly true that the prodelic concept is clearly in the forefront in the prefacing and concluding sections I have already quoted.[35] But in the inquiry proper, things are far from being so clear.

A first disturbing factor is that the prodelic concept of a *kritērion* covers both intellectual and perceptual immediate truths (7.25).[36] Is it enough for Sextus to be allowed to count as upholders of the *kritērion* (as he does in *M* 7.47) those philosophers who locate it in *logos*, as well as those who locate it in the "irrational evidences" (*en tais alogois enargeiais*)? In order to be true to the prodelic concept, one should find *logos* here construed as a power of intellectual intuition, able to grasp "rational immediate truths," and not as a discursive and argumentative faculty. But the concept of a rational immediate truth and the phrase *enargeia logikē* occur nowhere in Sextus, as far as I know; on the contrary, *enargeia* and *logos* are frequently contrasted (*PH* 3.82, 135, 266, 272, *M* 11.239). The early "inquirers into nature," who

35. *M* 7.25, 8.140, *PH* 2.95–96.
36. Heintz neglects this point.

are the historical illustrations of the identification of the *kritērion* with *logos* (*M* 7.89–140), are ratiocinators whose theories are based on a rational criticism of sensory evidence (7.89); the principles and elements they claim to be the foundations of the physical world offer a typical example of *adēla* entities (*M* 10.252). They cannot thus be saddled with views about the *kritērion* unless a strictly prodelic conception of this notion is left aside.

There are also occasions where statements about *adēla* being knowable or unknowable are explicitly classified by Sextus as views about the existence of a *kritērion*. Xenophanes, e.g., says that a true knowledge of gods is not allowed to man (DK 21B34); commenting on this fragment, Sextus says that the gods are here only a representative sample of the whole class of *adēla* (*M* 7.50). Xenophanes' doctrine may thus be summed up by saying that no man grasps the truth, at least in the field of *adēla* (*M* 7.51); and this is equivalent to denying the existence of a *kritērion* (7.52).[37]

In many other places, Sextus can be seen to be distorting or even breaking the conceptual frame that goes along with the prodelic concept of a *kritērion* (namely, the frame that opposes *enarges* and *adēlon*, *autothen* and *mē autothen*, *kritērion* and *sēmeion kai apodeixis*). He admits, at least as a theoretical possibility, that something *adēlon* might be true "from itself" (*autothen*), the other horn of the dilemma being that it might be true "as something proved" (*hos apodeichthen*, *M* 8.21). In *M* 8.379, he gives a syllogistic justification of the adelic conception of a *kritērion*: every *adēlon*, he says, needs a decision (*epikrisis*), and what needs a decision requires a *kritērion*. In *M* 8.26, he goes so far as to contrast immediate knowledge and knowledge through a *kritērion*: if anybody is claiming that this *adēlon* is true and that one false, those statements should come either "from themselves and without any *kritērion*," i.e., "immediately" (*ex het-*

---

37. Cf. also the first of the three κριτήρια attributed by Diotimus to Democritus (*M* 7.140).

oimou), or "with a *kritērion.*" No doubt a methodical search through the texts might collect many other such observations, but I think these few examples will be enough to show that the adelic concept of a *kritērion* is far from being as unobtrusive in Sextus as Heintz claims it to be; when we find the prodelic definition and the adelic one side by side in the first paragraphs of Book 7, we cannot dismiss this fact as a localized accident.

According to G. Striker, the paradox should be explained in a completely different way. She holds that the prodelic definition is the only one that Sextus inherited from previous history; despite the differences between the Epicurean concept and the Stoic concept of a *kritērion* (those differences are very well brought out in her book; but more on this later), neither school is supposed to define a *kritērion* as an instrument for grasping *adēla*. The adelic definition in Sextus should be construed as a kind of translation of the earlier prodelic definition into Skeptical language. According to the Skeptic, any assumption dogmatically asserted goes beyond what it is permissible to say, and thereby bears on something *adēlon.* What the dogmatist calls *enarges* and claims to grasp *dia kritēriou tinos* is exactly the same thing as what the Skeptic polemically calls *adēlon.*[38] Along the same lines, J. Barnes sees no escape from the paradox except by supposing a "systematic ambiguity" in the terms *adēlos, prodēlos, enargēs.*[39]

38. Gisela Striker's argument is as follows (n. 11 above), 106: "Neither the criterion of the Stoics nor those of the Epicureans can be defined in accordance with the terminology of these schools as 'measure of the grasp' of ἄδηλα. Through a καταληπτικὴ φαντασία one of course grasps an 'evident' fact (cf. *M* 7.25); and the criteria of the Epicureans can, as we saw, be used not just for testing statements about nonperceptible facts. The expression can most easily be explained in the context of the terminology of the Skeptics, according to whom nothing at all can be known and who therefore sometimes speak as if every seriously intended assertion refers to an ἄδηλον (cf. *PH* 1.200–202, 13, 16, 197–98). That would mean that it is a polemical formula, which reflects not the terminology of the philosophical schools but only the Skeptics' interpretation of their doctrines" (trans. A. A. Long)

39. Cf. Jonathan Barnes, "The Beliefs of a Pyrrhonist," *Elenchos* 4 (1983), 27 n. 74: "Sextus plainly states that the Pyrrhonist attack on κριτή-

This suggestion has the undoubted merit of drawing attention to some important features of the Skeptical stance. Sextus certainly does not take the widespread distinction between *enargē* and *adēla* at its face value, even if he is constantly making a dialectical use of it. In *M* 7.364, a definition of what is *enarges* that is substantially the same as the definition in *M* 7.25[40] is explicitly attributed to "our opponents" (*hupo tōn enantiōn*). Sextus claims on this occasion that nothing can naturally be grasped "from itself" (*ex heautou*); nothing can be said about the external world except by conjecture (*stochazomai*, 365), by inference from signs (*sēmeioumai*, 365; *sēmeiōsis*, 367). It follows that nothing is *enarges* (364) and everything is *adēlon* (368), so that the dogmatist would do better to call *adēlon* (in the terminology which he shares with his Skeptical opponent) what he calls *enarges*; the class of *enargē* is empty, de facto if not de jure.

It is no less true that the reason why the Skeptic construes the dogmatic assertions as bearing on *adēla*, even when the dogmatist does not say so, is that these assertions claim to express what things are in themselves, of their own nature. Any claim to *katalēpsis*,[41] let us say, immediately turns its object into an *adēlon*, however *enarges* it is said to be. As Sextus repeatedly asserts, giving one's assent to something *adēlon* is enough to land one in dogmatism (*PH* 1.16, 197, 210); conversely, it seems that being a dogmatist (speaking in a dogmatic tone or mood) is enough to turn what one claims to assent to into something *adēlon*.[42]

ρια undermines belief in τὰ ἐναργῆ (*PH* 2.95, *M* 7.25); he also expressly defines a κριτήριον as μέτρον ἀδήλου πράγματος (*PH* 2.15, *M* 7.33). I see no escape from that inconsistency—except the appeal to a systematic and unexpressed ambiguity in such terms as ἄδηλος, πρόδηλος, ἐναργής."

40. This definition runs τὸ ἐξ ἑαυτοῦ λαμβανόμενον καὶ μηδενὸς χρῆ-ζον εἰς παράστασιν.

41. In the strong (i.e., Stoic) sense of this word, of course, according to the distinction made in *PH* 2.4. Cf. above, p. 151.

42. Cf. *PH* 1.202 δογματικῶς, τουτέστι περὶ ἀδήλου, and Michael Frede, "Des Skeptikers Meinungen," *Neue Hefte für Philosophie* 15/16 (1979),

These arguments, however, do not, I think, entirely justify Striker's interpretation. Dogmatists and Skeptics disagree about the *reference* of the terms *enarges* and *adēlon*; this does not mean they disagree about the *meaning* of these terms and about their conceptual contrast. If the Skeptic believes the class of *enargē* to be empty, this does not imply that he takes the notion of an *enarges* as meaningless and freely substitutable by its contrary. When the question is how to define the concept of a *kritērion*, the referential equivalence between what the dogmatist calls an *enarges* and what the Skeptic calls an *adēlon* does not allow the latter to substitute *enarges* for *adēlon* within the definition; it is impossible to say that defining a *kritērion* as an instrument for grasping *prodēla* and defining it as an instrument for grasping *adēla* are equivalent, undifferentiated definitions. Of course Sextus might have made the mistake, but to be sure that he did not, it is enough to point out that in the definition in *M* 7.33, the *adēlon* object is mentioned as a *specific difference* that distinguishes *kritēria logika* from the other kinds of *kritēria*; the objects of those must thus be *enargē*. If both the terms *enarges* and *adēlon* did not keep a stable and distinctive conceptual meaning, the differences among the various classes of *kritēria* would vanish, and the whole classification (distinction [B]) would collapse. The

---

123: "Every opinion, whatever its content may be, can be dogmatic, just as, vice versa, every opinion can be undogmatic. So it is not the content of doctrines (although this too is not entirely irrelevant, as we shall see) that makes them dogmatic, but the attitude of the dogmatist, who thinks that his rational knowledge can answer questions and provide him with the sufficient grounds for his doctrines" (trans. A. A. Long). In order to prevent the states of affairs on which he expresses his opinions from turning into ἄδηλα, the Skeptic has to avoid the dogmatic traps hidden in ordinary language, above all in the verb "to be" (*PH* 1.19–20). He withdraws into ἀφασία, which is not muteness but a nonassertoric way of using language (*PH* 1.192); he employs the phrases "indicative of ἀφασία" put at his disposal by ordinary language—"perhaps" and the like (*PH* 1.195); he makes use of mental translation (*PH* 1.198), "co-signification" (*PH* 1.199), and κατάχρησις (*PH* 1.135, 191, 207). Cf. Charlotte Stough, "Sextus Empiricus on Nonassertion," *Phronesis* 29 (1984), 137–64.

substantive difference between the prodelic and the adelic conception of a *kritērion* looks thus to be irreducible.

How, then, to account for their being together in Sextus's text? I would suggest that it is, above all, a matter of conceptual inheritance, although to invoke history, in this circumstance, is not to give up trying to understand what happened. Striker's book, in this respect, offers all the materials required for an explanation which she nonetheless does not elicit. Let us look at the differences between the Epicurean and the Stoic concept of a *kritērion*, as they are pellucidly described in her book.

In Epicurus, the predominant use[43] of the notion is fundamentally based on an analogy between *kritērion* and *kanōn*. A *kanōn*, a ruler or a square, is paradigmatically right and allows the problematic rightness of a line or an angle to be tested. Similarly, a *kritērion* of truth is a purveyor of truths, immediately evident in themselves, that can be used to test the truth-value of opinions (or theories or hypotheses, etc.) that bear on not perceptible or not immediately known states of affairs, and thus are neither clearly true nor clearly false. Their being intrinsically true is what allows them to function as they do; but their value as a *kritērion* depends on their being used to test the truth-value of statements other than themselves.[44]

On the other hand, the predominant Stoic use of this notion[45] is no longer determined by the *kanōn*-paradigm. *Phantasia katalēptikē* is claimed to be a *kritērion*, not because it allows one to test something other than what it "presents," but because it al-

43. This qualification is needed, because Epicurus also employs the word κριτήριον in the sense of "power of judging" or "power of knowing": cf. *Ep. Herod.* 38, 51, and the comments by Striker (n. 11 above), 56 and 59. In order to mark out the predominant use, Striker writes "the 'Epicurean' meaning," in quotation marks; I do the same here.

44. Cf. Striker (n. 11 above), mainly 61–63, 73, 82.

45. Here again, it is only a matter of predominant use, which allows some occurrences of the word κριτήριον in the "Epicurean" sense (cf. Striker [n. 11 above], 98–99). In order to mark out this predominant use, I shall similarly write "the 'Stoic' sense."

lows one to state that something is the case, which is the very state of affairs "presented" by it (and causally productive of it);[46] what makes us know that something is the case is the same as what constitutes the criterion of this knowledge being true.[47]

There is, therefore, an obvious identity between the Stoic concept and what I have called the prodelic concept of a *kritērion*: the truths that *phantasia kataleptikē* is supposed to supply are immediate and evident. But, according to Striker, there is no such identity between the Epicurean concept and the adelic concept of *M* 7.33. Her reasons are the following.[48] The Epicurean *kritēria* can be used for other ends than just testing statements about nonperceptible states of affairs; indeed, they can play their role in confirmatory and nonconfirmatory procedures, designed to decide about perceptible cases, as well as in contestatory and noncontestatory procedures, which are designed to decide about nonperceptible cases. This observation is perfectly right, but does not establish the point at issue. The opinions tested by way of confirmation *ex hypothesi* bear on states of affairs that are potentially perceptible but not actually perceived. That is why they need confirmation; they are, Epicurus says, "waiting" to be confirmed (*prosmenon, Ep. Hdt.* 38, *KD* 24). The distinction ex-

46. I leave aside the question of whether φαντασία καταληπτική is only a matter of sense-perception (cf. Striker [n. 11 above], 107–10); let me just point out that according to Sextus it is not (cf. *M* 7.416–21) and that κριτή-ριον in its prodelic definition is not, either (cf. *M* 7.25). Φαντασία καταληπτική, as understood by Sextus, is thus a κριτήριον in exactly the same sense as he construes the notion of a κριτήριον when he adopts the prodelic concept of it.

47. Cf. Striker (n. 11 above), mainly 82–84, 90.

48. Striker (n. 11 above), 106 (quoted above, n. 38); the backward reference ("as we saw") is to p. 74. I leave aside another argument of a more general character, namely, the claim that the "Epicurean" sense of κριτή-ριον was fairly quickly supplanted, in the general use, by the "Stoic" sense (cf. 102, 107). This hypothesis does not at first sight look very plausible, because the modern use of *criterion* is, I think, "Epicurean" on the whole. But I have neither the space nor the capacity to discuss this point more accurately.

pressed in Epicurus by the pair *prosmenon/adēlon* is thus the same as what is expressed in another terminology (Sextus *PH* 2.97ff., *M* 8.145ff.) by distinguishing two classes of *adēla*: circumstantial *adēla* (*pros kairon*), which are such only de facto and for the time being, and *adēla* by nature (*phusei*), which are such by right and at any time. In the latter terminology, the "Epicurean" *kritērion* always refers to some *adēlon pragma*, and there is nothing to prevent us from identifying it with Sextus's adelic concept.

It remains to be understood how and why, without any explanation or even any indication that he was aware of them, Sextus left in his text those contradictory sediments of the conceptual history of *kritērion*. One might invoke, in quite general terms, his vacillating strategies when conceptual disagreements are at stake; we have seen many examples of this. But in the case of *kritērion*, a more specific reason may be suggested. In its "Epicurean" meaning, a *kritērion*, as such, bears on some *adēlon*; but it presupposes the grasping of some *enarges*, since it is in itself evidently true and it is neither possible nor necessary to certify this truth again, by applying a *kritērion*. It thus turns out that if the Skeptic succeeds in showing that no immediate truth is accessible to us, he will have killed two birds with one stone. He will have established that there is no *kritērion* in the prodelic (Stoic) sense, since to say that there is some *kritērion* in this sense is to say that we have some immediate knowledge. And he will also have established that there is no *kritērion* in the adelic (Epicurean) sense, since to say that there is some *kritērion* in this sense is to say that we can test *adēla* by referring them to some immediate evidence. Sextus's stance has thus some justification, even if it is still surprising that he did not make it explicit.

A.A. LONG

7

Ptolemy *On the Criterion*
An epistemology for the practicing scientist

The manuscripts of Ptolemy include a short essay entitled *On the Criterion and Commanding-Faculty*.[1] This title corresponds to the book's division into two unequal parts. Its first three quarters (sections 1–12) present an account of cognitive faculties and their functions, describe the different contributions of sense-perception and intellect, and outline the causes of dubious or erroneous judgment on the one hand and the secure determination of truth on the other. In the short final part (sections 13–16), Ptolemy appends an account of the relationship between body and soul,

This paper would not have been written without the stimulus and corporate work on Ptolemy of my Liverpool and Manchester colleagues. I thank them all, especially Anthony Lloyd. A translation of Ptolemy, *On the Criterion*, with notes, will appear in a volume of essays on *Truth in Greek Philosophy, in Honour of G. B. Kerferd*, edited by Pamela Huby and Gordon Kneale, for Liverpool University Press. This paper, though presented to the Dublin conference, was also written as a token of friendship for George Kerferd, and so it is included in that volume as well.

1. Περὶ κριτηρίου καὶ ἡγεμονικοῦ. Valentine Rose's doubts about the correctness of the attribution to Ptolemy were dispelled by F. Boll, *Jarb. f. klass. Philol. Sup. 21* (1894), 77–92. The text was edited by Boll's pupil, F. Lammert, as vol. 3.2 of the Teubner edition of Ptolemy's works (2d ed. Leipzig, 1961). I refer either to Lammert's section numbers or to the page and line of his edition.

locating the various cognitive faculties in different bodily organs on the basis of assumptions about the elementary or material constituents of body and soul. The upshot of the first part is a theory that scientific knowledge (*epistēmē*) is the systematic ordering of empirical data: intellect, though "more valuable" than sense-perception (14, line 17), depends on the senses for its primary contents, and both "principles" (*archai*) must be appropriately combined in any scientific study. In the second part, Ptolemy concludes that body and soul interact in the human constitution, the soul being "blended" with those regions of the body which contain its functions.

These are familiar answers to familiar questions; nor does Ptolemy's approach to them give any glimpse of new vistas to explore or unforeseen perils to avoid. The course he travels is short and flat, though sometimes obscure in description; and obscurity has been his essay's fate. The first translation into a modern language appeared only in 1980,[2] and little has been done as yet to elucidate the positions that Ptolemy defends and to explain why he writes as he does. Source-criticism rather than intellectual history has been the principal method applied to his work, giving the impression that Ptolemy wrote *On the Criterion* in order to satisfy diligent hunters for parallel passages from the various philosophers who provided his cultural background.[3] Two brief

2. Paola Manuli, "Claudio Tolomeo: il criterio el il principe," *RSF*, 64–88.

3. This assessment applies particularly to the most extensive investigations of this text, by Lammert, useful though these sometimes are for indicating features of Ptolemy's milieu: "Ptolemaios Περὶ κριτηρίου καὶ ἡγεμονικοῦ," *Wiener Studien* 39 (1918), 249–58; "Eine neue Quelle für die Philosophie der mittleren Stoa I," ibid. 41 (1920), 113–21; "II," ibid. 42 (1920–1921), 34–46; "Zur Erkenntnislehre der späteren Stoa," *Hermes* 57 (1922), 171–88; "Hellenistische Medizin bei Ptolemaios und Nemesios," *Philologus* 94 (1940), 125–41. See also the earlier work of Boll, *Studien über Claudius Ptolemäus* (Leipzig, 1894), 77–93. Manuli (n. 2 above), 64–74, strikes a better balance by seeing Ptolemy's essay as an example of "general philosophical culture."

points can be made in defense of a more generous reading of his essay. First, Ptolemy was a practicing scientist, not a philosopher with any declared allegiance to one of the established schools. Second, the breadth and nature of his scientific interests—astronomy, astrology, music, optics, geography—do much to explain why he found it useful to state his position on epistemology and psychology. How we interpret his eclecticism, or attitude to the cultural tradition, is a question to which both these points will be pertinent.

His empiricist thesis and his psychosomatic thesis—to refer back to Ptolemy's two principal claims in this book—were given an interesting prominence by the first modern editor, Ishmael Bullialdus, in a "brief note" at the conclusion of his 1663 edition.[4] Under the heading *Ad subtilissimi philosophi Renati Cartesii de animae specie intellectui impressa opinionem*, Bullialdus drew on both of Ptolemy's theses in a trenchant criticism of Descartes's most famous argument, a criticism that can be summarized as follows.

Ego cogito, ergo sum does nothing to shake the clarity and evidence of the principle *nihil est in intellectu, quod prius non fuerit in sensu*. Descartes's inference, though true and valid, does not support his claim that the soul exists quite independently of the body. The subject of his *cogito* is not *anima cogitans*, as he proposed, but *homo ipse cogitans*, which is a composite of body and soul. "Since it is man himself who thinks, and who cannot produce any actions except by the conjunct operation of his constituent parts, he will not be able to perform any function of reasoning or thinking except by the conjunct operations of the intellect and the bodily organs designed for receiving impressions of things and for containing spirits" (196). Accordingly, Bullialdus concludes, "the criteria established by Ptolemy, and ac-

---

4. Bullialdus's text and commentary were published by Cramoisy in Paris.

knowledged by universal agreement—sense-perception and in-tellect—will remain undisturbed" (196).

Bullialdus's recourse to Ptolemy as a weapon against Des-cartes is one of the forgotten cul-de-sacs of intellectual history, and comparable, one might say, to using a nut to crack a sledge-hammer. No committed idealist or skeptic would be converted to materialism or empiricism by reading Ptolemy's *On the Criterion and Commanding-Faculty*. His essay not only omits any reference to Academic and Pyrrhonian attacks on the foundations of knowledge, it also avoids the slightest suggestion that any con-troversy attends an account of the criterion of truth. Never hint-ing at any of the battery of available arguments for or against skepticism, which were commonplace in his day, Ptolemy writes as if the only issue is to settle the relative criterial contributions of sense-perception and intellect, from an implied basis of general agreement concerning human accessibility to how things really are. He advances no *aporiai*, develops no complex arguments, and indicates no questions that need fuller consideration. He names no philosophers either as supporters or as opponents, and his book is almost completely free from the generalized polemics which are so common in this kind of writing.[5] Neither of these omissions is his practice elsewhere. Here, however, his essay takes the form of a statement, to the effect that the facts are straightforwardly such as he describes them or at least may most reasonably be so construed.

These bland procedures would be disconcerting if Ptolemy were engaging directly with the issues that Sextus Empiricus re-cords in his arguments against all versions of the criterion of truth (*Adversus mathematicos* 7). Sextus devotes several pages to refuting the notion that what he calls the instrumental criterion is "intellect using sense-perception as its assistant" (*M* 7.354–68). This is just the thesis, in effect, that Ptolemy advances with-

---

5. Mild exceptions can be found at 8, lines 23–29, 13; 13, line 20; 22, lines 13–15.

out a hint of its being problematic. Whether or not either knew
the work of the other, a matter that the chronology seems to
leave completely open, Sextus's tripartite analysis of the criterion
in terms of "agent," "instrument," and "mode of application" (*M*
7.35–37) appears identical, apart from minor differences of terminology, to three aspects of Ptolemy's introductory scheme (3,
line 17–4, line 14). This division of the criterion, on which I will
have more to say shortly, is peculiar to Sextus and Ptolemy, and
there are innumerable other indications of their contemporaneity.
In order to understand Ptolemy's practice, however, we need to
compare his robust silence on skepticism with the attitude of
related intellectuals of his time, especially Galen, and to assess
his particular aims in writing this essay, its bearing on his scientific outlook, and his relationships to the various dogmatic philosophies which parallel and illustrate virtually every term and
idea he uses. For it should be emphasized that *On the Criterion*
owes any originality and independence it has to Ptolemy's organization and selection of standard concepts and strategies. It
would be difficult to find any text from the Roman Empire that
provides better material for testing the usefulness and limitations
of "eclecticism" as an index of a thinker's intellectual stance.

THE CRITERION OF TRUTH AND
PTOLEMY'S BACKGROUND

At the time of Ptolemy and Sextus it had become virtually de
rigueur for any thinker to state his position on the "criterion of
truth." By beginning his criticism of the "dogmatists" with an
extensive survey of their opinions on this subject, Sextus gives
the impression that this had always been so and that an entire
history of Greek philosophy could be written by detailing a
succession of doctrines answering to this concept. Nor is this
peculiar to Sextus. He reflects the common practice of the dox-
ographical tradition where "the criterion" had become a conve-

nient category for classifying what we would call different theories of knowledge.[6] In fact, as is now generally recognized, the criterion of truth only became an explicitly named and dominant subject of discussion in the Hellenistic period. First Epicurus and then the Stoics publicized the notion that a philosopher's primary task is to establish the foundations of our knowledge of the world, and to do so by setting out the canonical standards which are man's natural equipment for making secure discriminations between truth and falsehood or between what is and what is not. The paramount importance they attached to the criterion of truth should be seen as both a consequence and a cause of the contemporary development of skepticism. As moralists, Epicureans and Stoics looked to discoverable facts about human nature and the world at large as the grounds for their conceptions of happiness. Epicurus very probably elaborated his "canonic" as a rejoinder to the Pyrrhonian denial that there are objective or "natural" criteria for discriminating facts and values,[7] thus distancing himself from earlier atomist reservations about the cognitive reliability of the senses. The Stoics quite certainly were fiercely attacked by the newly skeptical Academy just as soon as Zeno of Citium promulgated the "cognitive impression" (*phantasia kataleptikē*) as a state of awareness that guarantees secure and accurate perception of its object.[8]

The Hellenistic debates between dogmatists and Skeptics were

6. Cf. ps-Galen *ap.* Diels, *Dox. Graeci*, 606, lines 8–10: "The criterion has three senses, general, special, quite special," a summary version of what Sextus gives at *PH* 2.14–15 and *M* 7.29–33 (see Brunschwig, Chapter 6 above, p. 160); Stobaeus 1.497, 21 Wachsmuth, on Aristotle, supported by Alex. Aphr. *In Aristot. De sensu* 111, lines 23ff. For Albinus and Galen, see below. The best account of the history of the "criterion of truth" in and before the Hellenistic period is Gisela Striker, "Κριτήριον τῆς ἀληθείας," *Nachricht. der Akad. der Wiss. in Göttingen*, Phil.-Hist. Kl. (1974), 2, 51–110.

7. Cf. Timon's account of Pyrrho, as reported by Aristocles in Eusebius *PE* 14.18.1–5, Diogenes Laertius 9.62. And see M. Gigante, *Scetticismo e epicureismo* (Naples, 1981).

8. Cf. Cicero *Acad.* 2.77–78, Numenius *ap.* Eusebium *PE* 14.6.12–13.

conducted in terms that became permanent features of the intellectual tradition, and the common property of all philosophers and scientists in the Roman Empire. Nothing about such a writer's school allegiance or sympathy can be inferred from his using such originally Epicurean terms as *enargeia*, "self-evidence," *prolēpsis*, "preconception," *epimarturēsis*, "attestation," or from his drawing from the much richer technical language of Stoicism such words as *katalēpsis*, "cognition," *sunkatathesis*, "assent," (*koinē*) *ennoia*, "(common) conception."[9] Within the Hellenistic period itself a common philosophical jargon had developed, and terms emanating from one school were frequently appropriated by another. What came to be shared, moreover, was not just words or concepts, but something we might call professionalism or expertise. Ptolemy and his contemporaries were writing for audiences who had been educated similarly to themselves, and whom they could expect to be familiar with an intellectual tradition characterized by a community of concepts, standard questions and answers, common argumentative methods and objections. Dialectical interchanges between the schools of philosophy and medicine, educational curricula, learned commentaries, and doxographical handbooks helped this process of unification quite as much as the merging of philosophical identities or eclecticism associated more specifically with thinkers such as Antiochus of Ascalon or Philo of Alexandria.[10]

This *lingua franca* is shared by Ptolemy and Sextus but, like any language, it is a blunt instrument. Ambiguities could arise

9. Here I am disagreeing with approaches to Ptolemy's "sources" to be found in Boll and especially in Lammert (n. 3 above). Many of Lammert's "parallels," as cited in his articles and edition of Ptolemy, turn out on inspection to be quite farfetched, particularly those he adduces for Ptolemy's supposedly Stoic inheritance. Moreover, most of the terms mentioned above are absent from *On the Criterion*; see n. 49 below.

10. For a further account of "eclecticism," which I have tried to complement rather than repeat, cf. M. Frede, "On Galen's Epistemology," in V. Nutton, ed., *Galen: Problems and Perceptions* (London, 1981), 67–72.

as technical terms became disseminated and detached from their original contexts. *Katalēpsis* is a case in point. In Stoicism, its original home, it signifies an infallible act of cognition based on the *kataleptic* impression, and such impressions refer primarily to self-certifying acts of sense-perception. Writers of the Roman Empire, however, frequently use *katalēpsis* as a synonym for *epistēmē* or *gnōsis*, mental apprehension quite generally.[11] Ptolemy, like Galen, complains about excessive fussiness over terminology, but he recognizes the importance of picking out the different properties of multiple items for which a single name is in use.[12] The criterion of truth itself is an example.

As a technical term, this begins its life, as I was saying, to describe the Stoic and Epicurean accounts of the natural means at our disposal for making utterly secure discriminations between truth and falsehood. The application of a criterion of truth, in this usage of the term, tests the existence of something or the truth of a proposition about something. Self-evidence (*enargeia*) from sense-perceptions or the clarity and distinctness of cognitive impressions (*phantasiai kataleptikai*) provided Epicurus and the Stoics, respectively, with incorrigible standards for judging what really exists; and the primary locus of both criteria was the phenomenal world. There are no precise analogues to these doctrines in earlier Greek philosophy. Hence it is an anachronism, in a sense, for Sextus Empiricus to identify the criteria of truth of philosophers from the whole preceding period—Heraclitus

---

11. For Sextus Empiricus's exploitation of a weak sense of κατάληψις, cf. Brunschwig, chapter 6 above, p. 151. A "Peripatetic" usage, stronger but non-Stoic, goes back as far as the late Hellenistic period: cf. Cicero *Acad.* 2.112 and H. Tarrant, *Scepticism or Platonism? The Philosophy of the Fourth Academy* (Cambridge, England, 1985), who makes an interesting (but not to my mind convincing) case for the Academic Philo of Larissa's use of a non-Stoic concept of "apprehension," 55–62.

12. Ptolemy, 8, lines 23–29; 15; Galen, e.g., *Meth. med.* 10.70, 81 Kühn, *Diff. puls.* 8.496 Kühn. On Galen's practice here and elsewhere I have benefited from reading an excellent unpublished paper by Jonathan Barnes, "Galen on Logic and Therapy."

and Parmenides down to Aristotle and Theophrastus. Throughout this time, however, philosophers had been preoccupied with questions concerning the cognitive value of our mental faculties, and particularly about the reliability of the senses as compared or contrasted with that of the intellect. In a context discussing Protagoras's dictum that man is the measure of all things (a likely precursor of the technical concept of the criterion of truth), Aristotle says: "We say that knowledge and sense-perception are the *measure* of things because our recognition of something is due to them" (*Metaph.* A1053a32–35).[13] This kind of remark about cognitive faculties could have been made by almost any philosopher from the time of Heraclitus and Parmenides onward. In designating sense-perception and intellect as "the measure of things," Aristotle was not anticipating the Stoic and Epicurean interest in a criterion that is an infallible means of judging particular matters of fact; he was making the much simpler point that sense-perception and knowledge are the mental faculties that furnish all our understanding of things. This claim does not imply that every application of these faculties to a particular problem will *eo ipso* settle the truth of the answer to it. To skeptical doubts of the Democritean variety, the Peripatetics responded by contrasting the sense-perceptions of the normal and healthy with those of the sick, a strategy too general to cover the indubitable judgment about particular states of affairs for which Epicureans and Stoics designed their specific criteria of truth.[14]

13. Cf. also Aristotle *Top.* 2.111a16, *A Po.* 2.99b35, *De sensu* 445b15; and Theophrastus *Metaph.* 19, fr. 13 Wimmer = Clement of Alexandria 1.301 Sylburg. Striker (n. 6 above), 55f., discusses Plato *Rep.* 9.572A6, *Tht.* 178B6, and Aristotle *Metaph.* K1063a3, the last two texts both referring to Protagoras.

14. For Aristotle, see my paper "Aristotle and the History of Greek Scepticism," in D. O'Meara, ed., *Studies in Aristotle* (Washington, D.C., 1981), 79–106, and, for Theophrastus, *De sensu* 69–72. Cicero, writing as a skeptical Academic, states the insufficiency of healthy senses as a condition for accurate perception, *Acad.* 2.8off.; cf. Tarrant (n. 11 above), 48f.

In Hellenistic practice, as Gisela Striker has well observed,[15] "criterion of truth" was used to include both of the cases just described—an infallible means of establishing particular matters of fact, as with the Stoics' cognitive impression, and also, quite generally, the cognitive faculties men have at their disposal. In this latter sense of the term, most Greek philosophers could be said to have stated opinions on the criterion of truth, as Sextus Empiricus maintains that they did, even though they did not use the expression or envisage anything comparable to its specific sense. Misrepresentation, however, could arise if the two senses were run together, so implying that an opinion on the value of our cognitive faculties committed its holder to an opinion about the infallible application of one or more of these, or that Aristotle, for instance, was concerned with just the same epistemological questions as the Stoics. Sextus in the doxography and criticism of *M* 7 does nothing explicitly to disambiguate these two concerns. To that extent his account of the views adopted on the criterion is misleadingly homogeneous as well as anachronistic. It is also ill suited to capture a position like that of Ptolemy, who is explicitly interested in both these senses of the criterion, but the second more prominently than the first;[16] for Ptolemy gives more attention to adjudicating between the cognitive contributions of sense-perception and intellect than to inviting the full Skeptical challenge by specifying the precise conditions under which complex facts can be infallibly determined. But even Sextus, by his practice, enables his readers to distinguish between theories about criterial faculties in general and theories about criterial applications in particular. This helps us to see that Ptol-

15. (N. 6 above), 53–55.

16. Cf. 15, lines 5–11: "So we must neither reject sense-perception as contributing little or nothing to the knowledge of what exists, nor on the other hand prefer its conclusion to that of thought, but we must attribute to each of them its proper function, and use each for the object which it is naturally suited to grasp infallibly."

emy belongs more closely with Sextus's view of the Platonic and Aristotelian tradition than with Stoicism or Epicureanism.[17]

It would be wrong to imply that questions about criterial faculties and questions about criterial applications had to be satisfied with different answers. Plato and Aristotle sometimes suggest that any properly functioning activity of intellect (*nous*) is immediately cognizant of the truth. Hellenistic philosophers, however, appear to have recognized the conceptual difference between these questions, or something like them, and to have distinguished different aspects of the criterion of truth accordingly. Potamo of Alexandria, who founded a so-called eclectic school of philosophy at the time of the emperor Augustus, is said to have distinguished between the "agent" and the "instrument" of the criterion of truth, identifying the former of these with the *hēgemonikon* (the Stoic term for intellect) and the latter with "the most accurate impression" (*phantasia*).[18] As we shall see from the fuller aspectual schemes of Ptolemy and Sextus, the relation of agent to instrument derives its context from activities like weighing, and measuring lengths. By analogy with these, the criterion of truth is represented as doing for putative facts what a weigher does for magnitudes with his scales. In Potamo's scheme, the intellect *qua* agent is the criterial faculty which passes judgment, and the "most accurate impression" is the instrumental standard which the intellect applies to make its judgment.

Potamo's identifications of agent and instrument are so specifically Stoic that his twofold distinction probably arose first in that school. Its suitability there is easy to show. In Stoicism, cognition (*katalēpsis*) results from assent to a cognitive (*kataleptic*)

17. Sextus discusses Plato, Speusippus, and Xenocrates at *M* 7.141–49, and Aristotle and Theophrastus at *M* 7.217–26. Minor differences apart, he attributes to them all a criterion that combines reason (*logos*) with evidence derived from the senses. The leavening hand of Antiochus is probably a powerful influence on these parts of Sextus's doxography; cf. n. 55 below.

18. Diogenes Laertius 1.21. Cf. Donini, Chapter 1 above, p. 16.

impression.[19] The distinction between agent and instrument clarifies this relationship by indicating that well-founded judgment is an act of the intellect using cognitive impressions as its instrumental standard. Moreover, the Stoic lists of criteria of truth specify cognitive faculties—knowledge, sense-perception, right reason[20]—as well as cognitive impressions, preconceptions, and common conceptions, any one of which is quite particular, as faculties are not, in its content.

Besides its acknowledgment of the two criterial aspects I have been discussing, Potamo's scheme has two further uses. First, it makes it possible to detect different sources of sound and unsound judgments. Faulty discriminations may be due either to unsound instruments (e.g., inaccurate sense-perceptions) or alternatively, or in addition, to the unsound minds or cognitive faculties that apply them. Second, his scheme is sufficiently general (recall his "eclectic" stance) to accommodate other accounts of the criterion besides the Stoics' and thus to provide a basis for classifying or reconciling different opinions on the subject.

Both of these points can be illustrated from the use to which the twofold criterial scheme is put in the compendium of Platonism by Alcinous or Albinus, a document roughly contemporary with Ptolemy and Sextus.[21] Albinus, as I will call him, reflects current practice by beginning his summary of Plato's philosophy with an account of the criterion. Like Potamo, he identifies the "agent" aspect with intellect or, as he says later, "the philosopher." The "instrumental" aspect in Albinus is different. He calls it "a natural criterion for judging truths and falsehoods" or, more summarily, "natural *logos*." Two subdivisions of this follow: first, a distinction between divine *logos*, absolutely accurate but inaccessible to man, and human *logos*, which is "infallible for the knowledge of things." Second, Albinus divides *logos* into "sci-

---

19. Cicero *Acad.* 2.145, Sextus Empiricus *M* 7.151.
20. Diogenes Laertius 7.54.
21. *Eisagoge in Platonis Opera*, ed. Hermann, vol. 6, 154–56.

entific" (*epistēmonikos*), whose domain is stable intelligibles, which it handles securely, and "opining" (*doxastos*) or "plausible," whose sphere is unstable sensibles, which it handles only conjecturally.

Albinus's scheme shows how the presumably Stoic distinction between criterial agent and criterial instrument could be applied to his version of Platonism. His division into scientific and opining *logos* (also found in Ptolemy and in Sextus's account of Xenophanes, Parmenides, and Xenocrates)[22] exploits the two criterial aspects effectively, for these enable him to show how a single agent, intellect, can make judgments of different epistemic value on the basis of two different criterial instruments, scientific and opining *logos*. Actually, however, Albinus ends up by blurring Potamo's sharp distinction between agent and instrument; he describes *logos* itself, as well as intellect, as a "judge," and thus assimilates criterial faculties to the instruments (opinion or science) that they apply in judging.

In Albinus's defense, it can be said that his distinction between intellect and *logos* is no more than a *façon de parler*, enabling him to indicate two different cognitive states of the intellect itself. Nevertheless, his procedure seems to illustrate the difficulty of applying a conception of the criterion designed for one philosophy to another for which it was not intended. Turning now to Ptolemy and Sextus, we find them starting from a more complex division of criterial aspects. Is it likely, I want to ask, that their schemes were prompted by a concern (not original to them) to expound the criterion of truth in ways that preserve Potamo's distinctions between agent and instrument, but do not risk conflating them, as Albinus does?

Ptolemy begins his book by elaborating a fivefold scheme, illustrated by analogy with the law court (*dikastērion*), to which

22. Ptolemy, 18, line 12–19, line 6; 21, lines 8–10; Sextus Empiricus *M* 7.110, 111, 147.

kritērion had been applied in Hellenistic Greek.[23] The first and fifth terms of his scheme—object of judgment ("what is") and objective ("truth")—are an inessential complication, which he probably introduced to assist with his probably original law-court analogy. His remaining three terms correspond broadly in thought, though not exactly in diction, to a threefold scheme which Sextus prefaces to his treatment of the criterion.[24] They agree with Potamo and Albinus in distinguishing agent from instrument, the weigher or measurer from his scales or ruler. Their interesting addition is what Sextus calls "mode of application" or simply "mode," and Ptolemy "manner" (literally "by which").[25] This third criterial aspect is analogous to the weighing or inclination of a balance that a weigher secures with his scales, or the alignment a builder secures with his rule.[26] It refers, in other words, to the actual judgment or decision the agent obtains through applying his instruments, i.e., the final outcome of the criterial process.

What this comes to differs, at least terminologically, in the two accounts. According to Sextus, the three aspects yield the following formula as the fully explicated criterion of truth: a man judges through the instrumentality of sense-perception or thought by the application of an impression (*phantasia*).[27] In Ptolemy the formula is stated like this: the intellect judges through the instrumentality of sense-perception by (the operation of) *logos*.[28]

23. On δικαστήριον, cf. Striker (n. 6 above), 52f.

24. Sextus Empiricus *PH* 2.14–17, *M* 7.35–37. Cf. Brunschwig, Chapter 6 above, p. 160, and my paper "Sextus Empiricus on the Criterion of Truth," *BICS* 25 (1978), 35–49.

25. "Mode of application," προσβολὴ καὶ σχέσις, is the elaborated equivalent in *M* 7 of καθ' ὅ in *PH* 2. Ptolemy's term is ᾧ, to be distinguished from δι' οὗ, the "instrumental" aspect.

26. Cf. Epictetus *Diss.* 1.17.7, 1.28.30, 2.11.13.

27. *PH* 2.16, *M* 7.37.

28. At 5, lines 11–14 οὐκ ἀλόγως ἄν τις ἐφαρμόσειεν τὴν μὲν αἴσθησιν τῷ δι' οὗ κρίνεται τὸ κρινόμενον, τὸν δὲ νοῦν τῷ κρίνοντι, τὸν δὲ λόγον ᾧ κρίνει τὸ κρῖνον.

Ptolemy's exclusion of thought as a criterial instrument is an idiosyncratic feature, to which I will return. Otherwise, the differences between him and Sextus are superficial rather than substantial. What Ptolemy means by *logos*, it emerges, *is* thought, *dianoia*, analyzed as "internal speech" (*endiathetos logos*); and this in turn is divided into knowledge and opinion. These are differentiated (cf. Albinus) by the systematic and utterly secure nature of knowledge and the simple, isolated apprehension of opinion.[29] Sextus's equivalent to Ptolemy's *logos* was *phantasia*. When Sextus comes to discuss this third aspect of the criterion, he does so exclusively by reference to the Stoic and Academic doctrines of "cognitive" and "convincing" impressions, of which the latter, though associated with the Skeptical Academy, has a Stoic origin.[30] In some accounts of Stoic theory, a cognitive (which will also normally be a convincing) impression is either a piece of systematic knowledge or a true but weakly held opinion, depending on whether it is the cognitive impression of a wise man or a fool.[31] Thus there is no incompatibility between Ptolemy's and Sextus's accounts of the third criterial aspect. Both their formulae allow the final stage of a criterial process to be the stable knowledge or unstable opinion which the mind arrives at by its application or its criterial instruments.

29. At 6, lines 3–11; cf. 18, line 11–19, line 6, and 21, lines 8–10. Ptolemy needs to distinguish between νοῦς, "intellect," and λόγος, "thought," in order to confine the former to the role of "judge," coupling the latter with sense-perception as faculties which serve the intellect's judicial function; cf. 5, lines 17–22. But this distinction between νοῦς and λόγος (or διάνοια) is not preserved when he deals in detail with the cognitive roles of sense-perception and intellect (sections 8–12). By then he has lost interest in the fivefold aspect of the criterion with which he started.

30. *PH* 2.70–79, *M* 7.370–445. For πιθανή as a species of Stoic divisions of φαντασία, cf. *M* 7.242ff.

31. Cf. Cicero *Acad.* 1.41; Sextus Empiricus *M* 7.151–52, which needs to be related to the Ciceronian passage in order to distinguish Zeno's position from Arcesilaus's polemic.

In itself this is scarcely a noteworthy claim. But now consider it in relation to the twofold scheme. There we found Potamo identifying the instrument with "the most accurate impression"—the scales, so to speak. But any one impression is an indication or apparent determination of some fact. And this— what the impression indicates—is not analogous to the scales themselves, but to the weight that they register. Furthermore, the threefold scheme, by distinguishing instruments from the mode of judgment they facilitate, highlights the judicial function of the third member, the intellect itself. It is the intellect's task to use criterial instruments for the production of its judgments. This point has special relevance to Stoicism, where a mark of the fool is precipitancy in assenting to impressions, an overhasty reading of the scales, as we might say.

This unavoidably intricate discussion of criterial schemes helps to elucidate Sextus's doxography and criticism, and the particular interests and contributions of Ptolemy. Sextus structures his criticism of the dogmatists around the three aspects of the criterion of truth, arguing against each of them in turn. Implicitly, it seems, he indicates the new developments of Hellenistic philosophy by identifying the criterion *qua* "mode of application" with *phantasia* and by confining his criticism to the Stoics and Academic Skeptics. Presumably he or his sources could find nothing comparable to the Stoics' "cognitive" or the Academics' "convincing" impressions in pre-Hellenistic philosophy. Hence his criticism of this aspect excludes everyone from the earlier period. The criterion *qua* "instrument," however, was entirely suitable for analyzing their views on the relative merits of sense-perception (*aisthēsis*) or opinion (*doxa*), on the one hand, versus intellect, etc. (*nous*, *logos*, *epistēmē*, or *dianoia*) on the other. These are the principal terms Sextus uses in this part of his doxography.[32] There he draws constantly on the twofold distinction

32. *M* 7.89–158, 201–26.

between agent and instrument, as, for instance, in his account of Plato making *logos* the criterion, in association with evidence received *through* sense-perception.[33]

For our understanding of Ptolemy and his milieu, we need to recognize that he is concerned both with the general and older question, "What are the respective contributions of sense-perception and intellect to our knowledge of the world?" and with the more recent and specific question, "What reliable criterion do we have for discriminating between particular truths and falsehoods?" In orthodox Stoicism the first question had been virtually reduced to the second: "cognitive impressions," as experiences of a mind that has no "irrational" faculty, are themselves "rational" and so transcend the old distinction between bare sensation and intellect.[34] Ptolemy's entire strategy is to preserve and elucidate this distinction. So he answers the first question as posed in the terms I have stated; but his response to it helps to provide his answer to the second question. He thus combines the two approaches to the criterion of truth that we have found in Sextus: the pre-Hellenistic interest in evaluating cognitive faculties, and the Hellenistic concern with the application of indubitable standards.

33. *M* 7.141–44, drawing on *Timaeus* 27D. Tarrant (n. 11 above) discusses this passage at length, 96–103, regarding it as a "garbled" and "probably abridged version of what Sextus had read in Antiochus." Certainly any doxographer who knew his craft could scarcely resist referring to Plato *Tht.* 184C, where the "instrumental" role (δι' οὖ) of the senses is for the first time carefully distinguished from the role of cause or agent (expressed by ᾧ); cf. M. F. Burnyeat, "Plato on the Grammar of Perception," *CQ* n.s. 26 (1976), 29–51. This Platonic passage was surely the origin of the two-fold criterion discussed above; but notice that in Plato ᾧ signifies the "agent," the mind, and not, as in Ptolemy, the mind's modus operandi.

34. Cf. Diogenes Laertius 7.49–51, and see M. Frede, "Stoics and Skeptics on Clear and Distinct Impressions," in M. F. Burnyeat, ed., *The Skeptical Tradition* (Berkeley and Los Angeles, 1983).

PTOLEMY'S EPISTEMOLOGY

Having elaborated his criterial scheme and introduced the concepts he will apply to its various aspects, Ptolemy concludes the main part of his essay (sections 8–12) with an account of his epistemology that loses little by being summarized as follows.

Intellect is posterior to sense-perception in its actualization and depends on the "transmission" (*diadosis*) of sense-impressions (*phantasiai*) for its primary cognition of objects.[35] But sense-perception is limited to the immediate experiences it undergoes, and it cannot pass judgment on any external objects as such.[36] Some of the ways it may be affected misrepresent external objects. It is also liable to confusion and impediment when it has to deal with properties common to more than one sense, or impressions from complex objects.[37] Yet it always tells the truth about the way it is affected; and its apprehension of its simple and specific objects—seeing colors, hearing sounds, etc.—when these are perceived under clear and normal conditions, is always veridical, or as infallible as a human faculty can be.[38] Under these circumstances, the senses are immediately cognitive of their proper objects and need no other foundation, so far as self-evidence itself (*enargeia*) is concerned.[39]

Intellect, though dependent on sense-perception for its starting-point, is the "more valuable" criterion, and it is not subject to the same limitations.[40] Through memory of percepts and the concepts it acquires thereby, intellect can pass judgment on sense-perception *and* on external objects; it adjudicates doubtful cases, classifies sensory evidence on the basis of its empirically

35. At 13, lines 4–8, 18–20; 14, lines 8–9.
36. At 13, lines 12–17; 15, lines 1–3.
37. At 15, lines 3–4; 17, lines 1–10.
38. At 15, lines 9–12; 16, lines 13–17.
39. At 17, line 17–18, line 4.
40. At 13, line 14–15, line 4.

derived concepts, and applies purely rational processes to its assessment of objects.[41] Intellect has an intrinsic and "infallible" capacity to discriminate among any impressions that it receives, in contrast with the confusion that may attend the senses.[42] Like these, it is liable to error when it has to pass judgment on complex objects—e.g., "man is the same as horse *qua* animal but different *qua* rational"[43]—but it has its own province of "proper" objects (theoretical and practical) about which it always tells the truth: e.g., same and different, equal and unequal, appropriate and inappropriate.[44] More generally, intellect, unlike sense-perception, functions by drawing inferences about objects. When these are one-off apprehensions, so to speak, or "detached" from a scientific disposition, the result is merely opinion (*doxa*). Science (*epistēmē*) is a stable and incontrovertible state of the intellect, consisting in self-evident and expert discrimination. More particularly, science works by analysis and synthesis, or collection and division, classifying existing things according to species and genera and dividing them accordingly down to indivisible particulars.[45]

Scholars have rung the changes in their choice of Ptolemy's sources or philosophical forebears. Boll argued for a late Peripatetic compendium; Lammert opted for the Middle Stoa, and especially Posidonius, who wrote a book *On the Criterion* (Diogenes Laertius 7.54); Manuli, acknowledging "a massive Stoic-Peripatetic presence," finds evidence in a number of cases to suggest "a more strict parallelism with Middle Platonism," as in Albinus.[46]

None of these proposals is patently false. Nor does any or even all of them together suffice to characterize Ptolemy's epis-

---

41. At 5, lines 20–26, line 14; 13, lines 14–16; 15, line 13–16, line 4.
42. At 14, line 21–15, line 4.
43. At 17, lines 1–16.
44. At 16, line 17–17, line 1.
45. At 18, line 9–19, line 6.
46. References in n. 3 above.

temology. A full genealogy of his terms and ideas would have to include Epicurus and the Academic Skeptics.[47] Nor, however, is it satisfactory to regard his position as one of undifferentiated eclecticism. If we had reason to think Ptolemy accepted a philosophical label,[48] Boll's assessment would be nearest the mark: Ptolemy's qualified empiricism is more obviously Aristotelian than Stoic, incorporating as it does the doctrine of specific and common sensibles and excluding the Stoics' self-certifying impressions of complex, empirical objects.[49] However, it is far better to let Ptolemy be his own man, and to regard him as culling the full resources of the philosophical tradition without carving it up into school categories in order to make the points he wants to make.[50] We have already seen that he does not attempt to combat Skepticism in the terms that the Skeptic lays down. His little essay should be read, I suggest, as a practicing scientist's statement of where he stands on the epistemological

47. Ptolemy's account of the development of language (7, lines 18–26) has its closest antecedent in Epicurus *Ep. Hdt.* 75f. His account of concept formation at 18, lines 4–9, employs processes attributed to Epicureans (Diogenes Laertius 10–32) as well as Stoics, and uses the distinctively Epicurean term εἴδωλον. The word ἀπερίσπαστος (10, line 19, and 16, line 15) is principally at home in reports of the Academic Skeptics; cf. Sextus Empiricus *M* 7.176ff.; Galen 5.778 Kühn, quoted below, p. 200.

48. In the preface to the *Syntaxis* Ptolemy starts from an explicitly Aristotelian division of the sciences.

49. Boll (n. 3 above) drew attention to striking similarities between Ptolemy's epistemology and Sextus Empiricus's account of the Peripatetics, *M* 7.217–26. Such reflections of Stoicism as Ptolemy does display (cf. Lammert, *Wiener Studien* 41 [n. 3 above], 176f. and ibid. 42 [n. 3 above], 184f.) are just what one would expect from the general diffusion of this philosophy at this date. What is surprising is Ptolemy's *not* using in *Crit.* such familiar Stoic terms as πρόληψις, κοινὴ ἔννοια, συγκατάθεσις (which he does use in *Harm.*; cf. Düring's ed., 9, lines 1, 27; 23, line 21), καταληπτικός. Other points that indicate his Aristotelian, rather than Stoic, ambience are his use of the actuality/potentiality distinction (14, lines 3–8) and the prominence he assigns to νοῦς in cognition. Stoicism is actually more prominent in the psychological part (sections 13–16); see below.

50. I find a similar sense of his controlling his philosophical inheritance

issues that arise in his day-to-day work. In a word or two, Ptolemy is concerned with the proper relationship between research or empirical observations on the one hand and theoretical or rational principles and generalizations on the other.

Ptolemy won his first editor's approval by making sense-perception the starting point of all concepts and cognitions. Although he at one point countenances objects peculiar to thought ("same" and "different" etc.: 16, line 8–17, line 1), the main burden of his doctrine supports Bullialdus's empiricist reading. Strikingly, in his preamble Ptolemy makes sense-perception the only criterial "instrument" (5, lines 12–13), and later he insists that the objects of sense-perception and thought are identical, though apprehended in different ways.[51] But Bullialdus understated Ptolemy's more prominent stress on the limitations of sense-perception as a cognitive faculty, and on intellect's sole responsibility for judging objects, whether by applying its concepts to the evidence of the senses or by using one sense to check another (13, line 20–14, line 3; 14, line 24–15, line 1; 15, line 13–16, line 4).

If Ptolemy's purpose in this book was to strike a balance between empiricism and rationalism, that would account for the selection of material we find it convenient to call Peripatetic, Stoic, etc. I have already explained why it would be mistaken to call his selection *eclectic* in any pejorative sense. Yet in a perfectly defensible sense his procedure is eclectic, though I should prefer to describe it as a methodology of optimum agreement. There are very close verbal and conceptual parallels between Ptolemy's account and the positions that Sextus, with some anachronism, attributes to Plato and the Peripatetics.[52] These do not show that

---

in the cosmology with which he starts the *Tetrabiblos*; cf. my paper "Astrology: Arguments Pro and Contra," in J. Barnes et al., eds., *Science and Speculation* (Cambridge, England, 1982), 178ff.

51. At 13, lines 10–16; cf. Aristotle *De an.* 3.432a5.

52. See nn. 17, 33, 49 above, and 55 below.

Ptolemy has simply cobbled his account together out of dox-ographical handbooks. Rather, they indicate that he presented his *own* views in a form that could invite a wide measure of agreement.

For the same reason, I surmise, he took over and elaborated the threefold scheme of the criterion, thus formulating his epistemology in accordance with the most up-to-date practice. Moreover, his use of that scheme enabled him to express his views in an arrangement that exhibited minimum disagreement with Stoicism. On Ptolemy's scheme, intellect uses *logos* (its conceptual apparatus) as its mode of adjudicating complex or doubtful observations, which it cannot resolve by sense-perception alone. In Stoicism, sense-perception or thought provides the mind with cognitive impressions, whose criterial power involves concepts that cause us to identify objects correctly.[53] The principal differences over details are due to different models of mind: the Stoics treat *phantasiai* from the sense-organs as rational (*logikai*), while Ptolemy prefers the more familiar notion of a division, mediated by *phantasia*, between raw (i.e., nonrational) data and the intellect's interpretation of these. At the level that concerns Ptolemy, he would not be unreasonable in regarding the Stoic account as a fine divergence from his own rather than a quite different treatment of knowledge. Even an Epicurean could find much to endorse in Ptolemy's account of the relationship and differences between sense-perception and rational judgment.[54]

Ptolemy's complete suppression of any skeptical worries or rejoinders can now be reconsidered. One of the Pyrrhonian Skeptics' principal strategies for discomfiting the dogmatists was to indicate their mutual "disagreement" (*diaphōnia*) and the ab-

53. For the causal role of cognitive impressions, cf. Frede (n. 34 above), 71ff.

54. Compare Epicurus *Ep. Hdt.* 49–51 on the truth of all sensations, as evidence of external properties, and the difference from true or false δόξαι about objects, with Ptolemy, 15, lines 11–14, etc.

sence of an agreed criterion to resolve it. By developing a view
of the criterion of truth that exploits optimum agreement between the schools, Ptolemy has an answer to this challenge. He
can maintain, as Antiochus of Ascalon did, that some apparent
differences between schools are terminological rather than doctrinal. Such a stance coheres completely with the impatience Ptolemy voices toward those who confuse questions of language
with questions about facts (9, lines 1–15). As a reformed Academic Skeptic, Antiochus had had the strongest of reasons for
playing up consensus in the philosophical tradition, as a foundation for defending his positive doctrines in ethics and epistemology. If this is a principal explanation of his so-called eclecticism, it motivates that practice in a manner not yet sufficiently
studied. Ptolemy's procedures certainly have an important precursor in Antiochus.[55]

PTOLEMY AND GALEN

Clearer still is Ptolemy's affinity to his contemporary Galen, a
point well emphasized, though not specifically on epistemology,

55. Shortly before this paper went to press I was able to read Tarrant's
very interesting book (n. 11 above). What is said in the paragraph above
would gain additional point if he is right (110) in regarding Antiochus's
Canonica as the source of Sextus Empiricus's doxography in *M* 7.89–260,
and that he wrote this work while still a member of Philo's Academy, to
defend "the right of 'what appears evidently to sensation and intellection'
to be the basic criterion of knowledge." Tarrant continues: "Like Galen
(*Plac.* 9.778) he [*sc.* Antiochus] could claim on the basis of the doxography
presented that such a criterion was acceptable to *everybody* from Carneades
to the Stoics themselves." I have commented (e.g., n. 49 above) on Ptolemy's
closeness to material in Sextus's doxography, and it seems entirely plausible
that he should have been strongly influenced by Antiochus's epistemology
in the *Canonica*, as reconstructed by Tarrant. But his "closeness" is certainly
not so great as to suggest anything like mechanical copying or lack of reasons he could give on his own account for writing as he does; cf. Boll (n. 3
above), 109f. The reader can ascertain this by comparing Ptolemy sections
8–12, and my summary above, with Sextus *M* 7.217–26.

by Paola Manuli.[56] Galen repeatedly indicates that the eclectic tendencies of his own approach to epistemology are grounded in his resistance to Skepticism. In *De optima doctrina* he attacks Skepticism quite openly. Against Favorinus, who had written three books in refutation of the Stoics' cognitive impression, Galen takes over the Stoic terminology, interpreting *katalēpton* to mean "securely knowable" (vol. 1, 42).[57] Apart from Pyrrhonists and Academics, he says, everyone agrees that they can distinguish between the illusions experienced in dreams or insanity, and perceiving truly; they take true perception to constitute secure knowledge, and everything pictured in dreams or insanity to be false. If the Skeptics refuse to concede this, the criteria of truth are utterly confounded (vol. 1, 43). Galen maintains that the existence of a "natural criterion" is plainly evident and that it serves as the source of such artificial criteria as compass, cubit, and scales (vol. 1, 48; *De plac. Hipp. et Plat.*, vol. 5, 723). The natural criterion that Galen proposes is *enargeia*, "self-evidence," whether of sensible or intelligible objects (vol. 1, 49).[58] Such evidence, he observes, cannot be judged by anything else. Galen cannot stop a Skeptic from disbelieving it; but such a desperate fellow will learn nothing from him.

Like Ptolemy, Galen accepts the extension of self-evidence to indemonstrable truths of reason, such as "things which are equal to the same thing are equal to one another," or "if equals are added to equals, their sum is equal" (*Meth. med.*, vol. 10, 36; cf. *Opt. sect.*, vol. 1, 108). Another way of describing self-evidence,

---

56. (N. 2 above), 65–73.

57. I refer to Galen by volume and page of Kühn's edition.

58. The extension of ἐνάργεια from perceptible to intelligible objects is already a feature of the epistemologies of Philo and Antiochus; see Tarrant (n. 11 above), 52, who gives further references to its use in Galen, 154 n. 61. He regards its attribution to Theophrastus by Sextus at *M* 7.213 as evidence of Antiochean influence on Sextus's doxography (n. 55 above), but I see no reason why Theophrastus should not have made such a claim for himself.

or what discriminates it from other criteria, is "the common conception of all people" (*Opt. sect.*, vol. 1, 109). Galen's examples of self-evident, indemonstrable, "commonly conceived" truths, not accessible to sense-perception, indicate the sense of Ptolemy's overly brief reference to the specific objects of the intellect (*Crit.* 16, line 17–17, line 1). More generally, Galen's recourse to self-evidence and common conception shows the same concern with optimum agreement, as a methodological principle, that we found in Ptolemy. By their time, *enargeia* and *koinē ennoia* are terms at home in all treatments of epistemology. As Galen remarks in *De plac. Hipp. et Plat.*, vol. 5, 778:

> The judgment on these things is referred to *phantasia*, as the recent Academics say, not only that which is convincing but also tested and undiverted, or cognitive as Chrysippus and his followers say, or sense-perception and self-evident thought as men in general say. In spite of the apparent difference of the terms, on careful scrutiny they have the same sense, as when someone says he begins from the common conceptions, and that he posits these as the primary and intrinsically reliable criteria of everything.

Here we find the same indifference to terminological and fine conceptual distinctions that Ptolemy exhibits. (Indeed the difference between the Academics' "convincing" impression and the cognitive impression of the Stoics could only be treated as a fine one by someone who was either philosophically inept or unconcerned, for his own purposes, with the distinction between the "apparently true" and the "certainly true." Galen knew the difference, but chooses here to ignore it.) Galen also likes to strengthen the case for an epistemological consensus by the device, so favored at this period, of citing the "ancient philosophers" (e.g., *Meth. med.*, vol. 10, 36).

Equally redolent of Ptolemy's doctrine and approach is Galen's treatment of the mind's criterial power in virtue of its concepts and capacities for inference. The characteristics of "natural criteria" are their universality and common nature. "I declare that we all have natural criteria, and I put this as a reminder, not as

an instruction or proof or personal statement." These are normally functioning sense-organs, "and in addition the mind or
intellect or whatever one likes to call it, *by* which" (recall Ptolemy's third criterial aspect) "we recognize the consistent and
inconsistent, and other things which belong to them, including
division and collection, similarity and dissimilarity" (*De plac.
Hipp. et Plat.*, vol. 5, 723). This recalls Ptolemy's procedures for
the scientific discrimination of objects (18, line 12–19, line 6).
Galen, though more philosophically ambitious than Ptolemy,
constantly underlines their common interest in asserting an
agreed tradition on the criterial contributions of reason and
sense-perception.[59] By advancing this tradition against the Skeptics, or quibbling dogmatists for that matter, Galen is explicit on
the strategy that Ptolemy quietly adopts. The effectiveness and
earlier history of this tactic can be assessed by comparing Sextus
Empiricus's doxography with his critical rejoinders. His unpolem-
ical reports of the criterion, especially those of Plato and the
Peripatetics, seem to reveal the leavening hand of Antiochus,
which has smoothed out most of the original differences.[60] Thus
these "ancients" can be associated with the Hellenistic consensus,
outside Skepticism, on the criterial roles of sense-perception and
intellect.

It would be misleading, however, to imply that either Ptolemy
or Galen adopted similar strategies to Antiochus's for precisely
similar reasons. Antiochus's interpretation of the philosophical
tradition, which we call his eclecticism, was chiefly motivated by
his dissatisfaction with the Skeptical interpretation of Plato that
had been current in the Academy; he tried to give an account of

59. Two examples of the ubiquity of the tradition: Philo of Alexandria
Ebr. 169, *Conf.* 127, and Porphyry *In Ptol. Harm.* 11.4–6 Düring: "the ancients made sense-perception and reason the criteria of all sensibles."
60. I wrote this sentence a year before reading Tarrant's careful justification of the point (n. 11 above, esp. 112–14). Antiochus is cited by Sextus
at *M* 7.162 and 201. For Antiochean anticipations of Ptolemy's epistemology, see Cicero *Acad.* 2.19–22.

Plato, and of the Peripatetics too, that would incorporate much of Stoicism, the leading doctrinaire philosophy of his day. Skepticism, though still alive in the time of Ptolemy and Galen, was not an issue they felt called upon as practicing scientists to confront head-on. Their broadly based epistemologies could be used to respond to Skeptics, as we see in Galen; but their most immediate purpose has more bearing on the history and philosophy of science than on philosophy construed more narrowly.

Galen, as is becoming clear from recent studies, steers a careful middle course between the extremes of the Empiricist and the Rationalist schools of medicine.[61] He finds the Empiricists' account of medical knowledge defective in their reliance on nonrational experience (*peira*) and in their efforts to base cures on memory of observable treatments and symptoms, to the total exclusion of investigation of underlying causes by analogical inference from the evident to the nonevident (*Subfig. emp.* 1–2, 7–11 = Deichgräber, *Empirikerschule,* 42, 44, 62–86). The Rationalists, however, while correct in combining experience with a rational method, turn out to make claims for the latter which they are unable to justify, disagreeing about their principles, legislating rather than proving (*Meth. med.,* vol. 10, 30–32). Galen himself takes the view that medical knowledge requires an appropriate blend of experiential and rational methods. He describes the rational one as the more powerful, but also insists that experience is the most reliable criterion (*Meth. med.,* vol. 10, 183; *Simpl. med.,* vol. 11, 456).

Galen's middle-ground epistemology serves to define his position in regard to the medical theory and practice of his day. With Ptolemy the case is similar in music. He begins his *Harmonics* with the claim that the criteria of harmony are sound (as matter and affection) and *logos* (as form and explanation; 3, lines

---

61. Cf. Frede (n. 10 above).

3–5).[62] *Logos* determines and completes the approximate discoveries of sense-perception (3, lines 6–15). The senses need a rational criterion, like that of the rule for a straight line, to settle any apparent discrepancies between observations and the facts (5, lines 1–10). That need is satisfied by "the harmonic canon":

> [It consists of] rational hypotheses [concerning musical intervals] that never contradict the majority's judgment about their sense-perceptions. This corresponds to the astronomer's task, which is to preserve the hypotheses about the celestial movements—hypotheses which are in agreement with the observed orbits, since they were themselves taken from what could be seen evidently and approximately, although they discovered by reason the particular details to the greatest possible degree of accuracy.
>
> (5, lines 11–20)

As in *On the Criterion*, Ptolemy views scientific knowledge in the *Harmonics* as combining reason and experience. Starting from sense-perception, reason discovers theoretical principles which, because they had their basis in experience, serve to ground and control all subsequent observations. Moreover, Ptolemy had an issue of his own to resolve in music, exactly like that of Galen's adjudication between Rationalists and Empiricists. The Pythagorean musicologists, he complains, worked too theoretically. They failed to give necessary attention to the actual experience of the ear, and thus produced theories so discrepant with the actual differences between sounds that they gave rationalism a bad name. Aristoxenus and his followers, on the other hand, made reason virtually superfluous by attaching too much importance to auditory experience. Their inappropriate application of numbers to the intervals of sounds and not to their differences contradicted reason and observation alike (5, line 27–6, line 10).

The epistemology of *On the Criterion* is put to work in the

---

62. I refer to page and line of Düring's edition, *Die Harmonielehre des Klaudios Ptolemaios* (Göteborg, 1930).

204 □ A. A. Long

Harmonics. First, an example of the Aristoxeneans' misapplication of the criteria:

> This discrepancy [arising from their account of the fourth] is not to be regarded as a fault of reason [i.e., mathematics] and sense-perception, but of their divergent hypotheses . . . and giving assent contrary to both criteria. For sense-perception practically bellows[63] its clear and unmistakable recognition of the fifth, in all cases when the canon indicates a ratio of 3:2, and of the fourth when the ratio is 4:3. These men, however, do not remain consistent with the canon.
>
> (23, line 19–24, line 1)

Second, an example of using both criteria correctly:

> Our present procedure is not one of generating the characteristics of familiar tones from mere theory, and then attaching them through the canon to the evidence from observations, but the reverse: first exhibiting the harmonies established through sense-perception on its own, and then proving thereby the principles [i.e., mathematical ratios] which are a consequence of the perceived identities and differences of tones of each kind.
>
> (42, lines 3–7)

This combination of induction and deduction recalls the "scientific disposition's" practice of collection and division from *On the Criterion* (18, line 13–19, line 6).

Nor are the clear echoes of that essay confined in the *Harmonics* to epistemology. Ptolemy also develops a scheme of correspondences between musical intervals and the divisions of the intelligent part of the soul; these divisions conform exactly to his analysis of the constituents of thought in *On the Criterion*.[64] This further relationship between the two books encourages the speculation that Ptolemy adumbrated his position on the soul's

63. μόνον οὐ κέκραγεν; cf. Sextus *M* 7.257 μόνον οὐχὶ τῶν τριχῶν . . . λαμβάνεται (*sc.* ἡ καταληπτικὴ φαντασία), in reference to "younger Stoics."

64. *Harm.*, 96, lines 15–30, and *Crit.*, 6, line 16–7, line 3; 5, lines 20–22; 21, lines 8–10.

"commanding-faculty" (*hēgemonikon*), following his discussion of the criterion of truth (sections 13–16), in order to provide the ground for any psychological excursions in his specialized scientific writings.

The principal points of Ptolemy's psychology are (1) the soul's elemental makeup and relation to the body, (2) the division and teleological significance of its functions, and (3) the bodily location of the commanding-faculty. He makes the brain the seat of the commanding-faculty responsible for cognition and "living well," and the heart the location of the commanding-faculty that controls "merely living."[65] Particular doctrines that he applies in his other books include: (4) the theory that bodily and psychological characteristics are co-determined by the ratio of their constituent elements; (5) the subordination of the senses to intellect; (6) the priority of vision and hearing above the other senses; (7) the conception of human rationality and its location as a microcosm of cosmic rationality and its location in the heavens. He invokes (5)–(7) in the *Harmonics* (7, line 15; 93, lines 11–24), and his treatment of ethnology in the *Tetrabiblos* presupposes the psychosomatic blending specified by (4).

In its relation to the philosophical tradition, Ptolemy's psychology, like that of Galen, can be represented as an eclectic amalgam of Platonic, Aristotelian, and Stoic features. More informatively, like that of Galen again, it involves an interesting series of decisions on controversial issues. Ptolemy sides with Plato against Aristotle and the Stoics in locating rationality in the head; yet he agrees with the latter in locating the basic principle of life in the heart. He is chiefly indebted to the *Timaeus* for his view of the bodily organs concerned with emotion and appetite, but his description of sense-perception, impulse, and thought is broadly in line with Aristotle and Stoicism. As to the vexed question of the soul's corporeality or incorporeality, Ptol-

---

65. At 22, lines 17–19. Boll (n. 3 above), 92, refers to the neo-Pythagorean division of the ἡγεμονικόν *ap. Dox. Graec.* 391.

emy was skillfully evasive in his first reference to the issue, where he argued that it is irrelevant to the division of functions between body and soul: "Everyone would agree that we conduct thought *with* [dative case] the soul and not the body. That this also holds good for sensory movements and all others, we would realize if we attended to the dissolution of body and soul in respect of quantity" (11, line 23–12, line 2). When he finally plumps for a version of Stoic materialism, or psychosomatic blending (19, line 15–20, line 13), a hard-line Platonist or Aristotelian would resist. But Ptolemy modifies his "Stoic" account by including "ether" as the exclusively "active" constituent of soul, which is wholly responsible for thought (20, lines 7–8, 15–16)—a fascinating compromise or concession to Aristotelian cosmology.[66]

PTOLEMY'S ECLECTICISM

Ptolemy's psychology bears out the interpretations I have given of his epistemology. In recalling these, it will be helpful to distinguish two senses in which his approach in both subjects is eclectic. First, like most of his contemporaries, Ptolemy works from within a tradition that is irreducibly composite, if viewed via its antecedents, but broadly unified in the perspective of its own members. We might call this unavoidable or undeliberated or cultural eclecticism. In another sense, Ptolemy is self-consciously eclectic, practicing the methodology I have called optimum agreement. This should be regarded as a dialectical strategy to give maximum credibility to the position he holds on the proper balance between empiricism and rationalism. He states his own convictions in a form that resists identification with any one school, while at the same time making it difficult for any school except Skepticism to argue against them, and implicitly pooling the dogmatists' resources against the Skeptics. His psy-

66. Cf. *Tetrabiblos* chap. 1 for Ptolemy's account of ether in his astrology.

chology is more obviously a compromise than his epistemology, but this was due to the nature of the inquiry. Ptolemy had to make choices over such controversial issues as the mind's location, parts, and relation to the body. Here too, however, his decisions are calculated to restrain disagreement as far as possible. For most of them, like Galen, he could cite the authority of the ancients.

Neither sense of eclecticism, however, is ultimately satisfactory as an account of *On the Criterion and Commanding-Faculty*. The first makes the patronizing point that Ptolemy was just a man of his time. The second, though much more informative, is limited to showing how and why he presented his thoughts in ways that could command general assent. What eludes eclecticism here, and perhaps anywhere else, is Ptolemy's evident commitment to the doctrines he presents—doctrines which still contain much that seems a reasonable approximation of the facts. That is what appealed to Bullialdus in the seventeenth century, and what source-criticism of Ptolemy's essay has tended to obscure. *On the Criterion* is the work of someone who has made up his mind on two issues of great complexity, but prefers to give us his decisions (the third aspect of the criterion of truth) rather than the instruments (the second aspect) he applied in reaching them.

8

Discovering the imagination
Platonists and Stoics on phantasia

The history of *phantasia* in Classical thought provides many examples of eclecticism. One of the most interesting of these involves the process whereby this Greek word was extended in its meaning from a term practically confined to technical philosophical debate in Plato, Aristotle, and the Stoics into something more like "fantasy" in the modern English sense, which can include in its range of meaning the notion of the creation of an unreal and even ideal world, visualized by the artist and shared with others for their pleasure and enlightenment, the world of the imagination. The clearest example of the extension, and indeed transformation, of the term occurs in a figure who lived at the end of the period we shall be considering, the Philostratus who wrote the *Life of Apollonius*. It is generally agreed that this Philostratus lived from about A.D. 170 to 250 and that his *Life of Apollonius* was not published until after 217.[1] There is also general agree-

---

1. For a good account of Philostratus, which includes older views and the more recent work of Solmsen and Lesky, see O. Schönberger, *Philostratos, Die Bilder* (Munich, 1968), 10–20. F. Solmsen's two essays on Philostratus (in *TAPA* and *RE*) are to be found conveniently in his *Kleine Schriften* (Hildesheim, 1968). See A. Lesky, *Geschichte der Griechischen Literatur*² (Munich, 1963), 893.

ment that Philostratus wrote, among other works, one called *Ei-kones*, which contains descriptions of sixty-five paintings and which was put into written form in Naples.[2] At some stage during his life he came to Rome and was accepted into the circle around the mother of Caracalla, Julia Domna, for whom he undertook to write the life of Apollonius of Tyana, a wonder-worker and philosopher of the first century A.D.[3]

The *Eikones* indicates a man who was interested in painting and the power it possessed, and above all in attempting to convey this power in words. The same interest is abundantly evident in the *Life*,[4] which, in spite of some possible historical content, we need hardly take as a critical biography. It does, however, allow Philostratus to show off his many-sided knowledge and skill. This freedom allows him to raise the question of the value of painting, through the mouth of Apollonius, and the discussion develops into a consideration of *mimēsis* (2.22). We learn from this that while all human beings have the power of imitation, artists have it in a more developed way, because of the skill that they have learned. It is because we all share in the power of imitation that we can appreciate the skill of artists, either in reproducing what we have all seen or in conjuring up what has perhaps never happened but can be imagined, as, for instance, the expression on the face of Ajax emerging from his delusion.

In this whole section there is no mention of *phantasia*, even though it is difficult to discuss the section in English without referring to the "imagination." Later in the *Life*, however, *phantasia* is specifically contrasted with *mimēsis* (6.19). Here, in a conversation with Thespesion, an Egyptian-Ethiopian Gymnosophist, Apollonius ridicules the manner in which the gods are

2. There is a slight complication in that another Philostratus also wrote a work called *Eikones*, but we need not dwell on this.

3. See, besides the work by Schönberger mentioned in n. 1, H. J. Rose's article in the *Oxford Classical Dictionary*[2] on Apollonius (12).

4. See the list of passages in E. Birmelin's "Die kunsttheoretischen Gedanken in Philostrats Apollonios," *Philologus* 88 (1933), 150–52.

represented in the local temples. Thespesion, somewhat annoyed, asks sarcastically if Greeks like Phidias and Praxiteles were so privileged that they could go to heaven and look around and use the gods there as models for the statues they make on earth. Oh no, Apollonius replies, they relied on something else. But what could that be other than *mimēsis*, asks Thespesion. It is something other, however, Apollonius replies: *phantasia*. *Phantasia* is a more skilled craftsman than *mimēsis*. "For *mimēsis* will produce only what she has seen, but *phantasia* even what she has not seen as well; and she will produce it by referring to the standard of the perfect reality." *Mimēsis* is often disturbed through terror, but nothing stops *phantasia* from its production. When someone wishes to produce Zeus, he must do it as Phidias did, and when Athena, he must conjure up (*ennoein*) armies and intelligence and the arts and how she sprang from the head of Zeus. Apollonius suggests finally to his hosts that it would be better to honor the gods by making no representations of them at all: they should leave the picturing of the shape of the gods to the worshippers because *hē gnōmē* (mind or imagination) makes better pictures and plastic representations than art.

We have, then, in this passage a movement from the praise of art based on mental vision to the exaltation of the mental vision itself, even if, or especially when, it does not issue in art. This sounds extremely Platonic, and so too does an earlier passage in 4.7. There Apollonius advises the people of Smyrna:

> Pay more attention to your own cultivation than to the appearance of the city, because a city which is adorned with good men gives more pleasure than one decorated with colonnades and paintings and gold. The cities which are beautiful through their works of art are like the statue of Zeus by Phidias in Olympia, sitting there. . . . But men who go everywhere are like the Zeus of Homer, who is presented in many forms by the poet and so is more wonderful than Phidias's Zeus of ivory. For he is seen only here on earth, but Homer's Zeus can be thought of overall in the heavens.

In other words, the less earthbound it is the more wonderful the art, and that is why literature is superior to painting or the plastic arts: it is a product of the mind and not tied to material place or time. The artist is not confined to reproducing existing reality: the power of *phantasia*, which is a higher one than that of *mimēsis*, creates what the eye has never seen but the mind has conceived.

It may seem a little ungenerous to cite these passages from Philostratus and then immediately start looking for the sources of his ideas, especially when they do look new and exciting, and when he has been credited with giving art a new standing.[5] It seems necessary to do so, however, even if we were to ignore the doubtful consistency of his views on *mimēsis*, which seems to indicate importation without assimilation.[6] That not all of Philostratus's ideas are original seems to be indicated by a passage in Cicero's *Orator*, written more than two hundred years before Philostratus, in which views remarkably similar to those of the sophist are put forward. The context (7ff.) is a discussion of the ideal orator. The supreme orator he is painting has perhaps never existed, says Cicero, and the eloquence we are seeking is at the very most suggested, now and again, in speeches, copies as it were of the perfect. We see various beautiful things, but none of them is so beautiful as that of which it is a copy.

> This cannot be perceived by eyes or ears or any sense: we grasp it only through thinking [*cogitatione tantum et mente complectimur*]. For example, in the case of the statues of Phidias, the most perfect of their kind which we can see, and in the case of the paintings mentioned [in 5, by Protogenes and Apelles], we can, in spite of

5. See E. Müller, *Geschichte der Theorie der Kunst bei den Alten* (Wroclaw, 1837), vol. 2, 316.

6. Birmelin attempted to trace Philostratus's sources in the two articles in *Philologus* 88 (1933) referred to in n. 4 above. See also B. Schweitzer, "Der bildende Künstler und der Begriff des Künstlerischen in der Antike," *Neue Heidelberger Jahrbücher* n.s. (1925), now most readily available in his *Zur Kunst der Antike* (Tübingen, 1963), vol. 1, 43ff.

their beauty, imagine something more beautiful.[7] That great sculptor Phidias, while shaping the image of Jupiter or Minerva, did not keep looking at some person from whom he drew the likeness, but in his own mind there dwelt a surpassing vision of beauty; at this he gazed and, fixed on this, he directed his art and hand to the production of a likeness of it. Accordingly, as there is something perfect and surpassing in the case of sculpture and painting, with the vision of which in the mind there are associated in the process of imitation those things which are never actually seen, so with our minds we conceive the ideal of perfect eloquence, but with our ears we catch only the copy.[8] These patterns of things are called *ideai* by Plato. . . . These, he says, do not "become"; they exist forever and are to be found in intellect and reason [*ratione et intellegentia*]; other things come into being and cease to be, they are in flux and do not remain long in the same state.

Here, as distinct from Philostratus, the reference to Plato is explicit, and the obviously Platonic "something perfect and surpassing . . . with the vision of which in the mind are associated in the process of imitation those things which are never actually seen . . ." corresponds to what Philostratus (in 6.19) says about *phantasia* and that which has not been seen. But this is precisely our difficulty, the use of the term *phantasia* in a *Platonic* context. If the context were Stoic, this term would be quite understandable, indeed expected. But it might appear unlikely that a Platonist would praise imagination as a faculty that would help us to create art—art, according to Plato, is an imitation of an imita-

7. My translation follows the general outline of that of the Loeb, but with occasional important modifications.

8. I follow the reading *Ut igitur in formis et figuris est aliquid perfectum et excellens, cuius ad cogitatam speciem imitando referuntur quae sub oculos ipsa non cadunt, sic perfectae eloquentiae speciem animo videmus, effigiem auribus quaerimus.* The greatest difficulty has been caused by *non* before *cadunt*. Sandys deletes it in his edition (1885). Kroll retains it, but says the resulting thought is impossible. H. Sjögren, "Kleine textkritische Beiträge," *Eranos* 19 (1919–1920), 163–66, argues for the retention of *non*. Cf. *Orator* 18: *Insidebat videlicet in eius mente species eloquentiae quam cernebat animo, re ipsa non videbat.*

tion—or that he would use *phantasia* as a term of approbation for a higher kind of insight.

It must be emphasized that it is with the use of the *term* in a Platonic context that we are concerned. It is not a matter of denying the real existence or employment of imagination, as we understand it, by Plato or within his system. Indeed, it might be maintained (and, on occasion, critically, as by Aristotle) that it is in this direction that Plato's theory of Forms leads us. With the imagination we stretch beyond the sensually verifiable and reach or create a world which we feel should exist, and which satisfies a longing that seems to us reasonable. It ought to exist, and we would like to say that therefore it does exist. Plato said that the world of Forms exists because it must exist. There must be something beyond the buzz of sensation that gives what we hear and see meaning and direction. Mind, too, gives a superior vision, particularly of beauty which, because beauty has degrees, points beyond itself and so creates a desire that cannot be satisfied by the seen. Longinus refers specifically to Plato in chapter 35 of *On the Sublime*, and even though he does not purport to be quoting him, he nevertheless puts forward views with which Plato would certainly not disagree:

> Nature has brought us into life, into the whole vast universe, there to be spectators of all that she has created. . . . Thus from the first she has implanted in our souls an unconquerable passion for all that is great and for all that is more divine than ourselves. For this reason the entire universe does not satisfy the contemplation and thought that lie within the scope of human endeavour; our ideas often go beyond the boundaries by which we are circumscribed, and if we look at life from all sides, observing how in everything that concerns us the extraordinary, the great and the beautiful play the leading part, we shall soon realize the purpose of our creation.
>
> (trans. Dorsch, Penguin Classics)

There is, then, to repeat, no question of denying that Plato was a great imaginative writer or of disputing the effective use he made of the imagination in the exposition of his philosophy. The question is, would a strict Platonist use the *term phantasia* approvingly, and would he use it for a faculty that produces even what it has not seen? It would scarcely seem so, judging by Plato's own description of *phantasia*. Let us consider briefly what this is. It is in Plato that we have the first occurrence of *phantasia* in Greek literature, in *Republic* 382E. There is some manuscript uncertainty about the occurrence of the word in that passage, and if genuine, there is some ambiguity in its use: it may mean that God does not deceive us by visions, *phantasia* being given a passive sense, or on the other hand it may mean that we are not to blame God for our wrong interpretations of sense-experience, an active sense of the word. This active sense is to be found in the *Sophist*, where the most explicit description of *phantasia* in Plato is given (260E–264A). There it is said that when assertion or denial occurs in the soul in the course of silent thinking, it is called *doxa*, and when *doxa* occurs, not independently but by means of *aisthēsis*, this is called *phantasia* (264A), referred to a few lines later as the "combination of sense-perception and opinion" (*summeixis aisthēseōs kai doxēs*). In the immediately preceding dialogue, the *Theaetetus*, where Protagoras is represented as playing a leading part, *phantasia* is deployed in a discussion of our knowledge of the sensible world. *Philebus* 38B–40A and *Timaeus* 27D–29 and 52 are also of interest, because even though the word does not occur in these last two dialogues, the same process is obviously being referred to. In the last-named, the changing world is the subject of *doxa* accompanied by *aisthēsis*.

Phantasia, then, in Plato refers to a cognitive state that depends directly on sense-perception and so is sometimes false. The term seems an unlikely candidate for exaltation in a Platonist context such as that of Philostratus or Cicero. If the context were Stoic, however, there would be no difficulty. For them, internal reasoning and the *phantasia* "which is capable of making a transition" are distinctive of human beings. Sextus Empiricus reports:

The Dogmatists [i.e., the Stoics] maintain that man does not differ from the irrational animals by speech taken simply as uttered [*prophorikos logos*] (for crows and parrots and jays produce articulated sounds), but by the reasoned speech which is internal [*endiathetos logos*]; nor does man differ by the simple *phantasia* only (for the animals too have *phantasia*), but through the *phantasia* of transition and composition [*metabatikē kai sunthetikē*].

(*M* 8.275–76)

This is illustrated elsewhere. Through various processes, from something that is actually present to us, concepts are also formed of what is not directly perceived. We form a concept of Socrates by resemblance, for instance, from a likeness of Socrates which is present to us. Others are formed by analogy: Tityos or the Cyclops, for example, by enlarging the normal man, the Pygmy by decreasing him, and the center of the earth through our experience of smaller spheres. Through transformation we get the notion of eyes on the chest, through composition that of the Centaur, and through contrariety that of death. Some notions come through transition, like the *lekta* (what can be expressed), and place. The notion of something just and good arises naturally (*phusikōs*). Finally, a notion might be conceived through privation, like that of "handless" (Diogenes Laertius 7.53).

The likelihood that in a Stoic context *phantasia* might be said to be capable of producing even what it has not seen is, I think, very high, while a context that was faithful to Plato's division of the two worlds, the mind and the senses, would be unlikely to use the term. Is it then possible that the presumed common source of Cicero and Philostratus has been influenced by Stoic theory, and that this source introduced, therefore, into a Platonic background a term, *phantasia*, which in strict Platonism would have been out of place? Passages in "Longinus," Quintilian, and Dio Chrysostom suggest that this was perhaps the case.

The "Longinus" who wrote *On the Sublime* (? first century A.D.) uses the term *phantasia* on a number of occasions (3.1, 7.1, 9.13, 43.3) but the central passage is chapter 15. There he seems to be using Stoic-influenced sources. He says: "*Phantasiai* contribute greatly to dignity, elevation, and power as a pleader. This is the name I give them; some call them manufactured images [*eidōlopoiiai*]. The term *phantasia* is used generally for anything that in any way suggests a thought productive of speech, but the word has also come into common currency in cases where, carried away by inspiration and emotion, you think you see what you describe, and you place it before the eyes of your hearers." From this we may conclude that "Longinus" was aware of the Stoic technical definition of *logikē phantasia* as one "in which what is presented can be conveyed in speech" (Sextus Empiricus *M* 8.70), and the associated definition of the *lekton* as "that which subsists in conformity with a rational impression [*logikē phantasia*]" (Sextus *M* 8.70 and Diogenes Laertius 7.63). "Longinus" wants to discuss *phantasia* not in philosophy but in poetry and in rhetoric, where its primary aim is to move the audience. The speaker has something vividly before his mind, and through his words he tries to bring it before his hearers. As an example of the use of *phantasia* in poetry "Longinus" gives the old instance of the Furies in the mad scene in the *Orestes*. This is so familiar because of the constant recurrence of the Furies as an example of delusion in Hellenistic epistemological discussion (see Sextus *M* 7.170, 244, 249, 8.63, 67). He praises all three of the great Classical tragedians for their use of *phantasia*. What he says about Euripides and the Furies is particularly interesting as a parallel to what Philostratus has to say on picturing the despair of Ajax and on *phantasia* producing even what it has not seen. "Longinus" says: "In these scenes the poet himself saw the Furies, and the picture in his mind he almost compelled his audience to behold." If "Longinus" is using Stoic sources, was the notion of *phantasia* "producing even what it has not seen" to be found in those same sources, mingled, perhaps, with the Platonism that was also present?

That ideas like those of "Longinus" were current is indicated by a passage from Quintilian, who may have been a younger contemporary but cannot be shown to have read him. He is explaining that we must have the capacity of feeling something ourselves before we try to move others. He says (*Inst. or.* 6.2.29) that the orator who will be most effective in moving feelings is the one who has acquired a proper stock of what the Greeks call *phantasiai* and we might call *visiones*, i.e., "those things through which the images of things not present are so brought before the mind that we seem to see them with our very eyes and have them before us." He goes on to urge us to turn a common vice into a rhetorical virtue. The vice is daydreaming. If we could turn this to our own service, we would deserve to be called people blessed with *phantasia*, people who can present fictitious situations or voices or actions as if they were real. The result of all this will be "self-evidence" (*enargeia*), Quintilian says, using the Greek word. This term is further discussed in 8.3.61ff. *Enargeia* somehow exhibits itself, for not merely must a speech reach the ears, but its contents must stand clearly before the eyes of the mind. One kind of *enargeia* is where the whole scene in question is as it were painted in words, for who is so weak in imaginative power that, when he reads a certain passage from the Verrine orations, he not only seems to be looking at the people involved, the place, and the rest, but even adds further details that are not mentioned?

Quintilian is talking about a capacity in the rhetor (and in his audience or readers), the power of *phantasia*, which consists of the ability to present through words vivid images to the mind's eye. Yet neither he nor "Longinus" is concerned with *phantasia* as such, as a psychological phenomenon, and certainly not as an epistemological one. Both are interested in it primarily because of its usefulness for effective speech. And this emphasis on effective speech might also explain one element in this complex of ideas so far seen only in Philostratus. This is the passage in *Vita Ap.* 4.7 where the Zeus of Phidias is compared unfavorably to the Zeus of Homer. This is at first sight surprising, in view of Philostratus's praise of Phidias elsewhere. Yet it is not the gratuitous slight it might seem: the elevation of literature over the visual arts can be understood as another statement of the value of the unfettered *phantasia*.

Phidias's dependence on Homer had become a topos[9] by the time of Philostratus. It is given full expression by Dio Chrysostom in his *Twelfth Oration*, given in A.D. 105 at Olympia, where Phidias's statue of Zeus was to be found. In the oration Dio concerns himself with the question of what shapes men's vision of the divine. There we have a large extension of the brief passage in Philostratus, but it obviously shares a large number of ideas with him. Under cover of an examination of sculpture Dio praises his own trade, words. As is only fitting in a speech supposed to be delivered in Olympia, which gloried in Phidias's masterpiece, he is more respectful than Philostratus toward his achievement. But in spite of the proposed justification of sculpture, he is saying essentially the same thing as Philostratus, and saying what we would expect from a sophist: literature, prose or poetry, is superior to the visual arts. Dio, however, says it in more detail and at much greater length. For him, even when the visual arts make use of symbolism, they are circumscribed. They have to restrict their object to one shape and to one place and time. Such is the tyranny of the eye that they can make little further use of any suggestion or illusion. Consequently, there is an inflexibility about the visual arts which makes them inferior to literature. Words are not earthbound: they can express every shift of thought, every movement of the soul, and they can indicate change over a period, instead of being tied to one single impression. Literature is more suggestive than the visual arts: it is not tied to a particular picture. It can suggest even what it does not

---

9. To be found in Polybius 30.10.6, followed by Strabo 8.3.30, and Plutarch *Aem. Paulus* 28, for whom it is already πολυθρύλητον. See J. Overbeck, *Die antiken Schriftquellen zur Geschichte der bildenden Künste bei den Griechen* (Leipzig, 1868), under Phidias, for further instances, including a couplet from the *Greek Anthology*.

state, and it is not detected when it is life-enlarging, because the ear is less tied to realism than the eye.

The chief points Dio has in common with the passages in Philostratus are obvious. Both Dio and Philostratus are concerned with representations of the gods, and that raises the question of whether it might not be better to have no representations at all. It certainly would be if the gods are to be represented in animal form. If they are to be represented, the representations should not be "realistic," naively imitative. Poetry is better than sculpture in suggesting the nature of the gods—as can be seen through the comparison of two leading representatives of these arts, Homer and Phidias—because it is less encumbered with the physical world and with what is obvious to the eye. The higher reaches of art are concerned with the unseen, and the less earthbound the medium of expression is, the less controlled by the eye, the better. As Philostratus puts it, the inspiration of the best craftsmen comes from what the eye has not seen, and that because of the power of *phantasia*. Dio does not, indeed, use the term *phantasia*, but he does, in 45, speak of something that, according to "Longinus" 15, is for some people an alternative to *phantasia*: he says that in obtaining a notion of a provident god, the visual arts for the most part followed the lead of the lawgivers and the poets whose pictures were the older (*presbuteran ousan tēn ekeinōn eidōlopoiïan*).

What Philostratus has to say, then, has been anticipated in one form or another by writers in the three centuries before him. Ella Birmelin has attempted to trace his sources in two articles in *Philologus* 88 (1933) entitled "Die kunsttheoretischen Gedanken in Philostrats Apollonios." I shall omit any consideration of her views on *mimēsis* and confine myself to what she has to say on the sources of Philostratus's notion of *phantasia*. This she sees as influenced partly by Aristotle, but more importantly by an Academic philosopher, Antiochus.[10] It is said of him in Cicero

10. For Birmelin, an important part of the process is what she calls the equivalence (*Gleichsetzung*) of Idea and Ideal in Cicero—the result, she says,

that "he was called an Academic, but in fact if he had made a few little changes, he was an absolutely genuine Stoic [*germanissimus Stoicus*]," or again, a little later, that he never followed his predecessors in the Academy, never moved a foot from Chrysippus (*Acad.* 2.132, 143). Sextus tells us that he tried to show that the dogmas of the Stoics are already present in Plato (*PH* 1.235). These three remarks come from opponents of Antiochus but must be taken seriously, especially when we also find in Cicero a source friendly to Antiochus putting forward the view that "the Peripatetics and the Academics differ in name but agree in substance, and from these the Stoics differed more in terms used than in actual positions" (*Acad.* 2.15). Birmelin, however, for the most part ignores the possibility of Stoic influences, largely, I suspect, because she overreacted to Schweitzer's article in which he asserted that Philostratus's notion of *phantasia* was Stoic but gave his reasons for this assertion in such general terms that the argument is not convincing even for one who wishes to agree with Schweitzer.[11] We must now try to see where the truth may lie.

From what context may Philostratus have taken his views on *phantasia*? I suggest that it was from a context like that which we find at such great length in Dio, a context where the question of our knowledge of the gods and of what shapes our vision of the divine was discussed. The philosophers of the Roman period

---

of a long development in the theory of Forms. She invokes the aid of Theiler: his *Die Vorbereitung des Neuplatonismus* (Berlin, 1930) mentions the most important supporters and opponents of his thesis that Antiochus put forward the notion of the Ideas as the thoughts of God. There is some interesting material in A. Oltramare, "Idées romaines sur les arts plastiques," *REL* (1941), 82–101, referred to by G. Luck, *Der Akademiker Antiochos* (Stuttgart, 1953), 28. J. J. Pollitt, *The Ancient View of Greek Art* (New Haven, 1974), has a short section on *phantasia*. E. Panofsky, *Idea*[2] (Berlin, 1960) is also of interest, as is Claude Imbert's "Stoic Logic and Alexandrian Poetics," in *Doubt and Dogmatism*, ed. M. Schofield et al. (Oxford, 1980).

11. See n. 6 above.

were extremely interested in theology,[12] and both Philostratus and Dio had an extensive literature to draw on. We need only glance at Cicero's *De natura deorum* to realize how far back the tradition went. But how did *phantasia* come into the context? Relevant passages in Maximus of Tyre and Philo of Alexandria suggest that it happened in a discussion or commentary on the *Timaeus*. One of the topics on which the philosopho-theological tradition dwelt was anthropomorphism, a question which had been at the center of theological debate since Xenophanes. There was, however, a point of view other than that of Xenophanes or Plato, represented notoriously by the Epicureans,[13] but certainly not confined to them. Here Maximus is of interest. He wished to be known as a *Platōnikos philosophos* but, like Dio before him, would have known and used other systems.[14] His second speech concerns the question of setting up images to the gods. Maximus is a tolerant man. He concedes that if men were really good, they would need no reminders of the gods. But men are weak, and wise lawgivers have realized what has to be provided. In this situation it is reasonable that the gods should be presented in man's shape, although Maximus is aware that the Persians, Egyptians, Indians, and so on do not share that view. The true god, the father and *dēmiourgos* of all things, is unseen by our eyes, and we cannot grasp his essence. We wish to catch a glimpse of him, but since in our weakness we cannot, we fall back on various aids to his presence, and the things we find beautiful remind us of him. Therefore, Maximus concludes, "If the art of Phidias stirs up the Greeks to the memory of the gods, and the honor done to animals the Egyptians, I shall find no fault in this variety."

Maximus here makes an obvious reference to the famous passage in the *Timaeus* on the father and maker of all; and even

---

12. See John Dillon, *The Middle Platonists* (London, 1977), 45.

13. See Diogenes Laertius 10.139, and the attack on Epicurean anthropomorphism in Cicero *ND* 1.71ff.

14. See Hobein in *RE* 14, 2 (1933), 2558.

much stricter Platonists than Maximus believed that God did reveal himself as an artist by the world he had made. The anti-anthropomorphic Plato and the Stoa[15] agreed on this point: the Stoa drew gratefully on Plato in their long expositions of God's concern for the world he had made.[16] God's making of the world was explained on the analogy of the human artist. An elaborate example of the process is provided by Philo in his *De opificio mundi*. Philo says (16) that when God wished to create this visible world of ours, he first formed the intelligible world (*noētos kosmos*) so that from this incorporeal model he might bring into being the corporeal world. It is wrong, however, to suppose that the intelligible world, formed from ideas, is in any place (*en topōi tini*; cf. *Timaeus* 52B). A parallel from our own experience will explain how it has been organized. When it has been decided to found a city, an architect first designs in his own mind all the parts of the city to be. Then, when he has engraved in his own soul, as it were in wax, the outlines of each part, he carries about within himself an intelligible city (*noētē polis*). He keeps the models alive in his memory and engraves ever more deeply on his mind the outlines. Then, like a good craftsman (*dēmiourgos*), he starts to build a city of stone and wood, his eyes fixed on his model (*paradeigma*), shaping the corporeal realities to each of the incorporeal ideas. In somewhat the same way we must picture God when thinking of founding the great city, the megalopolis. He first conceived the outlines (*tupoi*); from these he set together the intelligible world and, using this as a model, he completed the sensible world.

It is not surprising to find Philo here using the language of the *Timaeus*. The *Timaeus* was one of the best-known and most

15. The Epicurean can see no great difference between them on the matter in Cicero *ND* 1.20, and read the Stoic spokesman's support of Platonic views, 2.45ff. Cf. *SVF* 2.1009 on "Whence men have derived their notion of God."

16. See *SVF* 2.1106–86, the section on *providentia*, where von Arnim begins by referring the reader to Cicero *ND* 2.

popular of Plato's dialogues.[17] One of the questions raised by it, whether or not the world was created in time (*Tim.* 27D–29D), had been discussed interminably since the time of Plato's immediate successors and had by the second century A.D., as Festugière says, become a classic in the schools.[18] Commentaries on the *Timaeus* were multiplied,[19] and even when it was not a question of formal commentaries, its authority was constantly invoked on problems of creation, both by the ordinary Platonists and by those, such as Philo, Numenius, and the Christians, who knew the Jewish version.[20] The passage that was of interest for creation also contained an exposition (in 27D–28A; cf. 52A) of the doctrine of the two "worlds," the "world" that always is, to be grasped by intellection and reasoning, and the other that is always in a state of becoming and never really existing, which is the object of opinion accompanied by unreasoning sensation (*doxēi met' aisthēseōs alogou doxaston*). This was obviously useful as a concise summary of the core of Platonism and as such known, like the picture of the *dēmiourgos*, wherever Platonism had penetrated.[21]

17. Apuleius speaks for many: *Plato philosophus in illo praeclarissimo Timaeo* (*Apol.* 49).

18. A.J. Festugière, "Le 'Compendium Timaei' de Galien," *REG* 65 (1952), 101.

19. Galen complains of the neglect of medical questions by commentators on the *Timaeus* "even though many have written on other topics there, and some of them at more than due length" (*De plac. Hipp. et Plat.* 8.5). M. Baltes, *Die Weltentstehung des Platonischen Timaeus nach den antiken Interpreten*, 2 vols. (Leiden, 1976, 1978), provides a useful account of these commentators.

20. See J.H. Waszink, "Porphyrios und Numenios," now in *Die Philosophie des Neuplatonismus* (Darmstadt, 1977), esp. 171.

21. J.C.M. van Winden, *Calcidius on Matter: His Doctrine and Sources* (Leiden, 1959), 131, commenting on the intelligible-sensible distinction in Calcidius and the knowledge of the two worlds, draws attention to similar formulations in Apuleius and Albinus, and concludes, "Clearly this was a central theme in Middle Platonism." Similarly, Waszink in his commentary *ad loc.* Cf. Cherniss's note on Plutarch *Proc. an.* 1012D and references (Loeb Plutarch 13.1, 1976).

The Stoics would not agree with a two-world theory in this form, but that was not to prove an insurmountable obstacle. The notion of God as an artist shaping the world was entirely acceptable to them: for evidence we need only look at *SVF* 2.1132–40 under the heading *Naturam esse artificem*. They held, like Aristotle, that art imitates nature.[22] If God is like the artist, that the artist is like God seems a natural conclusion, even if our stricter swains might strain a little at it. It follows that in the discussion of human artistic creation in the Roman period the same authorities, especially the *Timaeus*, were used as in the discussion of divine creation. The comparison of different forms of artistic creation, especially the art of the word and visual art, had been going on since the time of Plato at least,[23] and we have seen the continuation of the tradition in the authors of the Roman period. It is not surprising, given the interest in theology in the period, that special attention was paid to the presentation of the gods, whether through the visual arts or words. What has come down to us of this debate has been presented by the artists in words, and they cannot be expected to be neutral. What they were upholding was the superiority of *logos*, with all the resonance, and ambiguity, of that word in Greek. Once again, it was a theme on which both Stoics and Platonists could unite. The Stoics said that God was the *spermatikos logos*, the seminal principle of the universe (Diogenes Laertius 7.136). He contains within himself the *spermatikoi logoi*, in accordance with which he produces all things. The history of the word *logos* in Greek meant that when a Platonist heard God described as *logos*, what

22. Aristotle *Physics* B2.194a21 ἡ τέχνη μιμεῖται τὴν φύσιν. For the interconnectedness, see Theophrastus *Met.* 8a19–20, where he says that if we are to understand matter we must in general proceed by making references to the crafts and by drawing analogies between natural and artificial processes. Seneca *Ep.* 65.2 says *omnis ars naturae imitatio est*. See Theiler in R. B. Palmer and R. Hamerton-Kelly, eds., *Philomathes* (The Hague, 1971), 30–31.

23. See Plato *Phdr.* 275D, Aristotle *Poet.* 1448a.

was suggested to him was that God was reason. Philo once more provides a good example of how the syncretism might be continued. He tells us (*Spec.* 3.207): "The soul of man is something precious. . . . The human spirit is godlike because it has been modeled on the archetype Idea which is the supreme *logos.*" It is easy to see how the *noētos kosmos,* the world of ideas, can become the world of the *logos* and the *logoi.*[24]

The combination of Platonist and Stoic on this topic was also assisted by the special ambiguity of *logos* in the Stoic system. The Stoics, of course, held that only bodies existed. *Logos,* the language which we speak and hear, is also material. When asked by their opponents what was the difference between a parrot and a man, they replied, as we saw, that it depended essentially on "internal *logos* and the *phantasia* which is capable of making a transition." The two notions are very closely linked, and this link explains why the *lekton* is described as "that which subsists in conformity with a rational impression [*logikē phantasia*]," and a rational impression as "one in which what is presented can be conveyed in speech" (Sextus Empiricus *M* 8.70). The *lekton* provided an easy opportunity for a link with the Platonists. It may be translated "what can or is to be expressed," i.e., what is meant: it is neither the word nor the object nor the thought, all of which are for the Stoics material bodies, but something connected with the external world, and between it and ourselves, because of the *logos* through which we can articulate reality. It is the connection we humans express through language. The *lekton* adds special ambiguity to *logos* in the Stoic system, because it is said to be incorporeal, one of the *asōmata* (Sextus Empiricus *M* 8.11–12).

It is easy, then, to conceive how a Platonizing Stoic (or Sto-

24. See Philo *Op. mundi* 20, where, following on the comparison with the architect, he says: "In the same way the world of Ideas will have no other place than the divine *logos* which has set these realities in order," and cf. 24–25. See Theiler (n. 10 above), 30–31, and Bréhier, *Les idées philosophiques et religieuses de Philon d'Alexandrie* (Paris, 1950), 89 ("bizarre syncretisme"), 154.

icizing Platonist) could argue for the superiority of *logoi* to the plastic arts, since a statue, however magnificent, is material and literally earthbound, whereas *lekta*, the meanings expressed by speech, are incorporeal, or, as the Platonists would say, spiritual, *noēta*. But what is perhaps most remarkable in a series of authors in the period is the insistence on the vision which the great artist, literary or plastic, must possess. Cicero in the *Orator* and Philo in *De opificio mundi* we have seen. The elder Seneca contrasts what the eyes see and the vision in the mind: "Phidias never saw Jove, but he nevertheless represented him as thundering; Minerva did not stand before his eyes, but his mind, that matched such superb technique, formed a concept of gods and put them on view" (*Contr.* 10.5.8, trans. Winterbottom, Loeb Classical Library). The younger Seneca, in a discussion of the "causes" (*Ep.* 65.4ff.), mentions the views of the Stoics and Aristotle and then says:

> To these Plato adds a fifth cause—the pattern [*exemplar*] which he himself calls the "idea"; for it is this that the artist gazed upon when he created the work which he had decided to carry out. Now it makes no difference whether he has his pattern outside himself, that he may direct his glance to it, or within himself, conceived and placed there by himself. God has within himself these patterns of all things.
>
> (trans. Gummere,
> Loeb Classical Library)

The great dramatist and orator must have the power of visualizing a scene and then placing it before the mental vision of his audience: that is why he must have *phantasia*, according to "Longinus" and Quintilian.[25] For Dio (12.69ff.) the sculptor and the

25. See the list of occurrences of the metaphor "eyes of the mind" given by Pease in his note on Cicero *ND* 1.19 (*Quibus enim oculis animi intueri potuit vester Plato fabricam illam tanti operis, qua construi a deo atque aedificari mundum facit?*). Pease comments: "The frequency of this metaphor is due perhaps to the fact that the phrase expresses what we mean by 'imagination.'"

poet may have the same vision: it is only the intractability of his material that hinders the sculptor.

In these passages, Philo and Seneca the Younger are obviously speaking from a Platonist background: if Philostratus's views on *phantasia* belong to the same background, a background where we do not expect the word *phantasia* as a term of commendation (for reasons already given), how do we explain its introduction? We may be able to gain some hint from a consideration of a few other authors. Let us take again Maximus of Tyre, the "Platonist philosopher," as we remember. In the eleventh discourse, where he discusses the question of Plato's god, he raises the question of the importance of vision. He says (Hobein, vol. 11, 3) that even Homer's famous description of Zeus in *Iliad* 1.528 (the description which is constantly quoted in the comparison of Homer and Phidias) is ridiculously inadequate. All such pictures are due to weakness of vision, dullness of mind: the painters, sculptors, poets, and philosophers merely present their vision of god after what seems to be the most beautiful, as best they can, borne up by *phantasia* (*exairomenoi tēi phantasiai*).

Maximus's usage is obviously very close to that of Philostratus. It occurs in a Platonist context. It is particularly worth noting that as a form of insight *phantasia* is inferior to the perfect vision of perfect beauty. Nevertheless, *phantasia* bears us upward, having a role that is closer to the Stoic *phantasia metabatikē* than to Plato's usage. Maximus's usage does not, however, indicate exactly how *phantasia* is introduced into the context. A second possibly helpful passage occurs in the *De spiritu sancto* of St. Basil, where, talking of the craftsman (*technitēs*), he says (76A): "He either designs the product in his mind beforehand and then applies his creative vision [*phantasia*] to the work of art, or looking at an already existing model [*paradeigma*] he directs his activity in accordance with its likeness." Basil lived a long time after Philostratus (from about A.D. 330 to 379), so we can use what he says here only as a *possible* source of enlightenment. Basil seems to be using the word primarily of the vision which the artist retains in his head to guide the execution of the work he has mentally designed for himself—not a Platonist view of *phantasia*. It is easy to see how this vision could be conceived as assuming an active directive character within him, becoming the creative imagination. Gronau, though not at all concerned with *phantasia*, wished to see Posidonius as the ultimate source of much in Basil, including this,[26] and Theiler draws attention to the parallel with Seneca *Ep.* 65.7–8 in his attempt to connect a number of doctrines with Antiochus.[27] (It is interesting also to note that Himerius [ca. 310–390], the rhetorician and eclectic "Philosopher" who taught Basil and Gregory of Nyssa, also wrote (a) on the superiority of the word to the plastic arts, (b) on anthropomorphism and Homer, and (c) on Phidias and the inability of the hand to follow the vision of the artist.)[28]

But the passage that, in my opinion, throws most light on how a Stoic *phantasia* might be introduced in a Platonic background is to be found in Calcidius's commentary on the *Timaeus*. (Calcidius, too, lived some time after Philostratus, in the fourth century, but we may use him as an indication of sources which he and Philostratus possibly had in common.) Calcidius comments on *Timaeus* 52A, where Plato is talking of the two "worlds": the second is that perceptible by the senses, which comes into being and is always in movement, comes about in a specific place and is to be grasped by belief accompanied by sensation (*doxēi met' aisthēseōs*). Calcidius comments that here Plato wants to give us an idea of

> the second *species* which comes into being when the artist conceives in his mind the outlines of the work that is to come, and, with the likeness of this fixed within him, on its model shapes what he has started on; it is therefore said to be in some place. . . .

26. Karl Gronau, *Poseidonios und die jüdisch-christliche Genesis-exegese* (Leipzig, 1914), 47.

27. N. 10 above, 23–24.

28. See Himerius, ed. A. Colonna (Rome, 1951): (a) 21.5, 48.14; (b) 47.7–8; (c) 32.12.

He says that this *species* is to be known through the senses, because the shape which is impressed on the work is seen by the
eyes of the people who look at it; and to be known by belief,
because the mind of the artist does not make this appearance come
into being from a firmly existing model but he takes it as best he
can from his own mind.

(chap. 343: p. 335 Waszink)

The artist, then, according to Calcidius, has a vision like that
of God looking at the Forms, but in the case of the artist the
vision is conditioned by the limitations of human capacity. He
draws from his own mind as best he can, that is, he relies not on
perfect knowledge but on "belief." The result of his artistic activities is perceived by the senses, of course. Therefore, says Calcidius, when Plato talks of the kind of cognitive state that is the
combination of perception and belief, he is thinking of the type
of vision that is to be found in the activity of the artist. What
Calcidius does not point out here is that the combination or mixture of belief and sense-perception is how Plato explained the
word *phantasia* in the *Sophist* and *Theaetetus*.

It is easy to imagine a commentator much earlier than Calcidius pointing out that Plato's *doxa met' aisthēseōs* is called by
him elsewhere *phantasia*. If he were a strict Platonist, he would
hesitate to expand the term beyond its Platonic meaning of fallible cognition. But by the first century B.C., and certainly by the
third century A.D., few Platonists were as strict as that. If he were
a Stoicizing commentator following the line that Calcidius does
here, it is easy to imagine him pointing out that there was no
serious divergence of opinion between Plato and the Stoics on
the question of the artist's vision. In both schools it is due to
phantasia, what Plato is referring to in the *Timaeus*, he would
say, even though he does not use the word. The word, he would
say, refers in Plato to the vision we have through the senses, the
type of vision that comes second after that of god. He would
explain that the Stoics too say that our sense-knowledge comes
through the *phantasia aisthētikē* and that the knowledge derived

from sense-experience is extended through other *phantasiai* which are not *aisthētikai*. The latter are to be thought of as making a transition and are, indeed, with the "internal reason" (*logos endiathetos*), the abilities which distinguish human nature. The commentator would add that in the Stoic system also, it is *phantasia* that is responsible for human works of art. For it is *phantasia* that enables us to transform what we have seen and to create even what has never existed, like the Cyclops or the Centaur. The philosophers also say that it is through *phantasia* that we can see god, and, also, that the best pictures of god are in words or thoughts, *logoi*.

That the transformation of *phantasia* into a term for the creative imagination was due to Platonic-Stoic syncretism of this type hardly admits of doubt, although objections have been raised to both philosophies in this connection. Birmelin, as was remarked before, plays down the influence of Stoics because of their alleged lack of interest in art: there at least she agrees with Schweitzer, who also holds that they have no theory of art and are even hostile to it.[29] This mistaken view is the result of an overliteral interpretation of Stoic moralizing, which must not be taken at face value. That a man must cultivate his soul before all else is a theme common to Plato and the Stoics. That such a commonplace will be developed by certain writers does not mean as a result that they will not be interested in theory of art. We saw Philostratus himself combining this sort of moralizing (*Vita Ap.* 4.7) with an interest in art. The consciousness of the comparative worthlessness of all things when set against the soul no more stopped Stoics (and Platonists) from having an interest in art than the consciousness of the ineffability of god stopped Middle Platonists and Neoplatonists from talking about him.

There is one final point. Solmsen rejected Birmelin's suggestion that Plato's theory of Forms was applied to art in Philostra-

29. Schweitzer (n. 6 above), 88.

tus.[30] On this issue I would side with Birmelin rather than Solmsen, even though her thesis cannot be accepted in its entirety, and it would be unwise to be too dogmatic on the matter. She felt sure that Antiochus's theory of art underlay *Vita Ap.* 4.7, particularly because of the parallel between Phidias's Zeus appearing on earth (*en gēi phainesthai*) and the phrase in *Timaeus* 52A (*gignomenon te en tini topōi*) contrasting the second order of reality with the world of Forms. She quotes *Timaeus* 52A, ending with the phrase about how this second order of reality is known: *doxēi met' aisthēseōs perilēpton*. As the Platonic source for "he [Plato] denies that they [the Forms] are generated" (*easque gigni negat*), etc., in Cicero *Orator* 10 she also quotes *Timaeus* 28A, where we are also told how the second order of reality is known: *doxēi met' aisthēseōs alogou doxaston*. She fails, however, to point out that both contain the formula for *phantasia*. If Antiochus really was the source, it is not unlikely that he would have pointed this out: his Latin readers would have translated *phantasia* here as *cogitatio*.[31] There are two main arguments in favor

30. Solmsen rejected all her suggestions in his article on the Philostrati in *RE* (see n. 1 above); I consider this treatment unduly harsh, and also misleading when he says against her that "the use of the Platonic theory of Forms in regard to artistic phenomena cannot really be demonstrated in Philostratus" (col. 153).

31. Reid goes a little too far when in his commentary on Cicero *Acad.* 2.48 (*ea ... quae cogitatione depingimus*) he says that *cogitatio* is "the only word in Latin, as *dianoia* is in Greek, to express our 'imagination.'" (He is wrong about both the Greek and the Latin.) Nevertheless, that *cogitatio* was favored in Latin to translate *phantasia* as a process is undeniable: see, e.g., Cicero *ND* 1.39 *cum mens nostra quidvis videatur cogitatione posse depingere*, "although our mind appears capable of imagining anything," 1.105 *si tantum modo ad cogitationem valent*, 3.47 *omnia quae cogitatione nobismet ipsis possumus fingere*. Cf. our passage in *Orator* 8, *cogitatione tantum et mente complectimur*, and *cogitatam speciem* in 9; and finally Apuleius *De mundo* 30, *rex omnium et pater quem tantummodo animae oculis nostrae cogitationes vident*. That *dianoia* is not the only Greek word to translate our "imagination" is part of my purpose here to show. Apart from *phantasia* itself, we saw *gnōmē* used in *Vita Ap.* 6.19.

To translate the result of the process, also called *phantasia* in Greek, Latin

of her suggestion. First, the two *Timaeus* passages were very well known. Second, the notion that the ideal world is not tied to a place had become a very popular theme: an instance is how Philo fastens onto this point at the beginning of his exposition in *De opificio mundi* 16.

The link between the phrases may appear too tenuous for us to feel certain that *Vita Ap.* 4.7 should be associated with a commentary on the *Timaeus*, in spite of Birmelin's arguments. One further consideration may be adduced, however, and it brings us back to Philostratus's statement on *phantasia*. There, in 6.19, he says that *phantasia* will produce even what it has not seen as well: "it will produce [the vision of the work of art to be] by referring to the standard of the perfect reality" (*hupothēsetai gar auto pros tēn anaphoran tou ontos*). By the time of Philostratus *pros ho* was listed as one of the causes to be considered in the making of anything, especially in the sense of "with reference to the Form."[32] And *tou ontos* here in Philostratus seems to be a deliberate echo of *Timaeus* 27E where "the everlasting reality" (*to on aei*), which is to be grasped by intellection and reasoning,

---

used *visiones*, as we saw in Quintilian, who also has *imagines*. Cicero says he will use *visum* for it (*Acad.* 1.40, 2.18), with which *visio* is interchanged (2.33). Schweitzer (n. 6 above), 90, says without proof that *species* is the usual translation of *phantasia*, as exaggerated a claim as is Reid's on *cogitatio*. Nevertheless, a glance at any Latin dictionary will show that *species* is frequently used for *phantasia*, especially in the sense of "appearance." Since it was also used for the Greek *idea*, a *correctio veteris Academiae* which consisted in a substitution of *phantasia* for *idea* was not impossible. Cf. H. Strache, *Der Eklektizismus des Antiochos von Askalon* (Berlin, 1921), esp. 17.

32. The Greek is awkward. The middle of the verb allows this translation without difficulty: see LSJ s.v. II and III: φαντασία proposes, the hands in the case of the sculptor or painter carry out the work. πρὸς τὴν ἀναφοράν causes some difficulty, but LSJ πρός, C III, supplies parallels, with meanings such as "in consequence of," "on the basis of." See Theiler (n. 10 above), 18ff. and in *Parusia*, ed. K. Flasch (Frankfurt, 1965), 215ff., on the "métaphysique des prépositions," as Arnaldez calls it in his edition of Philo *Op. mundi* (Paris, 1961), 153 n. On ἀναφέρειν and ἀναφορά in Plato and the Stoics, see M. Isnardi Parente, *Techne* (Florence, 1966), 295ff.

is contrasted with the world of change, which is approached through *doxa* with *aisthēsis*, the formula for *phantasia*.

We cannot be sure who Philostratus's ultimate source was or, indeed, whether Philostratus himself would have been able to name him. He seems, whoever he was, to have taken elements from Platonism and Stoicism and combined them. He seems to go back to at least the first century B.C. The present state of the evidence does not allow us to decide whether it was Antiochus or Posidonius or some unknown third person. What is undoubted is the importance of the idea he set in motion.

9

Discovering the will

From Aristotle to Augustine

It is clear that there is a problem about the will in ancient philosophy, but it is not so clear just what the problem is. At one
time it seemed that there was general agreement that the notion
of the will was *lacking* in Greek philosophy. But then there appeared a book entitled *L'idée de volonté dans le stoïcisme* (by A.J.
Voelke, Paris, 1973), and soon afterward there was one on *Aristotle's Theory of the Will* (A.J.P. Kenny, New Haven, 1979).
Actually the authors of these two books would probably accept
the view that the ancients did not have "our" concept of the will:
their books describe ancient theories that cover the same ground
that *we* would think of as belonging to the topic of the will. But

The bulk of the research on which this paper is based was carried out in
1979–1980 when I held a Guggenheim Fellowship and was Visiting Fellow
at Balliol College, Oxford. Tony Kenny welcomed me to Balliol with a presentation copy of *Aristotle's Theory of the Will*. I offered the tentative results
of my work at a Balliol research consilium in June 1980. But I could not
really formulate my conclusions until Albrecht Dihle's book appeared in
1982. I want to express here my gratitude to the Guggenheim Foundation,
to Balliol, to Professor Dihle—and not least to Tony Long for organizing
the Dublin colloquium on eclecticism in 1984 that gave me the happy occasion to gather all these threads together.

what is our concept of the will? That is a point which needs to be clarified before we start looking for traces of the will in antiquity, or looking for the gaps that show that this concept is lacking. For if we do not know what we mean by *the will*, we will not know what we are looking for.

Unfortunately, there is no *single* concept designated by *the will* in modern usage. Hence the historical problem of the emergence of the will is not a single problem, but a labyrinth of problems where different threads lead in different directions. As a first step towards unsnarling these threads, I will propose four different perspectives on the concept of the will, each of which might lead to a different account of the history of this concept. The first three perspectives are defined by different families of philosophical theories of the will; the fourth is defined by the special problem of "free will" as opposed to determinism.

1. The first classical theory of the will—or, rather, the first *family* of theories—is one that begins with Augustine and culminates in Aquinas and the medieval "voluntarists." In this tradition the theory of the will of God precedes and guides the analysis of the human will; the human will is thought of as modeled on, or responding to, the will of God. I call this the theological concept of will.

2. The post-Cartesian notion of will is the one most familiar to philosophers (and to nonphilosophers as well; for example, to jurists) in the English-speaking world. This essentially involves the notion of *volition* as an inner, mental event or act of consciousness which is the cause, accompaniment, or necessary condition for any outer action, that is, for any voluntary movement of the body. Of course there is some connection between this and the older, theological concept of will; Descartes is in touch with the theological tradition, and his links to Augustine are clear. But with Descartes something new comes into the world. Theories of volition from Hume to William James (and down to the contemporary doctrine of voluntary action in the law) are fundamentally conditioned by the Cartesian dichotomy between the mental and the physical: a volition is the mental cause (or ante-

cedent) of a physical act. This is the view that was ridiculed by Ryle in *The Concept of Mind* (1949), and which has had a bad press in the last generation of Anglo-American philosophy, though it may currently be undergoing a revival.

3. A quite different philosophical tradition begins with Kant's notion of the will as self-legislation and hence as the dimension within which we become aware of ourselves as noumenal, non-empirical entities. For this leads in post-Kantian philosophy to very strong theories of the will, notably to Schopenhauer's view that the will represents inner reality and vitality, "the thing in itself," whereas our rational cognition has access only to appearance, the outer mirroring of the will as an object for knowledge. Nietzsche's conception of the will to power belongs of course in this post-Kantian tradition.

4. Finally, there is the special topic of free will versus determinism, which cuts across all three of the traditions just distinguished and in fact precedes them all, since it can be clearly traced back to Aristotle and Epicurus. However, and this is paradoxical but nevertheless true, the question debated by Luther and Erasmus, whether the will is slave or free, was originally discussed by Greek philosophers without any reference to the will at all. We shall come to this in due course.

Now the historical emergence of the concept of will looks very different depending on which of these perspectives the historian takes as his guiding thread. Thus in his recent and extremely valuable Sather Lectures, Albrecht Dihle has adopted the perspective of the theological tradition.[1] His thesis is that the concept of the will as a factor or aspect of the personality distinct from, and irreducible to, intellect and desire or reason and emotion is completely absent from the Greek tradition but implicit from the

---

1. Albrecht Dihle, *The Theory of Will in Classical Antiquity* (Berkeley and Los Angeles, 1982). See especially 1, 4, and 6 for Dihle's statement of his thesis.

beginning in the biblical notion of obedience to the commands of God. To obey God is to do as He wishes, to comply with His will, although this will may be entirely inscrutable (as in the command to Abraham to sacrifice his son). The appropriate human response is to be seen neither in terms of rational understanding nor in terms of emotion and desire, but as a commitment of the whole person that calls out for the concept of will for its articulation. Dihle notes that neither in Hebrew nor in New Testament Greek is there any clear-cut terminology for this concept. But in what is for this nonspecialist a very persuasive reading of the biblical texts, and more generally of the Jewish and Christian literature down to Augustine, Dihle shows how the fundamental contrast between Classical Greek and biblical thought, in cosmology as well as in the analysis of human action, is first recognized by writers like Galen and Celsus in the late second century A.D. but gets its full philosophical articulation only in the fourth century—first in the Trinitarian debates, which provide a coherent doctrine of the divine will, and then in Augustine's theoretical reflections on his own experience of conversion and on the consequent need for clarifying his notion of the human will (*voluntas*) in the face of Manichean dualism. Dihle's book is a rich treasury of scholarship and insight; it could only be written by someone who is not only an outstanding classicist but who also has an intimate familiarity and deep sympathy with Hebraic and Christian literature from the inside. At the same time, his deliberate alignment on the theological perspective gives Dihle's picture of the intellectual development an Hegelian, even a providential structure, as if the history of Greek thought from Plato to St. Paul, from Philo to Plotinus, amounted to the gradual accumulation of a set of problems to which Augustine's theory of the will was to offer the definitive solution.

From the point of view of the history of philosophy, there is a serious disadvantage in stopping, as Dihle does, with Augustine. For Augustine begins but does not complete the task of working out a Christian theory of the will. Augustine was a religious genius, but he was not a professionally trained philosopher: he had neither the inclination nor the technical equipment to formulate his conception of the will within the framework of a systematic theory of human action. R. A. Gauthier is no doubt unjust to say that "if no one has ever defined the Augustinian conception of the will, that is simply because this conception does not exist: of all the traits of the 'will' in Augustine, there is not a single one that is not found earlier in the Stoics."[2] And it is surely eccentric of Gauthier to assign the originality in this domain to Maximus the Confessor in the seventh century (or to John of Damascus in the eighth), so that Gauthier is able to calculate that it took "eleven centuries of reflection after Aristotle to invent the will."[3] (If Augustine had done the job, it would only have taken *seven* centuries!) Gauthier may be exaggerating, but he is making a serious point. The point is that Augustine's concept of the will does not get a fully philosophical development until it is integrated within a theoretical model for the psyche, namely, Aristotle's. This synthesis of Augustinian will with Aristotelian philosophy of mind is the work of Thomas Aquinas. Gauthier's point about Maximus and John of Damascus is that the general lines of Aquinas's synthesis are indicated in a sketchy way by the two earlier theologians.

For the history of philosophy, then, in contrast with the history of religious ideas and *Weltanschauungen*, it will be more enlightening to compare two fully articulated theories: on the one hand Aristotle's, on the other Aquinas's, which is avowedly based on Aristotle's doctrine yet unmistakably contains a theory of the will that is not to be found in Aristotle. Such a comparison

2. R. A. Gauthier, *Aristote: l'éthique à Nicomaque*. I.1: *Introduction*, 2d ed. (Louvain, 1970), 259. Note that Gauthier's stimulating Introduction was not found in the first edition of his commentary on the *Ethics* but was added in the second edition.

3. Ibid., 266.

will permit us to specify, in a very precise way, just what is involved in the claim that Aristotle does not have a concept of the will.

Without attempting to compare the two theories in detail, let me briefly summarize the principal points of contrast between them and then sketch some of the major stages in the intervening development from Aristotle to Aquinas.

Aristotle's explanation of human action relies on two basic parts or faculties of the psyche: the rational and the nonrational, or the intellect and various forms of desire. Following Plato, Aristotle recognizes three kinds of desire: *epithumia* or sensual appetite, *thumos* or anger, and *boulēsis*, usually mistranslated as "wish," a rational desire for what is good or beneficial. The position of *boulēsis* is ambiguous: as part of the *orektikon* or faculty of desire it should belong to the nonrational part of the soul; but in its essential directedness to the concept of the good or happiness (*eudaimonia*) it is intrinsically rational. Other forms of desire are nonrational in that they may either obey or disobey the commands of reason. It seems that there is no corresponding possibility for *boulēsis* to deviate from whatever goal one's reason judges to be good. But this is a point that is never fully discussed by Aristotle and remains to be specified in later theories of the will.

A human being may act under the guidance of passion, that is, under the direct influence of anger or appetite; and for Aristotle such action is voluntary (*hekousion*) but not deliberate or "chosen." Deliberate action is the result of *prohairesis*, a rational choice or decision involving some deliberation as to the best manner of achieving one's goal. We can think of deliberation roughly as practical reasoning in Hume's sense: the selection of means for pursuing a desired end. But according to Aristotle the end in view is always rationally acknowledged as good or worth pursuing. Hence, in a formula that is probably oversimplified but convenient, Aristotle says that *boulēsis* sets the end and *prohai-*

resis determines the means to this end.[4] *Prohairesis* thus marks the point of confluence between our desire for a goal and two rational judgments: first, our judgment that the goal is a good one, and, second, our judgment that this action is the best way to pursue it. Hence, says Aristotle, *prohairesis* is "desiderative reason or rational desire, and it is as such a principle that the human being is the source and origin [*archē*] of his actions" (*NE* 6.2.1139b4). We can be held responsible for all our voluntary doings, for these are always "up to us" (*eph' hēmin*) to perform or to omit. But as rational agents we have assumed full responsibility only for the more limited class of deliberate actions, for those actions which include a rational moment of choice or decision (*prohairesis*).

Thus Aristotle's theory of action involves four distinct concepts, in additon to the notion of intellect or reason (*nous, logos*): (1) the notion of an action that is "up to us" (*eph' hēmin*), in our power to do or not to do; (2) the notion of an action that is voluntary (*hekousion*), i.e., done spontaneously, on our own initiative and intentionally, done neither in ignorance nor under compulsion. (These two domains, the voluntary and what is "up to us," are in principle coextensive; but they are defined from different points of view, since the designation "voluntary" specifies the intentional attitude of the agent.) (3) The narrower range of actions that are chosen, i.e., that result from *prohairesis*; and (4) the notion of *boulēsis* or desire for the end as the desiderative component in choice. To say that Aristotle lacks a concept of will is to say, first of all, that these four notions (or at least the last three) are conceptually independent of one another: there is no *one* concept that ties together the voluntary, *boulēsis* or desire for the end, and *prohairesis*, deliberate desire for the means. But it is precisely the role of *voluntas* in Aquinas to perform this work of conceptual unification. I list some of the principal respects in

4. *NE* 3.2.1111b26–29, 3.5.1113b3–4, etc.

which *voluntas* for Aquinas represents "the will" in a way that *boulēsis*, the corresponding term in Aristotle, does not.

1. *Voluntas* is established, since Cicero, as the standard Latin rendering for *boulēsis*.[5] And that seems both inevitable and correct, since *voluntas* is the verbal noun from *volo* "I want," just as *boulēsis* is the nominalization for the corresponding Greek verb, *boulomai*. But the secondary connections of the Latin noun are quite different, and these differences will weigh heavily on the philosophical career of *voluntas*. Thus in pre-philosophical Latin, to do something *voluntate sua* is to do it spontaneously, of one's own accord; and the adjective *voluntarii* is the normal term for "volunteers" in the army.[6] Hence Cicero naturally translated the Greek term *hekousion* as *voluntarium*, and as a consequence we today still call it "the voluntary." But this linguistic fact has important philosophical ramifications. Aquinas is simply thinking in Latin when he says "something is called *voluntarium* because it is according to the inclination of the will [*voluntas*]" (*Summa theologica* Ia.IIae.6.5; cf. 6.7). The mere translation of Greek terminology into Latin serves to link the voluntary in an essential way to *voluntas*, whereas nothing in Greek connects *hekousion* with *boulēsis*. In fact, Aristotle explicitly rejects this as an analysis of voluntary action.[7] (For him, an action is also voluntary if it proceeds from passion or appetite, without the intervention of *boulēsis*. Aquinas is aware of this doctrinal difference and tries to account for it by recognizing a broader use of *voluntarium*: Ia.IIae.6.2 *ad* 1.)

2. Corresponding to Aristotle's notion of "what is up to us" (*to eph' hēmin*) Aquinas has the category of "things in our power" (*in nostra potestate*) either to do or to refrain from doing,

5. Cicero *Tusc.* 4.6.12, cited in A.-J. Voelke, *L'idée de volonté dans le stoïcisme* (Paris, 1973), 57 n. 3.

6. Contrast the Greek term for *volunteer*, ἐθελόντης, which is unrelated either to ἑκούσιον or to βούλησις.

7. *Eud. Ethics* 2.7.1223b29ff.

and this is what he calls the domain of *liberum arbitrium,* "free choice" (*ST* I.83.3). But Aquinas partially identifies *liberum arbitrium* with *voluntas* or "the will" as the power to make decisions (*ST* I.83.4). He thus establishes a close connection between the will and the concept of freedom that is unparalleled in Aristotle or in any Hellenistic Greek discussion of *boulēsis.*

3. Strictly speaking, it is not the general faculty of *voluntas* that is free in Aquinas, since *voluntas* as the rational desire for good, or for whatever is believed to be good (Aristotle's *boulēsis*), is a necessary feature of human nature and is not subject to free choice: we can will to do evil *only* if we believe that it is in some way good for us (Ia.IIae.10.2 and 13.6; cf. I.82.1–2). What belongs to *liberum arbitrium* is not the selection of ends as such but the choice of contingent means leading to a desired end. But this is just Aristotle's notion of choice or decision, *prohairesis.* Hence, says Aquinas, "the proper act of free choice [*liberum arbitrium*] is *electio,*" his Latin rendering for *prohairesis* (I.83.3).

If we look back now from Aquinas to Aristotle, we see that something very remarkable has occurred. Aristotle analyzed the process of decision-making on the basis of three or four concepts that were only loosely connected to one another: the voluntary, what is in our power or up to us, *boulēsis,* and *prohairesis.* In Aquinas all four concepts are defined by reference to *voluntas,* the will. Of course Aquinas knows the *Ethics* inside out, and he retains all of Aristotle's distinctions in his own terminology: thus *boulēsis* as selection of the end (for Thomas this is *voluntas* narrowly conceived) and *prohairesis* as choice of the means (i.e., *electio*) are two different "acts" of the single power that is *voluntas* broadly conceived (I.84.4; cf. Ia.IIae.8.2). But where Aristotle's theory of action relies on a network of independent concepts, Aquinas presents a tightly unified account focused on a single faculty: *voluntas,* the will, which includes an essential reference to freedom of choice.

4. And there is more. In Aquinas willing (*velle*) stands next to

understanding (*intellegere*) as the two intrinsic operations of the soul as such, both of them capable of being performed without any bodily organ (I.77.5). Hence these powers remain in the soul after the destruction of the body (I.77.8). Needless to say, there is nothing corresponding to this in Aristotle (except for his enigmatic remarks about the Active Intellect). Thomas's notion of the soul as an independent substance with its own proper activities is influenced by Neoplatonic as well as by Christian ideas. And this notion of willing as a purely spiritual, incorporeal activity points ahead to the Cartesian notion of volition as a mental event causing a bodily motion. So here the contrast between Aristotle's psychology and the theological concept of the will represents a point of contact between the theological view and the post-Cartesian idea of the will as part of what is mental and non-physical. Cartesian dualism is prefigured in the Thomistic (and non-Aristotelian) dichotomy between rational and sensual desire: the latter but not the former is "the power of a bodily organ" (Ia.IIae.17.7).

5. Aquinas goes on to describe how the will is cause of motion both in the soul and in the body: "*Voluntas* moves the other powers of the soul to their own acts. For we use these other powers when we will" (*cum volumus*, Ia.IIae.9.1). The will and the intellect act causally upon one another in a complex way that need not concern us here. But a word on how the will causes bodily motion will show how in this respect again Aquinas partially lays the basis for the post-Cartesian notion of volition. The details are obscure, since they depend both on the notion of an act "commanded" by the will and also on the interaction between sensory desire and bodily movements. But it seems clear that the will does not give orders directly to the body; it issues its commands *to other psychic powers*. (To this extent we avoid any head-on confrontation with the problem of mind-body interaction). For Thomas the will controls bodily movement by inducing and inhibiting the emotions or "passions of the soul," the psycho-

physical processes which he describes as "movements of sensory appetite."[8] In other animals, bodily movement follows directly upon sensitive appetite; but a human being "awaits the command of the will. . . . The lower appetite is not sufficient to cause [bodily] movement unless the higher appetite consents" (I.81.3). This is the point at which human freedom and responsibility are located: "actions are called voluntary from the fact that we consent to them" (Ia.IIae.15.4). In this act of consent (in which the will and the reason collaborate) lies the control of the will over the body. But the direct efficient cause of bodily motion must be the sensitive appetite, which is itself a psychophysical phenomenon. The will intervenes only by its control over such appetite.

6. Finally, the will may also produce positive change by its effect on the emotions: "When the higher part of the soul is moved intensely toward some object, the lower part follows its movement" (Ia.IIae.24.3); "it is not possible for the will to be moved to anything intensely without a passion being aroused in the sensitive appetite" (Ia.IIae.77.6). In this Thomistic notion that the strength or intensity of willing can physically increase our control over our emotions, we can see the point of origin of the modern concept of strong-willed and weak-willed persons. This becomes clear in Thomas's discussion of *akrasia* (incontinence) and "sins which arise from passion," which he also calls "sins of weakness." In all such cases the will is involved, since "sin consists chiefly in an act of the will" (Ia.IIae.77.3). Thomas is speaking of "weakness of soul," not weakness of will, but it is some failure on the part of our will that is responsible for our weakness

8. Ia.IIae.24.3: *passiones* are all *motus appetitus sensitivi*. For the interaction between sensual desire and states of the body see Ia.IIae.17.7 *ad* 2. When the will is said to command the voluntary motions of the body, this is elliptical for the will commanding the relevant psychic powers, the *vires sensitivae* (Ia.IIae.17.9; see also 16.1). Thus "walking and talking are commanded by the will but executed by means of the power of locomotion" (Ia.IIae.6.4), that is, by a sensory desire located in, and causing physical changes in, a bodily organ.

in such actions. Hence although Aquinas does not actually use the phrase "weakness of will," it is easy to see how this formula could come to be applied to his analysis. There is nothing remotely comparable in Aristotle's description of *akrasia*, for which the term "weakness of will" is wholly inappropriate.

This comparison between Aristotle and St. Thomas permits us to identify half a dozen ways in which Aquinas has, and Aristotle lacks, a concept of will. And I have not mentioned what is perhaps the most profound difference of all between them, the point that is brought out most clearly in Dihle's book on the will. Aquinas's theory of the will is presented in his *Summa theologica*, and this theological orientation affects his treatment in a fundamental way. The theory of the human will stands in the shadow of a theory of divine will and an account of the divine creation of nature, including human nature. Thus we encounter the theory of the human will only in Q. 82 of Part One, after a long discussion of the will of God (in Q. 19) and the will of angels (in Q. 59). Aquinas's theory of the will is fundamentally conditioned by this fact that the will is, with the intellect, one of the two principles we share with God and with the angels. It is this "transcendent" status of the will and the intellect in Aquinas that makes it natural for him to claim that the soul can exercise these powers alone, without any bodily organ. (God and angels also engage in acts of willing, but they have no bodies.) This theological orientation for St. Thomas's philosophy of mind points to one more source for the Cartesian dichotomy between the mental and the physical.

If we turn back now to the historical development that takes place in the centuries between Aristotle and the rise of Christian theology, we can mark four major stages or landmarks in the emergence of this concept of the will as an essentially spiritual power exercising decisive control over our voluntary actions.

1. The first major innovation is the Stoic theory of action as worked out by Chrysippus in the third century B.C., in which the notion of consent or assent, *sunkatathesis*, plays a decisive role.

Sunkatathesis is not the act (as in Descartes) of the mind as an entity existing quite independently of the body, because the Stoics are materialists and all psychic activity is also corporeal: our assent occurs as some kind of change in the tension of the soul-*pneuma* located in the heart. But once the Stoic concept of "assent" is taken over into Neoplatonic and Christian views of the soul as an immaterial entity, Chrysippus's doctrine of assent will become the focal point of the concept of volition or "willing" that we find in Augustine, Aquinas, and Descartes. For *sunkatathesis* in the Stoic theory of human action plays exactly the same role that *consensus* and "the command of the will" play for St. Thomas.

The three essential factors in the Stoic theory of action are "presentation" or "impression" (*phantasia*), assent, and impulse (*hormē*).[9] It is impulse or *hormē* that is the direct cause of an external action, that is, of a voluntary movement of the body. But of course there is no problem at this point of mind-body interaction, since the *hormē* or impulse is a physical movement of the soul-*pneuma* in the heart, pointing us toward or away from a specific action. For the Stoics the inner "impulse" causes the outer movement in the same sense as today we would say the motion of our limbs is caused by nerve impulses from the brain. Freedom and responsibility—which was essential for the Stoics—must be located further back, at the point where the impulse itself is determined. This is where assent comes in.

9. *SVF* 2.73, 980, 3.169, etc.: the relevant texts are scattered throughout *SVF* 2 and 3. My account of the Stoic theory of action is based on chapter 3, "The Psychology of Action," of Brad Inwood's *Ethics and Human Action in Early Stoicism* (Oxford, 1985), which is the fullest and clearest exposition known to me. Thanks to his kindness I was able to consult both the earlier typescript of his dissertation and page proofs of the book. Inwood's account builds in turn on important studies by A.A. Long and A.C. Lloyd. Parallel accounts on the points that concern us here are found in Gauthier (n. 2 above), 245–47; F.H. Sandbach, *The Stoics* (London, 1975), 60. The treatments in Max Pohlenz, *Die Stoa*, 2 vols, 3d ed. (Göttingen, 1964), vol. 1, 88ff. and Voelke (n. 5 above), 32ff. are less satisfactory.

In animals an impulse is the automatic response to a *phantasia*, to an impression or "presentation" from the environment which suggests some appropriate action, for example, a glimpse of danger or the prospect of food. Both humans and animals will respond to such *hormētikai phantasiai*, presentations that stimulate impulse. But there is a difference: animal impulses proceed directly from presentations, while in humans an act of assent must intervene.[10] Recall St. Thomas: "In other animals movement follows at once the [sensitive] appetites ... but a human being awaits the command of the will" (*ST* I.81.3). For Chrysippus as for Aquinas, this is the locus of freedom. We are not masters of our *phantasiai*, the emotional and sensual impressions made upon us by the environment or by the condition of our body. But our *sunkatathesis* is a rational action that is entirely "up to us": as long as our behavior is controlled by the mechanism of rational assent, our behavior is in our own power.[11]

Every voluntary action involves this moment of assent, a moment at which we could rationally criticize the response suggested by the *phantasia* and refuse our consent to the proposed impulse: in human beings, impulse will not occur without at least an implicit act of assent. This is the moment when reason intervenes, or could intervene, to guide our conduct. Deliberation is not required, and for the Stoic Sage, deliberation would be superfluous. For Aristotle, man is the animal that deliberates and hence acts by choice (*prohairesis*). For the Stoics, man is the animal that acts from assent. They thus point the way to St. Thomas, who says: "Acts are called voluntary because we consent to them," and "Consent belongs to the will."[12]

2. The second major landmark in the emergence of the will is

10. See *SVF* 2.988 (p. 288, lines 1–26), with Inwood (n. 9 above), 54ff.

11. Cf. Inwood (n. 9 above), 44, 67.

12. *ST* Ia.IIae.15.4. For a partial attempt to integrate the Stoic *sunkatathesis* into an Aristotelian analysis of thought and action see Alexander *De anima* 72.13 to 73.22 Bruns. This no doubt helped to pave the way for John of Damascus and Aquinas. (I owe this reference to Pierluigi Donini.)

the translation of Greek philosophy into Latin. It has sometimes been claimed, most dramatically by Max Pohlenz, that the will was essentially a Roman invention, reflecting the fact that the Romans were such a strong-willed people.[13] More recently it has been observed that Roman originality in this domain is less a sign of national character than a reflection of certain peculiarities of the Latin language and the terminology it made available for translation from the Greek. Thus Gauthier speaks rather unkindly of the *maladresse* and mistakes of Cicero in rendering *hekousios* as *voluntarius*.[14] Dihle refers more generally to "a lack of psychological refinement in the Latin vocabulary."[15] One is reminded of Lucretius's complaint about the poverty of his native tongue. But whether it reflects linguistic poverty or strength of character, the fact is undeniable that *voluntas* and its cognates play a role in Latin thought and literature for which there is no parallel for any term in Classical or Hellenistic Greek. The best example of this is also the earliest occurrence of *voluntas* in philosophical Latin, in the famous discussion of the swerve of soul atoms in Lucretius Book 2. There are two very striking features of this text: (2a) It focuses on the term *voluntas*, which appears four times in forty-three lines, while there is no trace of any corresponding term in the relevant texts either of Epicurus or of any Greek Epicurean, and (2b) *voluntas* is described as *libera*, "free," in an apparent anticipation of the modern phrase "free will," whereas most ancient discussions of moral freedom, both in Greek and in Latin, do not present the will as the direct subject of freedom.[16]

13. Pohlenz (n. 9 above), vol. 1, 274, 319.
14. Gauthier (n. 2 above), 260f.
15. Dihle (n. 1 above), 133.
16. I take for granted the usual correction *voluntas* for *voluptas* (following *libera*) in Lucretius 2.257. For a recent defense of this reading see Don Fowler, "Lucretius on the *Clinamen* and 'Free Will,'" in *Syzetesis*, G. P. Carratelli, ed. (Naples, 1983), vol. 1, 334–36.

2a. Although we do not have Epicurus's own discussion of the swerve, we have two passages, one in the *Letter to Menoeceus* and one in papyrus fragments from a book *On Nature*, in which he is arguing against determinism (more exactly, against the fatalism of Universal Necessity). In the *Menoeceus* passage Epicurus contrasts "being a slave to the Fate of the natural philosophers" with the role of "what is up to us," which is "not subject to a master" (*to par' hēmas adespoton*, Diogenes Laertius 10.133). In the papyrus fragments the latter notion is referred to as "what we call the causal responsibility due to ourselves" (*di' hēmōn autōn tēn aitian onomazontes*) and "what we somehow perform through our own agency" (*to ex hēmōn autōn pōs prattomenon*).[17] All these phrases are only slight variants on Aristotle's formula "what is up to us" (*to eph' hēmin*) in contrast to the outcome of chance or necessity; and Chrysippus seems to have used the same terminology in discussing human freedom and responsibility for our actions.[18] These are the phrases Cicero renders as *in nostra potestate*, "what is in our power." Nowhere, as far as I can see, does a noun corresponding to *voluntas* appear in the Greek discussions of freedom and responsibility in Hellenistic philosophy, though of course the verb "to want" (*boulesthai*) is sometimes used together with other specifications of what it means for us to decide what is up to us.[19]

2b. We must wait a long time to find a strict parallel to Lucretius's description of the will as free (*libera . . . voluntas*). The expressions "free will" and "freedom of the will" are much more common in modern discussions of this topic. Although Augustine does occasionally speak of *libera voluntas*, the technical for-

17. Text from David Sedley, "Epicurus' Refutation of Determinism," *Syzetesis* (n. 16 above), vol. 1, 20, lines 46 (cf. line 38) and 52.

18. *SVF* 2.984, 998, 999, 1007.

19. See, e.g., *SVF* 2.998, 292, line 34, and 293, line 1. In the Latin of Aulus Gellius we find *voluntas* ascribed to Chrysippus, *SVF* 2.1000, 294, line 22, although in the Greek context that follows (lines 27–29) there is no corresponding noun.

mulations both in antiquity and in the Middle Ages follow a different vocabulary, and for good reasons. According to Aquinas, it would simply be a mistake to describe *voluntas* as free. In its narrow use as a translation for Aristotle's *boulēsis* (the desire for an end judged to be good), *voluntas* is *not* free: we desire necessarily, in virtue of our nature, whatever we judge to be good for us. It is only in regard to *prohairesis*, the deliberate selections of contingent means, that we enjoy *liberum arbitrium*, free judgment or free decision. (Similarly, God wills necessarily the good which is his own essence; but he wills freely, by *liberum arbitrium*, whatever he creates.) Although Augustine's doctrine is less fully worked out and less carefully expressed, his standard terminology is that adopted by St. Thomas: our freedom and moral responsibility lie in *liberum arbitrium voluntatis*; not in "freedom of the will," but in the exercise of "free choice" *by* the will.[20]

As far as I can see, Lucretius's phrase "free will," *libera voluntas*, found little or no echo in antiquity, even in Latin. (Augustine was certainly not following Lucretius!) I know of no detailed study of this terminology, but here are a few observations. When, in Roman times, Greek philosophy developed a technical expression for free will that went beyond phrases like "what is up to us," the term most generally employed is *to autexousion*, which simply means "what is in one's own power," as in Cicero's *in nostra potestate*. Just when this term was introduced, I do not know.[21] We find it, e.g., in Epictetus[22] and in Plotinus. Tertullian, writing shortly after A.D. 200, reports *autex-*

20. For the full phrase *liberum arbitrium voluntatis* see the first sentence of *De libero arbitrio* 2.1.1 and passim. When on the next page we find *libera voluntas* (five times in 2.1.3 for one occurrence of the full formula) we recognize this as a convenient abbreviation.

21. It is ascribed to Zeno and Chrysippus by Hippolytus in *SVF* 2.975, but that surely reflects the terminology of the later doxographer.

22. Five occurrences in Epictetus, according to Voelke (n. 5 above), 145 n. 8.

ousion as a technical term which he translates as *libera arbitrii potestas*, "the free power of decision."[23]

The metaphor of freedom, which was implicit as early as Epicurus's reference to our own responsibility in action as *adespoton*, "subject to no master," seems never to have hardened into a technical expression in Greek. Plotinus, in his famous essay on "the will [*thelēma*] of the One," uses the terms "what is up to us" (*to eph' hēmin*), "what is in one's own power" (*to autexousion*), and "what is free" (*to eleutheron*) as roughly interchangeable.[24] It seems that it was only in Latin, and above all in Augustine, that the terminology of freedom (*libertas*) became fixed as the standard formula for the human power of decision in virtue of which we are responsible for our actions.

3. Having moved ahead from Lucretius to Augustine by following the terminology of *libera voluntas*, we must return to the Stoics for our third stage. The first landmark, as we saw, was the focus on the volitional element of choice in the early Stoic theory of assent. The second landmark was the introduction of *voluntas* in the Latin translation of Greek theories by Cicero and Lucretius. The third stage will mark the convergence of these two influences in later Stoicism, to be illustrated first by the Greek of Epictetus and then by the Latin of Seneca. Although Epictetus was born about ten years before Seneca died, I take him first in order to distinguish the general atmosphere of late Stoicism from the special influence of Seneca's Latin vocabulary.

Epictetus is faithful to the orthodox Stoic view of assent as the decisive moment of rational control over action, but instead of expounding the classical theory of *sunkatathesis* (which was probably too technical for his taste), he prefers to develop two

23. *De anima* 21.6; cf. *arbitrii libertas* at 20.5. J. H. Waszink in his commentary on 20.5 (p. 288) suggests that the standard formula (*liberum arbitrium*) originates with Augustine.

24. See *Ennead* 6.8.4–6. The terms *boulēsis* and *thelēsis* both appear (6.13ff.) but neither is characterized as "free," *eleutheros*.

equivalent or closely allied notions which he can formulate in a personal way. The first is what he calls the rational "use of impressions," *chrēsis tōn phantasiōn*, which is just a more vivid phrase for the rational testing of impressions to see whether or not they deserve our assent. The other concept is *prohairesis*. This Aristotelian term apparently played no significant role in early Stoic theory but has become central for Epictetus. A few quotations:

> [*Discourses* 3.5.7] May death find me engaged in no other concern than with my moral choice [*prohairesis*], that it may be serene, unhampered, unconstrained, free. [1.22.10] Some things are up to us [*eph' hēmin*], some things not. Up to us are moral choice [*prohairesis*] and all the works of choice; not up to us are body, possessions, family ... [1.12.9] He is free for whom everything happens in agreement with his moral choice [*prohairesis*]. [1.1.23] [The tyrant says,] "I will put you in bonds." "What are you saying? put *me* in bonds? You will fetter my leg, but not even Zeus can conquer my *prohairesis*."

It seems clear that Epictetus has used this rather old-fashioned term to express a fundamentally new idea, much the same idea that Seneca had recently expressed by *voluntas*.[25] Epictetus's use of *prohairesis* serves to expand the notion of consent into the broader notion of moral character and personal "commitment" as shaped in our day-to-day, moment-to-moment decisions on how to deal with our inner feelings and outer relationships; and

25. From the point of view of moral philosophy Epictetus's use of *prohairesis* is old-fashioned, but Albrecht Dihle reminds me (in a letter) that it reflects the broad Hellenistic use of the term for one's character, attitude, or conduct, and for one's devotion to a person or a cause. See the passages cited in Dihle (n. 1 above), 193 n. 94. See also LSJ s.v. *prohairesis* 5–9; the Hellenistic use is prefigured in the citations from Demosthenes (ibid. 2–5). Epictetus is certainly relying on this idiomatic usage, but his own conception of *prohairesis* is radically new in its *Innerlichkeit* and in its central importance for the individual's own life. See also John M. Rist, "Prohairesis: Proclus, Plotinus et Alii," in *De Iamblique à Proclus*, Entretiens Hardt 21 (Geneva, 1975), 103–17, which has useful remarks on Epictetus's usage.

this notion is presented not only as the decisive factor in practical existence but as the true self, the inner man, the "I" of personal identity. By contrast, for Plato and Aristotle the "I" or true self was *nous*, the principle of reason most fully expressed in theoretical knowledge. This shift is a momentous one for the evolution of the idea of person and selfhood. For theoretical reason is essentially impersonal, and the Platonic-Aristotelian identification of the person with his intellect offers no basis for a metaphysics of the self in any individual sense. Epictetus, on the other hand, identifies himself with something essentially personal and individualized: not with reason as such but with the practical application of reason in selecting his commitments, in keeping his emotional balance, his serenity, by not extending himself to goals and values that lie beyond his control. This is a delicate operation of every waking moment, to be carefully monitored by periodic scrutinies of conscience, by steady application of the rule with which his *Handbook* opens:

> Some things are in our power [*eph' hēmin*], some things are not. In our power are judgment, impulse, rational desire, aversion, and, in one word, our own business. Not in our power are the body, property, reputation, political office, and in one word, what is not our own business. What is in our power is by nature free and unobstructed; what is not in our power is weak, enslaved, obstructed, and alien. . . . Test every *phantasia* by these rules, and if it concerns something which is not in our power, be ready to say, "this is nothing to me."

The life of the committed Stoic is thus a continual process of self-definition, of identification with the inner world that is "in our power," of deliberate detachment from the body and from the external world that lies beyond our control.

Traditional Greek terminology offers no appropriate term for this intense preoccupation with the inner life, the late Stoic parallel to a Cartesian *cogito* or focus on consciousness. So Epictetus takes an old word and fills it with his personal meaning. Perhaps if he wrote Latin he would have used *voluntas*, as Seneca did.

The official Greek equivalent for *voluntas*, namely, *boulēsis*, would have been much too narrowly technical and also too intellectual. By adopting *prohairesis* Epictetus locates the focus of his personal concern within the domain of choice, freedom, and responsibility.

More detailed study would show that in many respects Epictetus anticipates the spiritual attitude of a Christian like Augustine. He has never read the Gospel prayer "Our Father, thy will be done," nor heard the cry in Gethsemane, "Not my will, but thine be done," not to mention the Augustinian line from Dante: *in sua voluntat' é nostra pace*, "in His will is our peace." But Epictetus's version of the Stoic creed has moved surprisingly far in that direction. The old cosmic notion of Destiny and Providence as the law of Nature, the causal principle of the world order, is conceived by him as a personal "will of Nature" (*boulēma tēs phuseōs*) or "will of Zeus"; and his own *prohairesis* is described as "a part of God which he has given to us" (1.17.27). (Here again the principle of moral decision plays the role that reason plays for Plato and Aristotle, the divine element in human nature.) Hence Epictetus can find his own peace of mind in accepting the will of God as his own:

> In every case, I want and prefer [*mallon thelō*] what God wants. For I think what God wants is better than what I want. I attach myself to him as servant and follower, I share his impulse, his desire [*sunhormō, sunoregomai*]; I simply share his will [*haplōs sunthelō*].
>
> (4.7.20)

This is not the place to study the literary and linguistic nuances that differentiate Seneca's use of *voluntas* from Epictetus's doctrine of *prohairesis*. There are so many points of contact between the two that it almost seems that the Greek moral teacher is translating from the Roman essayist. For example, Seneca says:

> The body requires many things for health, the soul nourishes itself. . . . Whatever can make you good is in your power. What do you need in order to be good? To will it [*velle*].
>
> (*Ep.* 80.3–4)

And Epictetus says:

> There is nothing easier to manage than a human soul. What is needed is to will [*thelēsai dei*]; and the deed is done, success is achieved.
>
> (4.10.16)

The conception of spiritual exercise and training is so similar that one is tempted to think of direct influence, which is after all not out of the question, since Epictetus was educated in Rome immediately after Seneca's death. With or without direct contact, however, these two Stoics bear joint testimony to the development of introspective consciousness and its articulation in volitional terms in the last half of the first century A.D. But whereas the Greek philosopher, who is the more earnest and convincing of the two, articulates his doctrine around *prohairesis*, which echoes in the history of philosophy as a rather quaint term from the classical past, the Roman author launches his comparable message on the powerful vehicle of the future: *voluntas*, "the will."[26]

4. I conclude with a brief glance at Augustine's doctrine of the will, where Neoplatonic and Christian levels of spirituality are added to the Stoic and Roman conceptions of *voluntas* we have traced so far. From the Neoplatonists Augustine gratefully accepted the notion of a purely intelligible, noncorporeal domain of reality, to which the human will belonged together with the intellect. From St. Paul and his own experience of conversion he derived the sense of the divided self: "I do not do the good I will [*thelō*], but I do the evil which I will not [*ou thelō*]" (Romans 7:15). It was by meditation on these words of St. Paul that Augustine developed the notion of will that Kierkegaard found lacking in Socrates:

> Socrates explains that he who does not do the right thing has not understood it, but Christianity goes a little further back and says,

26. For parallels and translational equivalence between *prohairesis* and *voluntas* (in Cicero as well as in Seneca and Epictetus) see Dihle (n. 1 above), 133ff. with nn. 73–76, and references there to Pohlenz and Voelke.

it is because he will not understand it, and this in turn is because he does not will the right. . . . So then, Christianly understood, sin lies in the will, not in the intellect; and this corruption of the will goes well beyond the consciousness of the individual.[27]

The spiritual journey which Augustine reports in his *Confessions* is to a large extent his exploration of the concept of the human will and its responsibility for evil, and his own analysis is presented as commentary on the climactic episode of this narrative, in the conversion scene in the garden in Milan.

[I longed to imitate Victorinus but] I was held fast not by the iron of another but by the iron of my own will [*voluntas*]. The enemy held my will [*velle meum*] in his power and from it he had made a chain and shackled me. For my will was perverse and passion [*libido*] had grown from it, and when I gave in to passion habit was born, and when I did not resist the habit it became a necessity. . . . But the new will [*voluntas nova*] which has begun in me, so that I wished [*vellem*] to serve you freely and enjoy you, my God, . . . was not yet able to overcome the earlier will, strengthened as it was with age. So my two wills, one old, one new, one carnal, one spiritual, were in conflict and between them they tore my soul apart.[28]

I was frantic, overcome by violent anger with myself for not accepting your wish and entering into your covenant. . . . For to make the journey, and to arrive safely, no more was required than an act of will [*velle*]. But it must be a resolute and wholehearted act of the will, not some lame wish [*voluntas*] which I kept turning over and over in my mind . . . as I tore my hair and hammered my forehead with my fists; I locked my fingers and hugged my knees; and I did all this because I made an act of will [*volui*] to do it. . . . I performed all these actions, in which the will [*velle*] and the power to act [*posse*] are not the same. Yet I did not do that one thing which I should have been far, far better pleased

27. Kierkegaard, *The Sickness unto Death*, part 2 chapter 2, in *"Fear and Trembling" and "The Sickness unto Death,"* trans. W. Lowrie (Princeton, 1974), 226.

28. Augustine *Confessions* 8.5. I give the Penguin Classics translation by R. S. Pine-Coffin with slight changes.

to do than all the rest and could have done at once, as soon as I had the will to do it [*mox ut vellem, possem*], because as soon as I had the will to do so, I should have willed it wholeheartedly. For in this case the power to act was the same as the will [*voluntas*]. To will it was to do it. Yet I did not do it.

(8.8)

Why does this occur? . . . The mind [*animus*] orders itself to make an act of will [*imperat ut velit*], and it would not give this order unless it willed to do so [*nisi vellet*]; yet it does not carry out its own command. But it does not fully will to do this thing [*non ex toto vult*] and therefore it does not fully give the order. . . . For the will commands that an act of will should be made, and it gives this command to itself, not to some other will. The reason, then, why the command is not obeyed is that it is not given with the full will [*non plena imperat*]. . . . So there are two wills in us, because neither by itself is the whole will, and each possesses what the other lacks.

(8.9)

I will call attention only to three points in this doctrine.

4a. The sense of psychic conflict, which Plato captured by distinguishing three different factors in the soul (reason, *thumos*, appetite), is here described in terms of the fragmentation of a single principle, the will. The divided self is a divided will.

4b. The sense of alienation from one's true self, the frustration of not being able to realize one's deepest desire, is expressed in terms of a command of the will to itself, which the will itself does not obey. Note that whereas for Plato it is reason (*logos, to logistikon*) which should issue commands in the soul, here it is *voluntas* that gives the orders. Once again, one's "identification" with the positive aspect of oneself is expressed in terms of will.

4c. Finally, the will cannot be made whole, the self cannot be unified, by its own resources. Peace of mind comes only from reliance upon the will of the Creator: *inquietum est cor nostrum donec in te requiescat*. Historically speaking, the theoretical status of the Divine Will had been worked out earlier, by Athanasius,

Gregory of Nazianzus, and Marius Victorinus.[29] Augustine's own doctrine of human will is profoundly marked by this theological orientation, in two respects. On the one hand, the will of man, with its freedom of choice, provides the explanatory cause for evil and sin. (That is the theme of *De libero arbitrio*.) On the other hand, the will of man is the stage on which the drama of God's grace is to be acted out, as the *Confessions* aim to show us: "All you asked of me was to deny my own will and accept yours," *nolle quod volebam, et velle quod volebas* (9.1).

And so, at the end, we return to Dihle's thesis about the biblical and theological origins of the concept of will. That does not apply, however, to what we found in Chrysippus's theory of assent, in Lucretius's and Seneca's discussions of *voluntas*, or in Epictetus's doctrine of *prohairesis*. For even if Epictetus's conception does have some distinctly theological overtones, his basic notion of achieving moral invulnerability by restricting our concerns to what is in our power is essentially an ideal of rational autonomy that is man-centered rather than God-centered. The Stoic notion that the laws of nature represent the commands of God and that whatever happens follows from the will of Zeus must remain essentially figurative in a religious tradition where the philosophers do not believe that God speaks to man in any literal way. But of course the God of Abraham and Moses, of Jesus and St. Paul, issues his commands to mankind in no uncertain terms. Hence it is in this tradition that we naturally find a view of human will (as distinct from reason or desire) emerging as an overall attitude of obedience or disobedience to the will of God on the part of the whole person. And it is this view which is first fully articulated by Augustine and then integrated into a general theory of human psychology by Aquinas. The architectonic structure of Aquinas's *Summa*, where the psychological theory is presented within an account of God's creative action,

29. Dihle (n. 1 above), 116–18.

reveals the extent to which this view of the will has remained profoundly theological.

Nevertheless, there is another story to be told, as we have seen. When Augustine and Aquinas go to work, they draw not only on the theological tradition but also on the Stoic theory of assent, the Latin vocabulary that links *voluntas* to *voluntarium* and free choice, and the late pagan preoccupation with our inner life of self-examination and the effort toward self-perfection that we have illustrated from Seneca and Epictetus. Aquinas makes liberal use of Aristotle's psychology. And both authors rely on the Neoplatonic construal of psychic activity as the work of an immaterial substance.

Major historical developments are always overdetermined. Dihle has documented in detail what we always suspected: that the concept of the will as we find it developed in Augustine and Aquinas presupposes biblical religious experience as one of its indispensable conditions. But there were other conditions as well. The accounts of the will given by Augustine and Aquinas have proved to be two of the most powerful and durable examples of eclecticism in Western intellectual history.

Index of Greek and Latin philosophical terms

General index

This Index does not record all proper names found in the book. Modern scholars are included here only if their views are discussed in the main text or footnotes, or if they are cited for work central to the theme of each chapter. Many of the concepts discussed in the book may be identified by means of the Index of Greek and Latin terms.